CASE SUSPENSION AND BINARY COMPLEMENT
STRUCTURE IN FRENCH

AMSTERDAM STUDIES IN THE THEORY AND HISTORY OF LINGUISTIC SCIENCE

General Editor

E. F. KONRAD KOERNER

(University of Ottawa)

Series IV - CURRENT ISSUES IN LINGUISTIC THEORY

Volume 132

Julia Herschensohn

Case Suspension and Binary Complement Structure in French

CASE SUSPENSION AND
BINARY COMPLEMENT STRUCTURE
IN FRENCH

JULIA HERSCHENSOHN

University of Washington

JOHN BENJAMINS PUBLISHING COMPANY
AMSTERDAM/PHILADELPHIA

∞ TM The paper used in this publication meets the minimum requirements of American National Standard for Information Sciences — Permanence of Paper for Printed Library Materials, ANSI Z39.48-1984.

Library of Congress Cataloging-in-Publication Data

Herschensohn, Julia Rogers, 1945-
   Case suspension and binary complement structure in French / Julia Herschensohn.
      p.   cm. -- (Amsterdam studies in the theory and history of linguistic science. Series IV, Current issues in linguistic theory, ISSN 0304-0763 ; v. 132)
   Includes bibliographical references and index.
   1. French language--Case. 2. French language--Complement. I. Title. II. Series.
PC2221.H39   1996
445--dc20   96-2115
ISBN 90 272 3636 4 (Eur.) / 1-55619-587-7 (US) (alk. paper)   CIP

John Benjamins Publishing Co. • P.O.Box 75577 • 1070 AN Amsterdam • The Netherlands
John Benjamins North America • P.O.Box 27519 • Philadelphia PA 19118-0519 • USA

To Michael

PREFACE

Adapting relevant aspects of the minimalist program, this book investigates constructions with nonthematic external arguments and one suspended Case. It argues that the dual nature of internal Case in French correlates with a parallel limit on argument projection: a verb can have one subject and no more than two objects. The assumption of a Larsonian shell—a triple tiered VP containing the external and internal arguments—provides the theoretical justification for this proposal. Larson's single complement hypothesis allows the VP complement to be predicated of the sentential subject and the indirect object to be predicated of the direct object for a maximum of two internal arguments. The testing ground for the binary hypothesis is a collection of perplexing data concerning nonthematic subject constructions; these constructions are linked to a lack of internal Case according to Burzio's generalization. The existence of a class of psychological experiencer verbs lacking an underlying thematic subject, yet capable of assigning accusative Case, apparently contradicts the generalization. The book investigates the apparent dilemma of these accusative psych verbs, showing that dative as well as accusative is a structural, not an inherent Case in French, and that the generalization must be extended to accommodate suspension of either Case. Two classes of verbs with nonthematic subjects and suspended dative Case, psych verbs and inalienable verbs, support this claim. These *undatives*, parallel to *unaccusatives*, actually provide support for Burzio's generalization in its strongest form. The theoretical underpinning of the generalization—the linking of Case suspension and lack of an external argument—is reaffirmed by the demonstration that the suspension of either structural Case can be linked to a nonthematic external argument. Furthermore, the proposal of multivalent inalienable verbs, an explanation that falls out from the undative analysis, provides significant evidence for the structural nature of dative Case, for the extended generalization, and for the central thesis of the book, the binary nature of internal Case and argument structure. The binary limit thus provides not only a theoretically significant contribution to our understanding of grammar, but also a motivated explanation for a number of empirical problems.

I wish to express my appreciation to the University of Washington for release time and a summer grant that contributed to the research for this book; I am grateful to the College of Arts & Sciences for the first, and to the Graduate School Research Fund for the second.

I would also like to thank the anonymous readers of the original manuscript who offered pertinent suggestions and asked important questions. Likewise I express my gratitude to the following colleagues for fruitful discussions and comments on earlier drafts: Deborah Arteaga, Marc Authier, Heles Contreras, Joe Emonds, Fritz Newmeyer, Carlos Otero, Johan Rooryck, Lisa Reed, Yves Roberge, Hilary Sachs, Judith Strozer and Karen Zagona. In addition to reading earlier drafts, Heles Contreras, Fritz Newmeyer and Karen Zagona made very helpful comments on a final draft; they and Ellen Kaisse provided substantial extralinguistic support as well in the final stages, for which I am deeply grateful. For more general linguistic, collegial and moral support, I thank Jeanie Fleming, Robert Fronk, Randall Gess, Jürgen Klausenburger, Lynn Klausenburger, Marian Sugano and Laurie Zaring.

The following speakers of French were kind enough to provide grammaticality judgments (often on more than one occasion): Leon Bensadon, Jean and Babette Bourguignon, Katia Criqui, Anne George, Gwenaëlle Geslin, Marie Labelle, Maria Leon, Louise Lepley, Jean-Jacques Malo, Réjean Canac Marquis, Patrick Moreno, Martine Pettenaro, Johan Rooryck, Christine Tellier and Bernard Tranel. I gratefully acknowledge the generous help that E.F. Konrad Koerner, the series editor, has furnished me in my production of the final version of the book; he responded to e-mail queries seemingly within minutes. I also thank Cecile Kummerer for all the support she has offered over several years in areas of computation, formatting and friendship.

Finally, I thank the members of my family for their patience, encouragement, help and humor, especially during the final stages of the book preparation. Olivia's inspirational concern, Aram's computer expertise and Zachary's parodies of syntactic titles have made the production much more enjoyable. I have appreciated the interest shown by Syl, Peggy and Nick who have bolstered my spirits from afar. Most of all I thank Michael for his boundless enthusiasm, constant encouragement and very concrete help in preparing this book. It is to him that I dedicate the book.

Seattle, Washington, 28 October 1995   JH

CONTENTS

CHAPTER 1

MINIMALIST SYNTACTIC REPRESENTATION

Each language employs a limited number of sounds, forming a system of phonemes. An unlimited number would make the language unpronounceable and unintelligible. The same may be said of words. An infinite number of words, one for each sense experience, would make language impossible.

1.0 *Introduction*

Boas (1938:128) captures in this quotation the essence of what could be called the efficiency of language, the observation that language is parsimonious both in its tight structure and in its limited inventory. Of thousands of possible sounds, a human language uses a small subset—usually a few dozen—to constitute its sound system. The sounds are combined to create the units of meaning, words, whose number is kept to a list of several thousand in everyday usage. But this limited inventory would be unmanageable if there were no systematic means of combination. Words are combined according to strict syntactic principles to create sentences and longer discourse. The finite set of linguistic expressions combined grammatically is capable of describing experiential and abstract phenomena that are infinite in number. The system permitting combination is strictly finite and highly efficient. This frugality of linguistic system and inventory is significant in the consideration of language acquisition, for it can be argued that the underlying simplicity of language is one factor contributing to the relative ease with which children acquire a first language. Language is a well structured finite system capable of describing and categorizing a universe of infinite possibilities; it is both accessible and efficient, and thereby learnable.

Chomsky (1991:418) discusses the notion of economy in terms of the current generative model of syntax, pointing out that this system is biased toward tight integration because linguistic guidelines "have a kind of 'least effort' flavor to them, in the sense that they legislate against 'superfluous elements' in representations and derivations". The minimalist program explored in recent generative work seeks to elucidate the economical principles accounting for these properties of language. Adopting such a minimalist approach to a formal study of grammar, this book explores the question of abstract Case and its relationship to syntactic configuration. Section 1.1 presents the theoretical and empirical issues that motivate this book and outlines the chapters. Section 1.2 discusses the conception of language, its acquisition, and the theoretical presuppositions of the generative model as a framework of study. Section 1.3 introduces relevant innovations of the minimalist program that are used throughout the book.

1.1 *The determination of argument structure*
1.1.1 *The theoretical issue: Case and syntactic representation*

A topic of concern for generative linguistics has been the correlation between a verb's semantic actors (thematic roles), and the syntactic realization of these roles. Less attention has been paid to the relationship of abstract Case to argument and thematic (theta) structure because Case assignment has generally been treated as a surface phenomenon inconsequential to the deep lexical properties characteristic of thematic and conceptual correlates.[1]

Earlier studies such as Fillmore (1968) and Jackendoff (1972) sought to find systematic correspondences between syntax and semantics in an attempt to relate the referential universe to describe to the means of expression, the grammar. More recently Baker (1988:46) has proposed a one to one relationship between thematic roles and underlying syntactic relationships, the Uniformity of Theta Assignment Hypothesis, whereby identical thematic relationships between items are represented by identical underlying structural relationships. Such a systematic correspondence provides a theoretical rationale for the correlation between syntax and thematic roles. Indeed, recent work in this area suggests that many aspects of argument structure are determined by lexical information and thematic hierarchy. Grimshaw (1992:1) states:

> In the strongest possible theory the a[rgument] structure of a lexical item is predictable from its meaning, and the d-structure the item appears in is predictable from its a-structure in interaction with independent parametric characteristics of the language.

Hale & Keyser (1993b) flesh out an analysis of argument structure that portrays thematic roles as a function of lexical syntactic relations, the *lexical*

---

[1] The relationship between thematic theory and Case has mainly been studied in terms of inherent Cases (cf. Baker 1988); structural Cases are by definition not linked to theta role. For inherent Cases the assigner and assignee are lexically determined and syntactically inseparable; for structural Cases there is no necessary semantic / thematic relationship between the assigner and assignee. See Davis (1986) for a discussion of related issues.

relational structures that a head projects. The lexical relational structure includes syntactic and semantic information, much of which is derivative from general principles of lexical conceptual structure, and some of which is item specific. Their proposal redefines theta structure in terms of semantic and syntactic primitives that translate concepts into syntactic representation.[2]

The significant degree of congruence between lexical conceptual structure and its syntactic realization does not carry over to a correlation between Case and argument projection. A given type of argument (e.g. a direct recipient of the action of the verb) is not consistently associated with a particular Case (e.g. accusative) because arguments may be forced to move in the syntax in order to get Case (e.g. the passive construction) or arguments may be realized with variable Cases with the same verb (e.g. *load the wagon with hay / load hay on the wagon*). Nevertheless, even if there is no absolute congruence between Case distribution and the configuration of projected arguments, there exists a crucial linking of structural Case and potential argument position. Burzio (1986) was first to observe this in his generalization that the suspension of accusative Case (as with passive and unaccusative verbs) correlates with the lack of a thematic subject.

The present study explores the relationship between Case and available syntactic positions in a broadened investigation of nonthematic subject constructions. It argues that complement structure and Case, while not congruent, are codependent, and that a language's potential for assigning structural Case is linked directly to the potential complement structure of that language. It thus claims that argument structure is not a function of thematic or lexical relational structure alone, but is also delimited in part by Case theory. The relationship between Case and argument projection raises the following questions:

(1) a Is there a link between potential Case and argument position?
    b Can either Case or argument be missing?
    c Is the projection potential limited in any way?

This book presents evidence for an affirmative answer to these three questions in its examination of internal argument structure and internal Case in constructions with nonthematic subjects and suspended Case. In order to investigate these questions, the study concentrates on a single language,

---

[2] Zagona (p.c.) points out two issues related to the question of argument projection: the simplicity of the lexicon as opposed to the syntax, and the precise nature of the mapping from the lexicon to the syntax (how configurational in nature it is).

French, but many of the arguments are directly relevant to the other Romance languages, and may also be applicable to English. Presenting documentation of two structural Cases in French, the book argues, through an extension of Burzio's generalization, for a necessary linking of potential Case and argument position. Couched in terms of the minimalist program, this link is motivated by considerations of Case, configuration and economy of derivation. The specifier–complement relationship described by Larson's (1988) single complement hypothesis provides the theoretical motivation for a limit of two potential arguments.

The approach to French complement structure developed in this work has as an important element the binary hypothesis of Case. This hypothesis holds that duality, a crucial notion governing linguistic phenomena, is represented in French by two internal structural Cases, objective and dative, linked to two internal argument positions. An investigation of Case in French requires a clarification of Case theory to account for the complementarity of structural accusative and partitive Case and the structural nature of dative Case. The binary hypothesis entails an extension of Burzio's generalization to predict undative as well as unaccusative verbs with nonthematic subjects.

1.1.2 *The empirical issue: Nonthematic subject constructions*

In order to test the binary hypothesis it is necessary to look at syntax peripheral to that of standard transitive verbs. In French there exist a number of constructions with one defective or suspended internal Case which nevertheless allow two (but no more) internal complements. One of the internal arguments is forced to move to be assigned (nominative) Case. These constructions are said to have nonthematic or empty subject positions to which the internal argument moves. The subject position, assigned no semantic role by the verb, is sometimes filled by semantically empty expletives such as *there* in *there is a book*, but it is not always filled. It is precisely these Case defective constructions—unaccusative, psych, pronominal and inalienable—that provide a proving ground for binary complement structure and internal Case. The data investigated include syntactic constructions which are superficially unrelated, but which can be explained by the same principles.

French manifests a number of apparently paradoxical examples with respect to Case and internal argument structure; in (2)–(5) the *b* sentences are unexpectedly ungrammatical compared to the *a* sentences. Intransitive verbs usually do not accept direct objects, but can under certain circumstances (2a); the class of intransitive verbs represented in (2b), however, disallows direct objects under all circumstances.

(2) *Intransitive constructions*
    a   Il a pleuré toutes les larmes de ses yeux.
        "He cried all the tears of his eyes".
    b   *Il a/est resté un séjour agréable.
        "He stayed an agreeable sojourn".

Transitive verbs allow in French an affected dative pronoun with a benefactive or malefactive reading (3a); but the class of transitive verbs represented in (3b) disallows these indirect objects.[3]

(3) *Transitive constructions*
    a   Le vent lui a ballayé la cour.
        "The wind swept the courtyard to her [advantage]".
    b   *Les marionnettes lui ont amusé ses enfants.
        "The marionnettes amused her children to her [advantage]".

Pronominal constructions allow one clitic pronoun in addition to the *se* (4a); a certain class of pronominals disallows, however, a second clitic pronoun (4b) even if it is grammatical with the semantically equivalent nonpronominal form of the verb (4c).[4]

(4) *Pronominal constructions*
    a   Ils se les sont offerts, [les cadeaux].
        "They offered them [the gifts] to each other".
    b   *Le jouet se lui est cassé entre les mains.
        "The toy broke to her [disadvantage] in her hands".
    c   Le jouet lui a cassé entre les mains.
        "The toy broke to her [disadvantage] in her hands".

Inalienable possession is usually expressed in French by an indirect object pronoun rather than a possessive determiner with the body part (5a); a small class of verbs used with inalienables disallows this construction (5b).

---

[3] Affected datives, unlike those subcategorized by verbs of transfer and communication, are nonlexical in that they are not selected by the verb.
[4] Spanish, in contrast, allows the affected dative with pronominals of the same type.
    (i) Se le rompió [el juguete]. "[The toy] broke to her [disadvantage]".
See Chapter 5 for a discussion of clitic coocurrence restrictions in French.

(5) *Inalienable constructions*
   a   Marie s'est lavé les mains.
      "Marie washed her hands".
   b   *Marie s'est levé la main.
      "Marie raised her hand".

The *b* sentences of (2)–(5) present at once an empirical dilemma in their unexpected ungrammaticality, and a theoretical problem for an analysis which assumes that "there can be an indeterminate number of internal arguments" (Williams 1994:32). The approach expressed by Williams posits a negative answer to question (1c) concerning a limit on the number of arguments. The present study gives an affirmative answer to the question in substantiating the binary hypothesis of Case and argument structure in French. Through a close examination of the constructions in (2)–(5), it shows that the *b* examples are ungrammatical because they contain a third internal argument in contexts that already contain two. The subject in the *b* sentences is an internal argument that is forced to move when one internal Case is suspended, whereas the subject of the *a* sentences is an external argument.

1.1.3 *Outline of chapters*

    Chapter 2 establishes the necessary link between agreement nodes and argument positions implicit in the minimalist approach, a link required by Case checking, the triple tiered VP structure and the principle of shortest distance. The single complement condition and Larsonian shell furnish the theoretical justification for the binary limit on the link: a single complement may be predicated of the subject of the sentence, and a single complement may be predicated of the direct object of the verb. The claim of two pairs of linked nodes is proven in French by the existence of two structural internal Cases, objective and dative, which are shown to be linked to two potential argument positions. Chapter 2 proposes that the number of internal arguments cannot exceed two, a claim that appears trivial for transitive verbs (6), but which is shown to have predictive power for the more peripheral constructions involving verbs with nonthematic subjects (2–5b).

    (6) John gave Mary the book.

Case assignment, responsible for NP movement possibilities in constructions with nonthematic subjects, is closely linked to argument structure. It is shown that French verbs have dual Case assigning potential in that they may maximally assign objective and dative Case. The collusion of Case assignment and binary internal argument structure determines movement with nonthematic subject verbs: since both internal arguments cannot receive Case from the verb, one of them is forced to move to subject position with nominative Case.

The binary restriction predicts a limit to the number of internal structural Cases and potential internal arguments as well. In Chapter 2 empirical data is presented to bear out the theoretical predictions: it is argued that French requires two structural Cases, objective and dative. An investigation of objective Case reveals that the standard Case theory assumed by Belletti (1988) and Lasnik (1992) must be revised to account for Case assignment in French. Accusative and partitive do not constitute two different Cases, but are rather two realizations of Case on direct objects; accusative is the usual structural Case and partitive an objective Case that can save a derivation under very limited conditions when accusative is unavailable. The dual character of Case correlates with a dual restriction on internal arguments to be tested in subsequent chapters.

The third chapter explores the question of dissociability of the Case–argument link by clarifying the characteristics of Case defective arguments and Case marked nonarguments. Unaccusatives (2b) are prototypes of the nonthematic subject construction; they support the proposals on Case and argument structure in that they can allow partitive but not accusative Case, permitting, nevertheless, two internal arguments. The ungrammaticality of (2b) exemplifies the inability of these verbs to assign accusative Case although they must be analyzed as taking two internal arguments. Burzio's generalization is extended in light of the two Case proposal to predict a class of undatives parallel to unaccusatives. Affected dative clitics (Case marked nonarguments used in benefactive–malefactive ways as in (3a)) are introduced as diagnostics for dative Case assignment and hence for a class of undative verbs.

The next three chapters provide empirical evidence to support the theoretical claims developed in Chapter 2 and to argue for the existence of three other groups of Case defective verbs. The fourth chapter demonstrates operation of the Case / argument constraints with respect to one class of psychological experiencer verbs that have nonthematic subjects and are undative in their inability to assign dative Case. Like unaccusatives they have one defective internal Case yet take two internal arguments, one of which must move to subject position with nominative Case. Chapter 5 studies pronominal *se* in a range of constructions. It argues that the neutral / middle / psych uses are determined in the lexicon by the absorption of one argument, one theta role and accusative Case. These pronominals, constituting another class of Case defective verbs, contrast with referential reflexive *se* linked syntactically to its antecedent. The sixth chapter presents a fourth class of nonthematic subject verbs, inalienables (7).

(7) Marie a levé la main.
"Marie raised her hand".

It is argued that the superficial subject in (7) is underlyingly an internal argument and that *lever* is an undative verb; hence (5b) is ungrammatical because it contains one extra internal argument that cannot receive Case. Inalienable possession, expressed through the use of definite articles and dative clitics, provides further evidence for the proposed analysis of Case and argument structure. Unaccusative, psych, pronominal and inalienable constructions bear out the accuracy of the Case proposal. More importantly, the unusual syntactic configurations of these constructions are predicted by the binary approach to Case and argument structure.

1.2 *Principles and parameters model*
1.2.1 *Language acquisition*

Generative linguistics seeks to account for the creativity of language, the fact that—given a relatively small group of sounds, several thousand words, and a constrained syntax—a speaker is able to create an infinite number of stimulus-free sentences in a given language. The theory refers to the characterization of the speaker's idealized language system by the linguist as a grammar. Chomsky (1986a:27) uses the term I-language to refer to this capacity:[5]

> When we speak of a person as knowing a language, we do not mean that he or she knows an infinite set of sentences, or sound–meaning pairs taken in extension, or a set of acts or behaviors; rather, what we mean is that the person knows what makes sound and meaning relate to one another in a specific way, what makes them "hang together", a particular characterization of a function, perhaps. The person has a notion of "structure" and knows an I-language as characterized by the linguist's grammar.

---

[5] Contreras (p.c.) points out that Chomsky (1986a) in distinguishing I-language from grammar resolves the earlier ambiguities of the term "grammar" which had been used by linguists to refer both to the speaker's knowledge and the linguist's characterization of it.

Generative linguists have devoted their attention to analyzing this abstract knowledge of the speaker, rather than the speaker's performance, which often is an imperfect representation of his or her competence.

Chomsky's delineation of I-language attempts to account for the general perception that the child's rapid attainment of a facility in language cannot be attributed to a relatively limited stimulus (the sample of utterances actually heard). In a short period of time the child acquires the capacity to put together words and grammatical affixes to form adult-like sentences. The child's ability to create novel utterances cannot be predicted by an acquisition model based on imitation, but rather suggests a genetic basis to the language faculty. Recent generative research in various language types indicates that the child's internalized grammar comprises a limited number of principles and parameters whose values are fixed early in the acquisition process.[6] This genetically determined predilection is referred to as *universal grammar*. The maturation of an individual's linguistic capacity is viewed as an interaction of other modular systems with universal grammar: the environment acts as a catalyst to activate the genetic predisposition.

Knowledge of language may be compared to knowledge of a game such as chess: chess is not the particular instantiation of the game, but rather the abstract system underlying the game. The task of a scholar of games would be to deduce the rules of the game and the roles of the subsystems (for example, the type of move which each piece may make), just as the scholar of language must infer linguistic principles through observation of language instantiation. The grammar itself interfaces with other cognitive and external systems, such as perception and social interaction, in a modular fashion. In explaining the generative view of the autonomy of formal grammar, Newmeyer (1987:5) points out the relationship of grammar with the other faculties involved in language: "It is now well accepted that complex linguistic phenomena are best explained in terms of the interaction of these diverse systems".

1.2.2 *The system of levels and rules*

From a generative point of view the formal grammar consists of a lexicon (a mental dictionary with semantic, syntactic, morphological and phonological information about the words of the language), a highly constrained syntactic

---

[6] The investigation of syntactic principles and parameters in language acquisition has been the focus of work in the government–binding framework. Numerous articles and books have been devoted to elaborating this model, for example, Bley-Vroman (1988), Clahsen & Muysken (1986, 1989), Du Plessis et al. (1987), Flynn & O'Neil (1988), Goodluck (1991), Hyams (1986), Jaeggli & Safir (1989), Strozer (1994), White (1989).

component, and interpretive components related to sound (phonology) and meaning (semantics). These components of a principles and parameters model are graphically represented by a scheme in which the major levels of interface are the lexicon, PF (Phonetic Form) and LF (Logical Form). The lexicon provides the necessary semantic, phonological and syntactic information to determine the viability of concatenations of the words of the language. The underlying relationships or D-structures reflect the lexical information and provide input to the central syntactic operation, *move or affect alpha*. The output of this operation is the S-structure, in turn interpreted by two distinct components, PF and LF.

Movement is represented by the rule move alpha, which can apply at any level, and restricted by syntactic principles that constrain the output that can be generated. The levels of D-structure and S-structure are in large part derivable from lexical properties, characteristics of syntactic categories and otherwise needed syntactic principles. The syntactic output is an instantiation of the X-bar theory of syntactic category projection.[7] Syntactic relationships are determined by the lexicon and represented at subsequent levels by chains which trace the paths of moved elements; the base syntactic relationships are thus recoverable. Syntactic linking is further delimited by a number of principles which define the configurations permissible for such links. Syntactic outputs are interpreted by Phonetic Form and Logical Form, the inputs to articulatory and conceptual performance systems respectively.

The lexicon is the repository of information about the words of a language: their meaning, pronunciation and the contexts in which they can be used. Speas (1990:9) explains: "The lexicon includes a list of entries for all words and affixes, and [...] every lexical entry includes four types of information: 1) a phonological representation; 2) semantic information; 3) syntactic information; 4) morphological information". One important aspect of the semantic information in the lexicon concerns *theta roles*, the semantic relationships determined by lexical items; the roles include notions such as 'agent', the performer of an action or 'goal', the indirect recipient of an action. The necessary environment for a given lexical item is described by its s[emantic]–selection and its c[ategorial]–selection. C-selection or sub-categorization describes the syntactic environment determined by the item.

---

[7] Earlier generative models describe the base as consisting of the lexicon and phrase structure (PS) rules that generate P[hrase]–markers. PS rules are essentially subsumed by the X–bar theory coupled with the information in the lexicon.

Some information is idiosyncratic and must simply be provided for a lexical item, such as the irregular plural of *mouse, mice.*[8]

Drawing on elements of the lexicon, the syntax is capable of generating sentences of the language. Its basic input is determined by the X-bar schema which at once defines lexical categories and licit syntactic relationships. The syntactic category 'X' is representative of the major syntactic categories N (noun), V (verb), A (adjective) and P (preposition). These categories can be characterized in binary terms by the features [+/–N ,+/–V]: noun [+N–V], verb [–N+V], adjective [+N+V], preposition [–N–V] (cf. Chomsky 1986b:2). The categorial head N, V, A, P projects a phrase which can combine to create complex sentences. In addition to *lexical heads* such as N and V, there are nonlexical *functional heads* such as C (complementizer), T (tense) and Agr (agreement). A head is can be modified by a *specifier* (Spec) and extended by a *complement*, according to the following schema (8).

(8) X'' *projection*
$X'' \rightarrow \text{Spec}_X \; X'$
$X' \rightarrow X \; \text{Comp}_X$

The projection of a category X is labeled according to three levels of projection— X^0, the zero level or head; X', the intermediate or complement level; and X'' (XP), the phrase level or maximal projection of X. Two kinds of relationships are defined by the X-bar scheme, specifier–head and head–complement. The specifier and complement are expandable as maximal phrases, whereas the head is always an X^0 level lexical item or feature bundle. Expansion may be either rightward or leftward, a parameter determined by the language in question.

1.2.3 *Regulatory principles*

X-bar theory both defines and delimits the syntactic configurations possible in a given language, but it alone does not determine the possible outputs. Another assumption is that syntactic derivations (input to LF) contain *traces*, empty categories that trace a path of moved elements to their syntactic

---

[8] The lexicon includes not simply a listing of disparate facts about lexical items, but also indicates phonological, morphological, syntactic and semantic regularities. Grimshaw (1992:3) notes, "The position taken in much earlier work, that the lexicon is idiosyncratic and is acquired piece by piece, simply cannot be maintained. It fails to explain the high degree of regularity of the lexical system as well as how children come to acquire lexical information".

origin.[9] These linked traces constitute two types of chains, A[rgument]-chains and A-bar (non-argument) [A']-chains. The former contain a head in an argument position and its trace(s) in the original position from which it receives its theta role, but not Case (for example, passive sentences whose superficial subject is the selected direct object of the verb). The latter contain a head in a non-argument position (for example relatives or interrogatives in the CP) and its trace(s) in its original position.

The syntax is further constrained by other subtheories and principles such as *Case theory*, requiring that noun phrases receive abstract Case (usually from verbs or prepositions), and the *Theta Criterion* allowing only one theta position per chain. The theory of *government* defines locality relations. Chomsky (1986a:162) describes the essence of the government relationship: "Let us say that a category α governs a maximal projection X'' if α and X'' c-command each other; and if α governs X'' in this sense, then α governs the specifier and the head X of X''. Thus, a head α governs its complements". C-command is defined as in (9) (cf. Aoun & Sportiche 1983).

(9) *C-command*
     A c-commands B iff A does not dominate B and for every maximal projection C, if C dominates A then C dominates B.

The notion of government is crucial to other modules such as Case, theta role assignment, and binding. A preliminary and informal description of *binding theory* shows three principles defining limitations on chains (10).

(10) *Binding theory*
     a   Anaphors must be bound in a minimal domain
     b   Pronouns must be free in a minimal domain
     c   R[eferring]-expressions must be free

The components of and principles regulating the formal system describing linguistic competence are considered universal and thus help account for the learnability of language.

---

[9] The constraints of X–bar theory and the existence of traces guaranteeing recoverability of syntactic relations reflect the Projection Principle (Chomsky 1981:36), which holds that representations at each syntactic level are projected from the lexicon.

1.3 *The minimalist program*

Pursuing the direction set by the principles and parameters paradigm, Chomsky (1993, 1994, 1995) puts forth a model of the grammar that is reduced to its minimal essentials, a model that attempts to eliminate redundancy and to motivate theoretically the elements and functions of its computational system.[10] Incorporating theoretical advances such as a more explicit structure of functional categories (cf. Fukui & Speas 1986, Pollock 1989), he proposes a grammar pared down to the minimum: the lexicon, the interpretive components PF and LF, and two operations, *Move* and *Merge* that push forward the computation / derivation of syntactic structures. The levels of D-structure and S-structure are seen as superfluous. Invariant linguistic principles determine possible derivations, and cross linguistic variation is limited to parts of the lexicon and certain properties of lexical items. An overview of the minimalist program is presented in the following sections.

1.3.1 *Categories and computations*

A significant feature of the minimalist program distinguishing it from earlier models is the requirement that elements and functions of the computational system be *motivated* by an evaluation metric, economy of derivation. The principles and parameters model embodied a shift from an earlier rule driven (and thus language particular, structure specific) grammar to one that was regulated by cross-linguistically valid principles (e.g. the Projection Principle). Noting the characteristic efficiency of linguistic derivations, the minimalist program extends the principles and parameters model by reevaluating the role of its elements and by seeking reasons for their interaction.

In minimalist terms the grammar is a mechanism capable of generating a set of admissible derivations, computations which are not simply grammatical as determined by interpretability by PF and LF (that is, whether the derivations 'sound right' and 'make sense'), but which are also derived in the most economical manner, according to principles of 'least effort'. From the perspective of language learning and language use, it would be reasonable to assume that direct and succinct linguistic computations would be preferable to lengthy and redundant operations. The reduction in components and

---

[10] The following references give relevant overviews and discussion of this framework, some with particular reference to Romance: Arteaga (1995), Epstein (1995), Lasnik (1993, 1994), Longobardi (1994), Manzini (1994), Marantz (1995), Moritz & Valois (1994), Olarrea (1994).

elimination of redundancy can thus be seen as desirable on grounds of learnability and processing. Furthermore, the emphasis on interface levels as opposed to abstract D-structure and S-structure reflects the intuitive sense that language links sound and meaning. PF represents the perceptual–articulatory sound system, while LF represents the conceptual–interpretive meaning component.

The lexicon furnishes for each lexical item its phonological, morphological, syntactic and semantic coordinates. It therefore provides the necessary information concerning the base syntactic structures into which the lexical item can enter and the features it possesses or requires for checking. The fact that the lexical item virtually projects the base syntactic structures into which it can enter obviates the need for a level of D-structure. The derivation exploits the operations Move and Merge to check morphological features (e.g. subject–verb agreement, Case assignment): morphological feature checking drives the derivation which consists of chains linking the moved elements to their base positions. Because the chain accesses lexical information (e.g. selectional properties) at any point, the Projection Principle is essentially a given. The point at which phonological features are "stripped away" leaving input to LF is called *Spellout* (Chomsky 1994:8). This operation may take place at any point in the computation, eliminating the need for a level of S-structure. If the derivation can be interpreted at the interface of the syntax with the interpretive components, it is said to *converge*. It must converge at both PF and LF, or it *crashes*. The derivation can crash at any point in the computation, preinterface because of an incompatibility of features, or postinterface by violation of *Full Interpretation* by PF or LF (Chomsky 1995:Section 1). The derivation is subject to output conditions.[11]

The grammar allows the following operations (Chomsky 1995:Section 2): *Select*, the choice of a lexical item from the lexicon; *Merge*, an operation that takes a pair of syntactic objects and combines them into a new object; *Move*, raising by either adjunction (head movement) or substitution (movement of a maximal projection); and *Delete*, the operation that deletes matching features as they are checked off in the course of the derivation. A chain formed by Move meets the conditions of c-command (therefore only raising is allowed), uniformity (only head or maximal projection may move), and *Last Resort*, one of the guiding principles of the minimalist program. Move is animated by feature checking since the matching of morphological feature is the engine by

---

[11] Chomsky (1986a:98) proposes that every element of PF or LF must receive an appropriate interpretation, "must be licensed in the sense indicated. None can simply be disregarded".

which the derivation proceeds (Chomsky 1995:Section 4). Morphological features may be *strong*, requiring that the lexical item raise overtly; or they may be *weak*, requiring that the features alone raise after Spellout, to be interpretable at LF but inaudible at PF.

There are several principles that determine the necessity and economy of a derivation (Chomsky 1995:Section 4). The requirement that morphological features (e.g. Case) be checked off is accommodated by two complementary tendencies, *Last Resort* and *Procrastinate*. The former requires overt raising of an element to check off a strong feature, a costlier measure than no movement at all, but a necessity for convergence. The latter is less costly and to be preferred for covert movement (feature raising alone). For example, main verbs in French possess strong tense features that require prespellout overt raising whereas English verbs possess weak tense features requiring that the verbs procrastinate and not raise. French verbs that do not raise fail to check off the strong tense features that persist unchecked at LF; English verbs that do raise violate Procrastinate; both derivations would crash for those respective reasons. Another economy principle that guides derivations is the *Minimal Link Condition* holding that moves prefer the shortest distance. In terms of feature checking, the motivator of movements, an element raises to a feature checking node only if there is no intervening node that would suffice.

Many components of the principles and parameters model are no longer required in the minimalist format because they are accommodated by another mechanism. The Projection Principle is not necessary since lexical information is available throughout the derivation and is an integral part of it. Government, Chomsky (1993:10) says, "would be dispensable, with principles of language restricted to something closer to conceptual necessity: local X-bar theoretic relations to the head of a projection and the chain–link relation". Chomsky (1994:9–10) reviews X-bar theory, claiming "there are no such entities as XP or X⁰ [...] though we may use these as informal notations, along with X‴".[12] Theta theory is complementary to movement and thus has little role in the overt syntax. Theta roles are not formal features, they are assigned, but do not enter into the syntactic computation (Chomsky 1995:Section 6).[13]

---

[12] Kayne (1994), in his investigation of linear order and syntactic hierarchy, argues that "X–bar theory is not a primitive component of UG. Rather, X–bar theory in essence expresses a set of antisymmetric properties of phrase structure" (p. 3). His antisymmetric Linear Correspondence Axiom claims that c–command maps into linear precedence, creating a hierarchy with specificiers before heads and with complements following them. See Chomsky (1995:Section 8) for a discussion of Kayne's proposals.

[13] Contreras (p.c.) points out that failure to assign a theta role to an argument causes a derivation to crash.

1.3.2 *Spec–head agreement*

Chomsky (1993:7) adopts an approach to Case theory whereby "all these modes of structural Case assignment be recast in unified X-bar theoretic terms, presumably under the Spec–head relation". Previous treatments have considered nominative Case assignment to be an instance of Spec–head agreement between the inflectional head of IP, I and its specifier subject NP, while objective Case is assigned by the V under government. Chomsky assumes that the external argument is generated predicate internally (cf. Zagona 1982, 1988; Contreras 1987; Sportiche 1988; Burton & Grimshaw 1992) and that the projection of the predicate includes a hierarchy of functional nodes (cf. Emonds 1978, Pollock 1989).[14] He redefines the sentential subject position as a specifier of sentential agreement, Agr_S, parallel to a position for objective agreement, Agr_O. Agr_S'' corresponds then to S[entence] or IP [Inflection Phrase], and is embedded under CP.

For example, according to Chomsky's proposal a transitive verb such as *laver* "to wash" can be represented as in (11). The expansion in (11) respects binary branching and general conditions of X' theory. Agr_S'' corresponds to IP (or S), its Spec containing the sentential subject position which is checked for nominative Case by the head Agr_S to which Tense raises and adjoins. The subject originates in the predicate, in the Spec of VP_1, and raises to the Spec of Agr_S'' position. All lexical items are fully inflected and possess several kinds of features that may be [+/– interpretable]; non interpretable features such as Case must be checked off before LF or the derivation crashes. Because nominative Case features are strong for finite tense, the subject must raise in English and French. In (11) the nominative Case is checked off (and then deleted, becoming invisible at LF) after the subject has raised to Spec Agr_S. Clitic pronouns in French show strong features (reflected in the explicit morphological marking of Case) so they also require raising for the strong features to be checked off before LF.[15] Direct object DPs, on the other hand, obey Procrastinate in not raising overtly. In (11) the direct object originates in the Spec of VP_2 position, raising covertly to the Spec of Agr_O'' to be checked for objective Case.[16]

---

[14] See Contreras (1991, 1995) for a discussion of functional categories and their features, and Williams (1994) for a critical discussion of the arguments for the VP internal subject (p. 141–153) and for verb raising (p. 164–178).

[15] See Otero (1995), Sportiche (1992, 1993), Uriagereka (1995) for a discussion of clitics.

[16] "In the general case, V will raise to Agr_O forming the chain $CH_V = (V,t)$. The complex [V Agr_O] raises ultimately to adjoin to Agr_S and therefore shares relevant features with it, and the subject in [Spec, Agr_S] is in the checking domain of Agr_S, hence agrees indirectly with V" (Chomsky 1993:45, fn 16).

(11) Marc lave la voiture.
     "Mark washes the car".

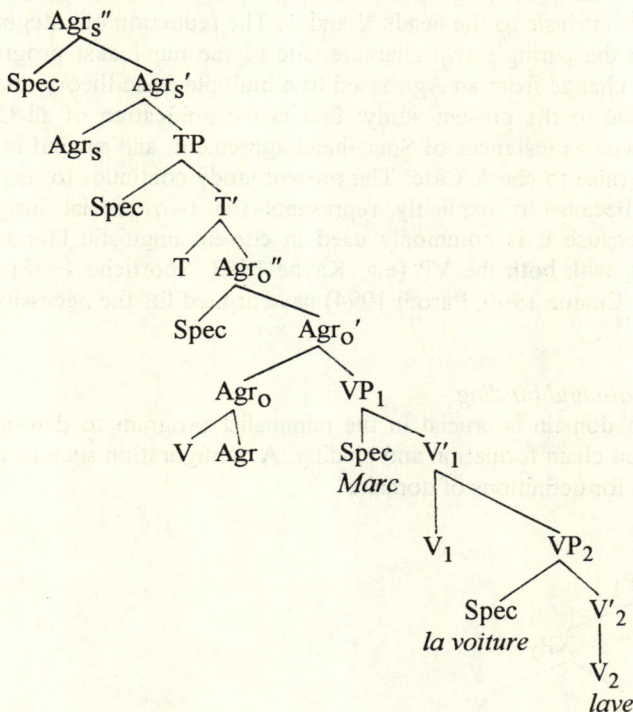

```
                    Agrs"
                  /      \
              Spec        Agrs'
                        /      \
                    Agrs        TP
                              /    \
                          Spec      T'
                                  /    \
                                 T      Agro"
                                      /      \
                                  Spec        Agro'
                                            /      \
                                        Agro        VP1
                                       /    \      /    \
                                      V   Agr  Spec      V'1
                                                Marc
                                                       |
                                              V1        VP2
                                                      /    \
                                                  Spec      V'2
                                               la voiture    |
                                                            V2
                                                           lave
```

In subject–verb–object languages the two kinds of structural Case marking, nominative and objective, appear to be asymmetric: nominative Case on the subject precedes the Case assigner, the inflected verb; objective Case on the verb's direct object follows the Case assigner, the verb. The proposal of two agreement nodes Agr$_s$ and Agr$_o$ makes both kinds of Case checking parallel. Case is checked as an instance of Spec–head agreement in the Agr nodes. The subject in Spec Agr$_s$ has nominative Case checked by its head Agr$_s$. The object in Spec Agr$_o$ has objective Case checked by its head Agr$_o$. The strong nominative subject in English and French raises overtly to the Spec Agr$_s$ whereas the DP object usually raises covertly. The asymmetry between the superficial distribution of the two kinds of Case marking (nominative Case precedes the Case assigner, objective Case usually follows in SVO languages) is obviated in a system which requires raising, both overt and covert, of arguments to the agreement nodes.[17]

Chomsky (1995:Section 10) considers the possibility of eliminating the Agr nodes in favor of a VP projection headed by a light V, since, he says, Case assignment is intrinsic to the heads V and T. The reduction of categories is consonant with the paring down characteristic of the minimalist program. His contemplated change from an Agr based to a multiple Spec theory retains two insights crucial to the present study: first is the unification of all Case checking phenomena as instances of Spec–head agreement, and second is the concept that DPs raise to check Case. The present study continues to use the term Agr both because it explicitly represents the two crucial insights described, and because it is commonly used in current linguistic literature. Linguists working with both the VP (e.g. Kayne 1993, Sportiche 1992) and the NP / DP (e.g. Cinque 1990, Parodi 1994) have argued for the necessity of agreement nodes.[18]

1.3.3 *Domain, chain and binding*

The notion of domain is crucial in the minimalist program to determine Case checking, licit chain formation and binding. A configuration such as (12) serves as a model for definitions of domain.

(12)

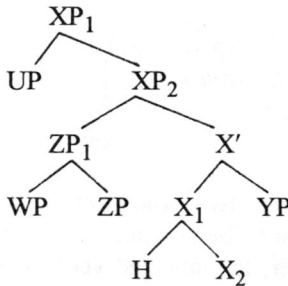

---

[17] Marantz (1995:Section 4) gives a very readable discussion of word order, pointing out how the requirement of strong nominative is a way of implementing the Extended Projection Principle requiring an explicit subject. Sportiche (1992) discusses French clitic placement and related issues in a very compatible framework.

[18] There is no difference between the terms NP and DP that is crucial to arguments or data presented in this book (except Vergnaud & Zubizarreta's distinction referred to in Chapter 6). Both terms are used, but usually NP is used in a discussion that contains material predating the common use of DP.

The *minimal domain* of X is {UP, ZP, WP, YP, H}, or everything within the maximal projection except the head and its higher projections. The *minimal complement domain* or internal domain of X is YP, that is, the internal argument of the head. The *minimal residue* of X is {UP, ZP, WP, H} or the minimal domain minus the internal domain. It is the minimal residue that serves as the *checking domain* for the verification of inflectional features. Sentence (13) demonstrates the checking domain of the verb.

(13) Marc *l*(a)   'a   lavé+*e*.
     Mark it [+fem, +acc] has washed+fem "Mark washed it".

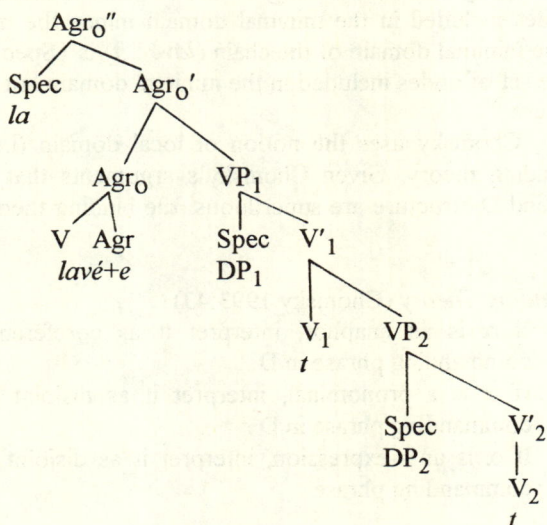

Sentence (13) demonstrates these definitions of domain for a sentence comparable to (11). The clitic *la* is feminine accusative, and in the *passé composé* the past participle must Agree in gender and number with the preceding direct object. In terms of the VP complex, the minimal complement domain of V_1 is the projection of VP_2, containing its internal but not external argument, while the checking domain of V_1 is DP_1. The DPs and V of the VP complex are required to raise in order to verify agreement features and Case marking. In terms of the Agr_0 complex, the minimal domain of Agr_0 is Spec Agr_0, V and the projection of VP_1; its checking domain is Spec Agr_0 and V. Given this checking domain of Agr_0, the object pronoun in Spec of Agr_0 must be marked with feminine singular accusative Case and the past participle in V must agree in gender and number with the preceding direct object. The proposal of an Agr_O node accounts quite simply (and in a parallel manner to Agr_S) for Case marking and past participle agreement in French.

The relations depicted in (13) represent chains linking raised elements through a path to the foot of the chain. One chain links the subject *Marc* (not shown, but in the Spec of Agr_S) to its trace in DP_1. Another chain links the direct object *la* ([+fem, +acc]) to its trace in DP_2. Clitics are overtly present in Spec Agr_O in French, whereas lexical DPs (11) raise only covertly.[19] A third chain links the past participial V to its traces in VP_2 and VP_1. The notion of domain is understood derivationally in terms of chains rather than just representationally in terms of categories. The minimal domain of a chain is the set of nodes included in the minimal domain minus the moved item and its traces. The minimal domain of the chain (*lavé ...t*) is {Spec Agr_O, DP_1, DP_2}, that is, the set of nodes included in the minimal domain but excluding the verb and its traces.[20]

Finally, Chomsky uses the notion of local domain (i.e. "D" in (14)) to restate binding theory. Given Chomsky's arguments that the notions of S-structure and D-structure are superfluous, the binding theory holds at the LF interface.

(14) *Binding Theory* (Chomsky 1993:43)

    a   If α is an anaphor, interpret it as coreferential with a c-commanding phrase in D

    b   If α is a pronominal, interpret it as disjoint from every c-commanding phrase in D

    c   If α is an r-expression, interpret it as disjoint from every c-commanding phrase.

The revisions proposed by Chomsky will be examined in the light of the constructions in French to be studied throughout the book. The present study both draws on and strengthens the theoretical framework of the minimalist program. The postulation of a VP internal subject, a Spec–head formulation of agreement, and a Larsonian VP shell is necessary for French on both empirical

---

[19] Chomsky (1991) suggests this analysis of Romance clitics. The derivation in (13) assumes a treatment of clitics along the lines of Roberge (1990), that they represent a Case spell–out licensing *pro* in argument position.

[20] Chomsky provides a guideline for evaluating the economy of a derivation by comparing shortest movement to shortest number of moves in a given configuration. Distance is not measured, however, in a given domain: "If α, β are in the same minimal domain, they are equidistant from γ" (1993:17).

and theoretical grounds (Sportiche 1988, Pollock 1989, Kayne 1993). This study will provide further support for these aspects of the minimalist program in its demonstration of the necessity of two internal Cases and their linking to specific nodes of the Larsonian shell.

1.4. *Conclusion*

This chapter has put forth the major thesis of the book, the binary hypothesis regarding internal Case and complement structure in French. This hypothesis proposes that internal argument structure and Case assignment in French are binary in nature, a limitation responsible for determining the syntax of typical transitive verbs as well as a number of constructions involving nonthematic subjects. The study thus aims to confirm the importance of syntactic considerations as well as thematic relationships in determining argument projection.

The chapter has also outlined the major presuppositions of the principles and parameters model and relevant innovations brought by the minimalist program. This program lays the groundwork for a reappraisal of Case defective constructions in French. Chapter 2 argues that there are two structural Cases in French and two linked Agr nodes. The object agreement nodes maximally allow two internal Cases and consequently no more than two internal arguments. The binary hypothesis theoretically derives from the minimalist program and empirically supports that program, as evidence throughout the book will demonstrate.

CHAPTER 2

CASE AND ARGUMENT STRUCTURE

2.0 *Introduction*

The central question posed in the first chapter concerns the determination of argument structure, the complements selected by a head. Certain theorists (e.g. Baker 1988, Belletti & Rizzi 1988, Grimshaw 1992) suggest that primitive semantic notions shape syntactic configurations and that argument structure corresponds to thematic structure. This congruence approach is theoretically appealing in its unifying the two structures and is empirically supported by the most obvious data.[1] However, Zubizarreta (1985:249) asserts that "it is not always possible to predict the syntactic frames in which the internal arguments of a verb are realized". The theta roles of *rob* are distributed differently from those of the semantically very similar *steal* (1).

(1) a   We robbed Mary of her watch.
    b   We stole the watch from Mary.

This chapter claims that a limit on the number of core internal arguments constitutes an a priori syntactic restriction on argument projection that indirectly constrains distribution of theta roles. It argues that the duality of internal Case corresponds to a parallel limit on the number of internal arguments, a linking that is empirically and theoretically motivated within the framework of the minimalist program. The duality hypothesis proposed here does not exclude the influence of thematic or lexical conceptual structure on argument structure, but focuses instead on the limitations imposed by the syntax. A first section of this chapter reviews the standard account of theta roles and argument structure. Section 2.2 discusses the standard treatment of Case before proposing an approach holding that French has two internal structural Cases. It argues that there is a theoretically necessary link between

---

[1] Newmeyer (p.c.) points out that it was long assumed that the most obvious data did not support this congruence (e.g. Chomsky 1957:Chapter 9), a fact that was taken as evidence for the autonomy of syntax.

structural Case and argument structure not previously observed. Sections 2.3–2.4 present arguments bearing out the proposal of two structural Cases in French, objective and dative. Previously unresolved questions concerning the nature of partitive Case are answered by the solution that accusative and partitive are two realizations of Case on the direct object.

2.1 *Argument structure and thematic roles*
2.1.1 *Thematic theory*
Within the generative model the area of thematic relations or theta theory deals with the basic semantic roles assigned by the head of one syntactic category to its complements, for example, by verbs to their NP arguments. A theta role may also be assigned compositionally by the VP to its subject. Jackendoff (1972) develops ideas of Gruber (1965) concerning the syntactic expression of semantic roles. These include *agent* (2a), "identified by a semantic reading which attributes to the NP will or volition toward the action expressed" (Jackendoff 1972:32); *experiencer* (2b), the human psychological focus of the verbal activity; *goal* (2c), the recipient or location of action received; and *theme* (3), the NP understood as undergoing the action or whose location is asserted;

(2) a *John* threw the ball.
    b *Mary* worries a lot.
    c John gave flowers to *Mary*.
(3) a John washed *the clothes / the dog / the baby*.
    b *Mary* arrived on time.

Jackendoff (1987:378) elucidates the place of theta roles in a later generative model pointing out that "theme, agent, etc. are not primitives of semantic theory. Rather they are relational notions defined structurally over conceptual structure".

The central principle of thematic theory has been the Theta Criterion holding that there is a unique relationship between arguments and theta roles (4).

(4) *Theta Criterion* (Chomsky 1986a:97)
    Each argument α appears in a chain containing a unique visible θ-position P, and each θ-position P is visible in a chain containing a unique argument α.

This criterion expresses the intuitive notion that each argument has one semantic role and each theta role designated by a lexical item must be assigned to an argument. Baker (1988:46) goes further in attempting to relate theta theory to syntax by proposing the UTAH (5).

(5) *Uniformity of Theta Assignment Hypothesis (UTAH)*
Identical thematic relationships between items are represented by identical structural relationships between those items at the level of D-structure.

His hypothesis proposes a one to one relationship between thematic roles and underlying syntactic (structural) relationships. He hints at a link between Case and argument structure in the Case Frame Preservation Principle (6).

(6) *Case Frame Preservation Principle* (Baker 1988:122)
A complex X^0 of category A in a given language can have at most the maximum Case assigning properties allowed to a morphologically simple item of category A in that language.

This principle limits the number of arguments in grammatical function changing constructions, but does not address limitations in absolute terms.

Specific thematic relations such as *agent, theme* have been used to discuss basic syntactic operations or constructions such as the relationship of passive and active sentences. Nevertheless, "the use of theta role labels has been criticized by researchers, primarily because of the lack of consensus concerning the appropriate set of theta roles and the criteria for determining what theta role any given argument bears" (Rappaport & Levin (1988:8).[2] Research dealing with arguments and their lexical representation has examined the interrelation of argument structure, theta roles and lexical conceptual structure in an attempt to link semantics to syntactic expression.[3] Williams (1994:26) speaks of the "incidental" use of theta terminology whose "role in

---

[2] While it might be desirable to limit the number of theta roles in order to constrain the grammar, the very flexibility of language seems to allow additional semantic relationships requiring additional theta roles. For example, Guéron (1986) proposes primary and secondary theta roles. The articles in Wilkins (1988) cover a range of theta roles.

[3] See for example, Keenan (1976), Hopper & Thompson (1980), Williams (1981, 1994), Di Sciullo & Williams (1987), Zubizarreta (1985, 1987), Hale & Keyser (1986, 1988, 1993b), Jackendoff (1987), Levin & Rappaport (1987, 1994), Safir (1987), Baker (1988), Speas (1990), DiSciullo (1991), Dowty (1991), Mithun (1991), Grimshaw (1992), Demonte (1992), Pesetsky (1995).

the theory remains to be determined" while Speas (1990:16) points out that "the role labels themselves are just convenient mnemonics for variables in particular positions in the lexical conceptual structure [...] It is quite likely that this [thematic] hierarchy derives from some principles of 'cognitive prominence', although far too little is known about lexical conceptual structures even to speculate on the nature of such principles".

Pushing even further the question of how to define theta roles Hale & Keyser (1993b:68, henceforth H&K) claim "there *are* no thematic roles. Instead there are just the relations determined by the categories and their projections". Theta roles are then an epiphenomenon resulting from the limited relations that are defined by argument projection and the syntactic principles regulating it. Presenting a convincing body of arguments for a syntactic view of lexical relational structure, Hale & Keyser elaborate a model of argument projection that is regulated by the same syntactic principles that operate in the overt syntax. They propose that structural relations (e.g. c-command, complementation) associate with the notional content of the lexical items to contribute to the semantic interpretation of the whole derivation. This can be exemplified by the semantic relation of implication embodied in the [V VP] structure "of what is commonly called the *causal* relation" (ibid.:69). They assert that the DP specifier of the VP will logically be construed as an agent of the caused action. Although H&K recognize the small inventory of theta roles (they ask "Why are there so few thematic roles?") and the parsimonious projection of arguments, they do not specifically account for a limit on the number of internal arguments.

2.1.2 *Arguments and adjuncts*

The argument structure of a verb refers to the external (e.g. subject) and internal (direct, indirect, prepositional, clausal, etc.) arguments that the verb must or may take. Williams (1981) makes that structure explicit in proposing a distinction between *external* and *internal arguments*. Discussing maximal projections of heads, he states (1981:84) "all of the arguments of that head must be specified internal to the maximal projection, except for the one external argument—that is, the item that is located external to the maximal projection but with which the maximal projection is coindexed". The most common external argument, that of agentive verbs, is the subject. Only one external argument is permitted since it is coindexed with the maximal projection, whereas the internal arguments constitute an "unordered list" (ibid., 83). The distinction of external from internal arguments is relevant in a variety of constructions (e.g. passive, causative) where the two kinds of arguments show differing distributions. "Internal arguments are lexically identified as being linked to a syntactic frame. Therefore, an internal argument must be syntactically realized. Only an external argument may remain unrealized syntactically" (Zubizarretta 1985:253).

Grimshaw (1992:7) extends Williams's and Jackendoff's discussions of argument structure by proposing an argument hierarchy, *structured a[rgument] structure*. "My proposal is that the hierarchy [(7)] is properly understood as the organizing principle of a-structures. Argument structures are constructed in accordance with the thematic hierarchy, so the structural organization of the argument array is determined by universal principles based on the semantic properties of the arguments".

(7) Agent > Experiencer > Goal / Source / Location > Theme

Williams (1994:26) points out three features characterizing the relation 'argument' of an NP to a verb: it is obligatory, unique and structurally local. The relation is obligatory in that an NP must be an argument of something, and a verb often must take an argument (intransitive and optional object verbs aside). The relation is unique in the thematic sense, "there must be an NP to fill a certain 'argument of' relation" (ibid.:27), and it is local in that internal arguments are direct complements Case marked by the verb. Although Williams is not working in the minimalist framework, his comments underline the redundancy of certain aspects of the principles and parameters model as well as the relationship of argument, theta role and Case. Williams's three features can be seen to involve the Projection Principle, the Case Filter and the Theta Criterion. The necessity of an NP to be an argument means that it must have a theta role and be Case marked. In the minimalist framework semantic feature information is part of the lexical projection and Case checking is the driving force in the derivation; so an NP's semantic role and Case are features initially provided by the selectional properties of the verb and verified by feature checking and LF interpretability. Conversely, a verb's projection is by definition its lexical legacy throughout the computation, a characteristic that obviates the Projection Principle. The uniqueness feature reduces to Full Interpretation since an NP with too few or too many interpretations would be uninterpretable.

While selected arguments are obligatory to the proper interpretation of a derivation, it is quite common for a syntactic representation to have additional optional expansions. Indeed, the supplemental clauses and phrases that can elaborate each major category are quintessential examples of the creative aspect of language. They often contrast with the selected arguments in explicit syntactic ways, and the contrast is categorized as the difference between an argument and an adjunct. For example, adjuncts resist long distance *wh* extraction (8a) whereas arguments allow it (8b).

(8) a   *Where did you wonder [why Jane spoke t]
    b   Who did you wonder [why Jane kissed t]

Syntactic tests to distinguish obligatory selected arguments on the one hand and optional adjuncts on the other exist in varying degrees of reliability and number for the major syntactic categories.[4] Nevertheless there exists a hazy area of complements, particularly PPs, whose role is somewhat compromised between obligatory and optional. A phrase that modifies another phrase must logically fit, so there are certain instances when it is difficult to distinguish arguments from adjuncts.

As for Case marking, it is traditionally assumed that internal arguments of a verb receive Case from that verb, and that the external argument receives nominative Case from tense. There are exceptions, instances in which arguments are Caseless and must seek Case elsewhere.[5] Two examples that will not be examined in this book are exceptional Case marking verbs that assign accusative Case to the lexical subject of an embedded infinitive (e.g. *want* in English or verbs of perception in French), and raising verbs whose embedded lexical subject of infinitive raises to get nominative Case in the matrix clause. This book will examine other instances of Caseless arguments and argumentless Case.

2.2 *Binary Case and argument structure*

Morphological marking is the most explicit clue to Case in French. Franks's (1995:16) position, which is adopted here, holds that:

> Morphological case is not fundamentally distinct from abstract case, but rather reflects its language-particular realization. The problem of relating abstract case to morphological case should therefore be attacked from the opposite direction. Case theory must first and foremost be able to account for morphological case properties.

---

[4] Radford (1988) devotes several chapters to this issue, using evidence such as ellipsis, coordination, anaphora and morphological affixation for the distinction in English. Many of his diagnostics are applicable to French, and other diagnostics can also be adduced for French.

[5] CP complements may be arguments of the verb, but are not usually Case marked (exceptions are discussed in Kempchinsky 1992a, Zaring 1994). Demonte (1992a) presents a class of verbs that she argues takes a prepositional accusative (a prepositionally Case marked direct argument of the verb).

The development of Case theory has taken into account Rouveret & Vergnaud's (1980:25) Case Filter requiring all lexical NPs to carry abstract Case and Vergnaud's (1985:Chapter 2) extensive discussion of the formal aspects of Case. Section 2.2.1 reviews standard assumptions concerning Case and its treatment in the minimalist program. Sections 2.2.2 and 2.2.3 propose a binary approach to Case and argument structure in French.

2.2.1 *Standard assumptions concerning Case*

It is generally assumed that abstract Case is assigned either structurally or inherently. Chomsky (1986a:193) draws the distinction between two manners of Case assignment: "we distinguish the 'structural Cases' objective and nominative, assigned in terms of S-structure position, from the 'inherent Cases' assigned at D-structure [...]. Inherent Case is associated with theta-marking while structural Case is not". According to this view certain Case assigning properties of verbs are lexically determined whereas other Cases are structurally determined. Freidin & Sprouse (1991:396) use the terms "configurational" and "lexical" rather than "structural" and "inherent" while Baker (1988:113ff.) distinguishes "structural" (e.g. nominative), "inherent" (e.g. genitive), and "semantic" (Cases which correlate consistently with theta roles, e.g. ablative in Estonian). Franks (1995:40–41) divides "default" (e.g. nominative, accusative) Case assigned at S-structure from "configurational" (e.g. dative) and "quirky" (e.g. governed instrumental) assigned at D-structure. Both Baker and Franks note that the bipartition of Case into structural and inherent does not adequately describe Case distribution in richly inflected languages.

In earlier systems the agreement features of inflection (tense) assign nominative Case, while the verb itself assigns objective Case under government. Under the minimalist program, the two structural Cases are entirely parallel: Agr_S and Agr_O are two functional categories whose role is to check nominative and objective Case respectively (Chomsky (1993:8). Case assignment is mirrored by agreement, and both are accomplished (checked) by the Spec–head relationship. For Agr_S nominative Case is mirrored by subject–verb agreement, and for Agr_O in French objective Case is mirrored by agreement of the past participle with the direct object which has overtly passed through the Spec of Agr_O (Chomsky 1993; Kayne 1989, 1993).

(9) a

$$Agr_S''$$

Spec Agr_S'

DP_{su} Agr_S TP

T Agr_S
[+nom]

b Agr_O''

Spec Agr_O'

DP_{ob} Agr_O VP

V Agr_O
[+acc]

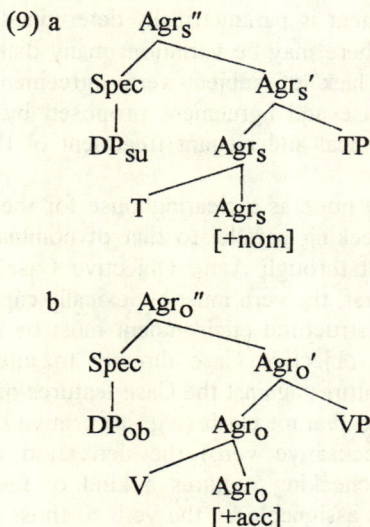

In (9a) the subject DP (which has raised from VP internal position) in the Spec is checked for nominative Case by the head Agr_S; the head agrees in number with the DP_{su} (10a). In (9b) the object DP (which has overtly raised from Spec VP_2) is checked for accusative Case by the head Agr_O; the head agrees in gender and number with the DP_{ob} (10b).

(10) a   Elle-*s*   dorm-*ent*.
        they-fem-pl   sleep-pl
        "They are sleeping".
    b   Il *les*   a   pris- *es*   [les photos].
        he them-fem-pl has   taken- fem-pl the photos
        "He has taken them [the photos]".
    c   *Madame* est mort *e*
        "Madame has died".
    d   *La glace* s'est brisé *e*.
        "The mirror broke".

The past participle agreement rule in French is reduced to Spec–head agreement of the verb in Agr_O with an A chain whose tail is in the Spec of VP_2 and which has a link in Spec Agr_O. This rule accounts for agreement with preceding direct object (transitives (10b)), agreement with unaccusatives taking *être* (10c), and many cases of *se* (10d), when the DP must be part of a chain linking Spec Agr$_O$.[6] Overt agreement is parametrically determined, so even among certain dialects of French there may be variation: many dialects ignore past participle agreement and lack of subject–verb agreement is reported.[7] The unitary treatment of Case and agreement proposed by the minimalist program furnishes an economical and elegant treatment of these phenomena.

The proposal of an object agreement node as a clearinghouse for the VP permits an account of internal Case checking parallel to that of nominative Case checking of the external argument through Agr$_S$. Objective Case can only be realized under two conditions: first, the verb must be lexically capable of assigning that Case and second, the structural environment must be met. Under this proposal a verb assigning objective Case directly to internal arguments raises to Agr$_O$ to check its features against the Case features of the raised DP object. As long as there is no feature clash (e.g. accusative Case assigned to the argument of an unaccusative verb) the derivation goes through, otherwise it does not. Case checking requires a kind of feature harmony, that is, a matching of features assignable by the verb to those of a selected complement of the verb.

Case checking also requires a linking of structural positions, the Spec VP$_1$ to the Spec Agr$_S$ and the Spec VP$_2$ to the Spec Agr$_O$. Chomsky (1995, Section 5.6) demonstrates the necessity of matching features in an example of improperly Case marked accusative subject or nominative object. These improperly marked DPs would cause the derivation to crash because their Case features would not be checked off before LF. The Case checking engine of the derivation couples with the proposed structure to engender the specificity of linking of Agr to VP. The raising thus manifests a leap-frogging pattern (e.g. the object crosses the trace of the VP internal subject) because, Chomsky (1993:19) claims, "crossing and not nesting is the only permissible option in any language". The specificity of Case to structural position is

---

[6] Kayne (1989:85) spells out a detailed analysis of past participle agreement arguing that it "must be mediated by an empty category that intervenes between the clitic or WH phrase and the past participle". Kayne (1993) discusses past participle agreement in Romance dialects that allow variation from the typical situation described here. Chomsky (1995:Section 7.3) discusses difficulties that have been pointed out in Kayne's analysis.

[7] According to an anonymous reader, Old Mines, Missouri and Ontario French show variable subject–verb agreement. In the two dialects mentioned, the agreement morphology is apparently being lost. The same reader points out that some dialects show past participle agreement with a following direct object. In these cases the agreement would obtain with covert as well as overt raising of the direct object.

demonstrated by past participle agreement in French: only the DP originating in Spec VP$_2$ passes through Agr$_O$ and triggers agreement.

2.2.2 Binary Case

The notion that binary choices are central to linguistic theory is supported by the pervasive character of this kind of duality in the language system. Early work in phonology done by members of the Prague School pointed up the importance of binary choices in the establishment of distinctive features (e.g. Trubetskoy 1949, 1968). More recently, linguistic theory has delineated *two* types of syntactic category, *functional* and *lexical*. The pivotal character of binary choices in language does not appear arbitrary either for the system itself or for its role in language acquisition, for a limitation of the grammar should facilitate the acquisition process. "By restricting variation possibilities to a finite number of parameters, each with a finite number of values, the learning problem is simplified" (Gibson & Wexler 1994:407).[8] Systemically the value of a binary limit can be demonstrated by a brief discussion of the tenet of binary branching.

Kayne (1984:Chapter 7) argues convincingly that structural representation of syntactic sequences must be limited to binary branching. He shows that only binary (or no) branching of syntactic configurations produces what he terms "unambiguous paths". Kayne (1984:131) points out that such a direct link between two nodes is necessary to the interpretation of anaphoric relations: "An anaphor that falls under the binding principles must be connected to its antecedent by an unambiguous path".

(11)a 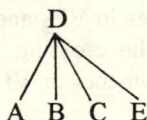   b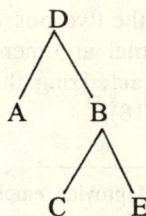

---

[8] Gibson & Wexler (1994:408) continue "Given a relatively small number of parameters—say forty—along with a least two possible values for each parameter, a space $2^{40} \approx 10^{12}$ possible grammars results. This is an enormous search problem if every parameter setting combination must be considered in turn". A value of greater than two would increase the options exponentially, but a value of one permits only one setting.

In (11a) A, B, C and E all c-command one another, but are not connected by unambiguous paths. An anaphor seeking a c-commanding antecedent would be unable to 'find' one unambiguously. In (11b), an example of only binary branching, nodes A, B, C and E can unambiguously pick out an antecedent: A and B mutually c-command each other; A c-commands C and E but is not c-commanded by them. Kayne argues that binary branching is also necessary for government relations. The restriction of X' theory to binary branching is theoretically desirable because it establishes unambiguous paths for anaphoric relations and also because it constrains the grammar.

Internal Case in French also reveals a dual pattern, since two Cases are available to verbal complements, objective and dative. Lexical DPs show no morphological mark for objective Case and are marked by *à* for dative.[9] Pronouns show a morphological Case distinction between accusative *le–la–les* "him–her–them" and dative *lui–leur* "to him–them".[10] In the minimalist framework dual Case can be understood in terms of a Larsonian shell. Chomsky (1993:13) proposes a tiered VP with three levels of arguments: the external argument in Spec VP_1 that moves to Spec Agr_S, with nominative Case; the first internal argument in Spec VP_2 that moves to Spec Agr_O, with objective Case; and the second internal argument in Spec VP_2. In French, just as objective Case targets the argument in Spec VP_2, dative Case targets the argument in Spec VP_3. Dative Case is indicated by dative *à* on the indirect object noun phrase or is morphologically realized on the clitic pronoun. In order to accommodate Case checking and dative clitics, the Agr_O node must be doubled to echo the two possible internal arguments in VP_2 and VP_3 (12). The raising of internal arguments in (12) reflects the crossing rather than nesting pattern characterizing the movement of arguments in VP_1 and VP_2 (Chomsky (1993:8, 18).[11]

---

[9] Sections 2.3 and 2.4 provide empirical justification of these two Cases; Section 2.2 furnishes the theoretical framework to accommodate the empirical data.

[10] Locative phrases have a clitic variant *y* and are sometimes obligatory (e.g. with *mettre* "to put"), but do not meet other tests of structural Case (Section 2.3, 2.4).

[11] Masullo (1992:22) proposes a double Agr_O node for Spanish. "In Spanish two Agr_O nodes should be postulated, one for accusative NPs [...] and one for dative NPs". Sportiche (1992:60) also proposes an indirect object agreement node for French, with the suggestion "to treat the dative voice not as a clitic voice but rather as the dative equivalent of Agr_O or Agr_S, i.e. as the locus of assignment or checking of dative Case, in effect then Agr_{io} (indirect object agreement)". Sportiche does not consider the specificity of Agr to VP that is discussed here.

(12)

```
            T'
          /    \
         T     Agr_O2"
             /      \
          Spec      Agr_O2'
                  /      \
             Agr_O2      Agr_O3"
                       /      \
                     Spec     Agr_O3'
                            /      \
                        Agr_O3     VP*
```

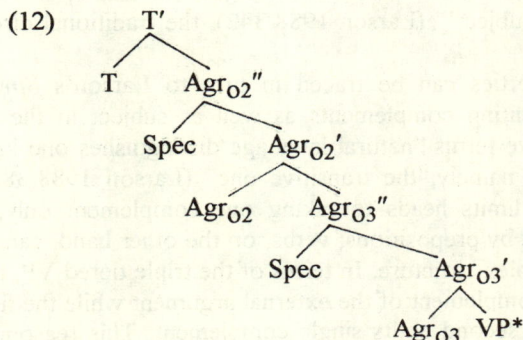

The specificity of VP tier to corresponding Agr is guaranteed on both syntactic and semantic grounds. Given minimalist assumptions, the crossing pattern of raising is required. As the discussion of objective and nominative Case above has pointed out, the Agr nodes are in a sense 'programmed' to check a specific Case. For example, it is the strong nominative feature of tense (which raises to Agr_S) that forces raising of the nominative subject in French and English (the overt manifestation of the Extended Projection Principle in those languages). Furthermore, considerations of economy can be adduced to support the specificity of movement. Since the grammar evaluates every derivation in terms of the overall computation, and since "two targets of movement are equidistant if they are in the same minimal domain" (Chomsky 1993:18), only the crossing pattern provides an equally short distance for all three DPs that are raised from the triple tiered VP. Each DP raises to the closest unfilled Spec of Agr position. The semantic reasons for the specificity are examined in the next section.

2.2.3 Binary argument structure

The minimalist program provides an account of Case because it uniformly treats all instances of structural Case as Spec–head agreement. This proposal accommodates Case checking through the Larsonian shell with its specific links to the Agr nodes, it motivates movement in terms of economy of derivation, and it explains parametric differences in word order as a function of covert or overt raising. The syntactic cohesion of this model is complemented by the semantic advantage advanced by the Larsonian approach. On semantic grounds the c-command relations imposed by the Larsonian shell predict the predicational properties of the triple tier VP. Just as the traditional VP (here VP_2 and VP_3) is predicated of the external argument (here in Spec VP_1), the verb plus indirect object (here in Spec VP_3) is "predicated of an 'inner subject'" (Larson 1988:342), the traditional direct object (here in Spec VP_2).

The predicational properties can be traced in turn to Larson's *Single Complement Hypothesis* limiting complements as well as subject in the X' expansion to one. In intuitive terms "natural language distinguishes one kind of relation as fundamental, namely, the transitive one" (Larson 1988:381). This hypothesis essentially limits heads to taking one complement only, a characteristic well illustrated by prepositions; verbs, on the other hand, can be associated with a more complex structure. In terms of the triple tiered VP, the traditional predicate is the complement of the external argument while the first internal argument takes the second as its single complement. This reasoning limits the number of internal arguments then to two.[12] The specificity of agreement node to VP tier is not to be seen simply as a fortuitous response to the syntactic necessity of convergence; the specificity has structural properties that impinge on the interpretation of the arguments and their relationship to one another as well as to the verb. The number of agreement nodes could not then be multiplied indefinitely; they are theoretically limited. The constructions examined throughout the book will corroborate the importance of the Larsonian structure in a nonarbitrary manner.

The theoretical linking of agreement node to VP tier raises again the questions posed in Chapter 1, repeated here.

(13) a   Is there a link between potential Case and argument position?
     b   Can either Case or argument be missing?
     c   Is the projection potential limited in any way?

The syntactic and semantic justification for the linking discussed above lead to an affirmative answer to (13a). As for (13b), while selectional properties of a verb should assure that its arguments get Case, there exist defective syntactic configurations where a selected argument doesn't get Case or where Case is assigned to an unselected argument.[13] It is these configurations that will be

---

[12] Hale & Keyser (1993b:67) describe this consequence of X' theory in terms of unambiguous projection: "The theory of grammar does not include a stipulation to the effect that all branching must be binary [...] merely that projection must be unambiguous". See also Kayne (1994:30, 136).

[13] Franks (1995:31) notes that in certain instances Slavic structural Case represents a thematic tie between a verb and its argument and in other instances Case is strictly configurational. "The default accusative, however, arises on arguments of transitive verbs

examined in detail in the following chapters, for they will bear out an affirmative answer to (13c).

Given the arguments presented for single complements, the answer to (13c) should theoretically be affirmative. However, the difficulty of distinguishing arguments from adjuncts has contributed to the perception voiced by Williams concerning the indeterminate number of internal arguments. The specificity of Agr to VP nodes argued for above implies that the number of arguments allowed should be linked to the number of Cases available: extra arguments could not be projected without Cases available for them. This line of reasoning leads to two conclusions for French, an affirmative answer to (13c), and a privileged status for accusative and dative Case. The present study excludes from consideration prepositionally governed arguments that are selected by the verb and Case marked inherently, and CP arguments that are not Case marked.[14] It will indeed be argued that accusative and dative are privileged structural Cases in French, linked inextricably to potential argument positions.

Although PP arguments are outside the scope of this study, a few observations will indicate that they might also support the proposal put forth here. The exclusion of multiple accusatives or datives should not entail the impossibility of an indeterminate number of PP arguments. However, it appears that even PP arguments respect a kind of dual limit. Informal surveys of French verbs taking PP arguments show a marked preference for no more than two complements. Willems (1981:87) notes that verbs that show the *construction multiple* fall into two groups: 241 verbs are of the type V+NP_1+à NP_2 (e.g. *donner le livre à Marie*) and 204 verbs are of the type V+NP_1+de NP_2 (e.g. *recevoir un livre de Marie*). There are no examples of V+NP_1+P NP_2+P NP_3 (+P NP_4 etc.). Likewise, of the 750 verbs listed by Zamir et al. (1992) only seven (all of which contain intrinsic clitics) appear to select more than two arguments.[15] A related set of evidence involves variable

---

with open case features and on nonargument time and distance phrases with potentially all classes of verbs".

[14] An example parallel to the prepositionally governed arguments for highly inflected languages would be quirky inherent Cases governed by certain verbs. For Slavic languages Franks (1995:30–41) privileges accusative and dative as structural Cases of V: accusative is assigned to sisters of [–N]^0 categories and dative to sisters of [V']. Instrumental is assigned structurally to sisters of VP.

[15] The seven include mostly pronominals: *s'accrocher avec qn sur qch, se brouiller avec qn pour qch, se confesser de qch à qn, se décharger de qch sur qn, s'en référer à qch, s'en revenir de qch, en vouloir à qn de qch* "to hook up with s.o. on s.t.; to break up with s.o.

verbs of the *spray / load* type; while they allow variable syntactic position for a given semantic role, they seem to obey the binary limit (e.g. *rembourser qn de qch / qch à qn; délivrer qch à qn / qn de qch* "to reimburse s.o. with s.t. / s.t. to s.o.; to deliver s.t. to s.o / s.o. from s.t"). Even PP arguments seem to be limited in number to two complements, a fact that might be accounted for by assuming that the triple tier VP limits internal arguments to two whether they are Case marked structurally or by a preposition.

Binary internal Case entails a corollary limit on internal argument projection. Theoretically, the limitation to two internal arguments is implicit in much linguistic work.[16] Indeed, a limitation on the number of internal arguments at once describes the observed generalization that ditransitive verbs maximally select two arguments and provides a principle for constraining the syntactic expression of thematic relations. This limitation, proposed here only for French (but very possibly available in other languages), requires binary internal argument structure. The present study will bear out this proposal in examining constructions where the internal arguments are limited to two whether or not the verb assigns two internal Cases. These constructions permit up to but no more than two internal arguments. Crucial to the testing of this hypothesis is the existence of verbs whose Case assigning properties are defective, verbs which are incapable of assigning accusative or dative Case.

2.3 *Structural objective Case*

It is generally assumed that direct objective Case is structural, that is, configurationally defined (cf. Belletti 1981, Chomsky 1986a, Baker 1988). Like nominative Case it does not require an overt preposition, it applies in default configurational situations, and in French it is manifested on clitic pronouns (Suñer 1988). In addition to marking the direct object of transitive verbs, it applies in instances of exceptional Case marking in causative constructions and in raising from small clauses.[17] In minimalist terms,

---

about s.t.; to confess s.t. to s.o.; to unburden s.t. onto s.o.; to refer to s.t. about s.t.; to be put aright from s.t.; to hold a grudge against s.o. about s.t".

[16] Emonds (1985:31) alludes to this possibility. "I have no stake in limiting the number of internal arguments to two. Possibly three or even more are sometimes required, but I know of no absolutely convincing cases such as a transitive verb with two idiomatic prepositional complement phrases". See also Burzio (1986:186).

[17] These constructions have been extensively documented in the linguistic literature; examples of configurational accusative and partitive in causative and small clauses are shown in (i) and (ii) respectively.

(i) a   Paul fait courir Marie. Paul la fait courir. "Paul makes Mary / her run".

objective Case targets the Spec of VP_2 and is checked by Agr_{O2}. The status of objective Case appears straightforward from a theoretical perspective, but some work has pointed up questions regarding accusative and partitive Case, both of which are objective. It is essential to clarify the nature of objective Case for a study of nonthematic subject constructions since Case is suspended in these environments.

In the following sections partitive and accusative Cases are shown to be two variants of direct object Case checked through the Agr_{O2} node. The following sections argue that partitive is a DP internal redemptive Case, available to save a derivation lacking accusative Case, while accusative Case is the usual objective Case. The reexamination of partitive Case is organized as follows: Section 2.3.1 looks at the definiteness effect, Section 2.3.2 presents diagnostics for distinguishing partitive from accusative, and Section 2.3.3 shows that accusative and partitive Case are both noninherent.

2.3.1 *Accusative, partitive and the definiteness effect*

The definiteness restriction refers to the stipulation that presentational existential sentences (e.g. *there is...*) require that the postverbal DP be determined by an indefinite, a quantifier or a cardinal number, that is, definite DPs are excluded from this position. The presupposition of existence and uniqueness entailed by definites restricts their use in these existential constructions which *assert* (and do not *presuppose*) the existence of a partially specified set. The restriction may be more aptly described as a specificity effect since it is more accurately *specific* DPs that are prohibited.[18] Two apparent exceptions to this restriction are definite DPs with a list reading (14a) and those that are nonspecific qualified indefinites (14b).

(14) a   Qui est dans la cuisine? Il y a la mère, le père, et le fils.
       "Who's in the kitchen?
       There's the mother, the father and the son".

---

    b   Paul considère Marie intelligente. Paul la considère intelligente.
         "Paul considers Mary / her intelligent".
   (ii) a Paul en fait courir plusieurs. "Paul makes several of them run".
       b   Paul en considère certains intelligents.
         "Paul considers some of them intelligent".

[18] Lasnik notes a similar phenomenon in Turkish pointed out by Enç (1991): "Specific objects are accusative, whereas nonspecifics have no overt Case marker" (Lasnik 1992:398). The feature [definite] is the crucial distinction between accusative and partitive in French, as the object clitic diagnostic shows. See Kayne (1975:110) for a discussion of this distinction and Longobardi (1994) for a discussion of reference.

　　b　Il y a la plus merveilleuse table chez l'antiquaire.
　　　　"There's the most wonderful table at the antique dealer's".

Milsark (1976:127) describes the 'list' (14a) as a hypothetical set projected by the members of the list. The qualifiers as in (14b) include superlative, restrictive relative, *unique, same,* etc.[19]

Belletti (1988) and Lasnik (1992, 1994) discuss the problematic nature of partitive Case.[20] Belletti (1988:2) assumes that while nominative and accusative are structural Cases "partitive Case is an inherent Case". She uses Chomsky's distinction between inherent and structural Case (cf. Section 2.2.1); structural Case is assigned configurationally at S-structure, while inherent Case, associated with theta marking, is assigned at D-structure. The distinction is different under the minimalist program since there are no levels of D or S-structure; structural Case is checked off by Agr_O whereas inherent Case is checked off by an inherent Case marker such as a preposition. Belletti convincingly argues that unaccusative verbs (including *be*) appear with partitive Case in a variety of languages, and thereby she accounts for a broad range of data including the definiteness effect noted in existential constructions with expletives. She maintains (1988:5–6) that definite determiners are incompatible with partitive Case, "given our interpretation of partitive Case as implying a reading of the NP to which it is associated as 'part of a set'". Furthermore, her proposal of partitive Case eliminates the need to assume transmission of nominative Case from subject to postverbal noun phrase in expletive constructions.[21]

Lasnik (1992, 1994) also argues for Case assignment over Case transmission in expletive constructions and suggests that the difference between structural and inherent assignment may be parametrically determined. He provides additional evidence to support Belletti's proposal of partitive Case and her rejection of Case transmission in expletive constructions. After discussing extensively the distinction between structural and inherent Case, he concludes (1992:401) that "it is difficult to find facts internal to Italian (or to

---

[19] The set may contain a single member as in (i), cited by Postal (1986:345).
　　(i)　Il me reste vous. "There remains to me you".
[20] Belletti & Rizzi (1988) propose that accusative may exceptionally be either structural or inherent; this proposal is addressed in Chapter 4. Chomsky (1995) discusses the Belletti and Lasnik proposals.
[21] Cf. Chomsky (1986a:94) "it follows from the visibility condition that an expletive element linked to a non-Case marked argument must have Case. The argument must have Case transferred to it by the linked expletive if it is to receive a θ-role, so that the expletive element must be in a Case-marked position".

English) to determine which of the two general approaches discussed above provides the appropriate characterization of partitive Case assignment in those languages, particularly since neither language provides any overt morphological indication". Section 2.3 provides morphological evidence from French that clarifies the characterization of partitive and the nature of objective Case.

Generally, French data support most aspects of Belletti's proposals concerning partitive Case. However, in contradiction to Belletti's and Lasnik's assumptions regarding the structural vs. inherent distinction, morphological inflection and Case distribution indicate that partitive Case is not completely distinct from accusative, nor is it inherent. Accusative Case, while usually linked to the direct object of the verb, is impossible in certain environments whereas partitive Case (also structurally limited to the direct object) is grammatical in those same environments. The reconsideration of objective Case presented below proposes that partitive Case, always characterized by the preposition *de*, can 'save' a derivation lacking accusative Case, because the indefinite–quantificational structure of the DP manifesting partitive Case provides sufficient agreement marking to permit the noun phrase not to move despite a lack of accusative Case.

2.3.2 *Morphological diagnostics and Case assignment*

Since accusative and partitive Case both appear on the direct object of the verb, the major distinction between them is that partitive can only be indefinite, i.e. subject to the definiteness restriction. There is no way to distinguish accusative from partitive Case in the context of normal transitive verbs. The only context where the difference is not neutralized is that of existential sentences. The term 'partitive' is used here only in the sense of Belletti (1988) with respect to Case marking. It overlaps with but is not equivalent to the term 'partitive' meaning part of a whole, quantified; this term may be applied to both definite and indefinite DPs (cf. Giusti 1991b, Lobeck 1993).

Partitive Case in French, as it shows up in existential sentences, is always indicated by the indefinite, often accompanied by quantifiers. Indefinite determiners and quantifiers are always followed by *de*, either overt or covert. Partitive *de* is not overt with cardinal numbers and certain quantifiers, as, for example, in *une pomme* "an apple", *plusieurs hommes* "several men" or with pronominal *en*.[22] This lack of overt *de* with partitive is similar to dative *à* that

---

[22] Quebec French does not include the overt *de*:

   (i)   J'en ai pris une, pomme. "I took one of them, apple".

is not overt with clitic pronouns (e.g. *lui, leur* "to her / him, them"). The prepositions show up, though, in dislocation structures.[23] Giusti (1991b:453), following Belletti, argues that prepositional *de* assigns Case in partitive constructions: "indefinite quantifiers assign partitive Case to their complement NP". Partitive Case becomes significant when accusative Case fails, targeting the Spec VP_2 as does accusative Case, and thus rescuing the objective noun phrase. Partitive Case, while checked in the same manner as accusative, is not assigned by the verb, but is a DP internal Case assigned by *de*. The role of quantification and the internal structure of the DP are related issues that have been profitably explored by several linguists (see Milner 1978, Tellier 1991, Valois 1991, Tellier & Valois 1993).

Because partitive is mutually exclusive with definite, there are three categories of morphological marks—determiners, pronouns and agreement—which serve to delineate accusative and partitive in French. Bare noun phrases are usually ungrammatical in French; the noun phrase may be determined either by a definite determiner (e.g. definite article or demonstrative) or an indefinite determiner (e.g. indefinite article or quantifier).[24] This same alternation occurs in the pronominal system, with the definite pronouns *le (m) / la (f) / les (pl)* correlating with acccusative noun phrases and indefinite *en* corresponding with partitive noun phrases. Finally, the accusative / partitive distinction partially shows up in the agreement of the past participle which must accord with a preceding clitic direct object in gender and number if it is accusative, but not partitive. Both definite and partitive DPs are acceptable with the accusative assigning transitive verbs (15).

(15) a Jean a rendu *la cassette*.
        "John gave back the cassette".
     b Jean *l'*a rendu*e*.
        "John gave it back".
     c Jean a rendu *plusieurs cassettes*.
        "John gave back several cassettes".

Tranel (1992:274–278) discusses grammaticality judgments of several variants of this construction in continental and Quebec French.

[23] Examples of right dislocation are given below.
  (i) Je lui ai donné le bouquin, à elle. "I gave her the book, to her".
  (ii) J'en ai pris une, de pommes. "I took one, of [the] apples".

[24] Idiomatic expressions constitute an exception permitting bare noun phrases, for example, *rendre justice, porter plainte, avoir faim, porter assistance, avoir tort* "to render justice, bring complaint, be hungry, bring assistance, be wrong".

Cassette is a feminine noun which triggers the final *-e* agreement marker on the participle (15b).[25] Both partitive and accusative Case are found on direct objects as Belletti points out. Determiner and pronoun choice act as diagnostics to discern accusative from partitive Case assignment in French existential sentences.

2.3.3 *Partitive as the redemptive objective Case*

Belletti proposes that partitive is an inherent Case assigned by unaccusative verbs. Implicit in her position is the claim that partitive is a distinct Case governed by certain verbs (here unaccusatives) much as instrumental is governed by a class of verbs in Slavic. She does not deal with instances of partitive in other nonaccusative environments such as presentational passive and middle voice constructions. This section argues for a different analysis, that partitive and accusative are but two Case realizations of the direct object of the verb. Since the distinction between them is neutralized in the context of accusative verbs, even in exceptional Case marking, the only environment where a difference between them shows up is when accusative Case is suspended (passive, middle voice, unaccusative). In these environments with an expletive subject, partitive is grammatical whereas accusative isn't.

The crucial piece of evidence that Belletti uses to argue for the inherent character of partitive Case is its inability to Case mark the subject of a small clause. As footnote 17 has noted, this evidence does not hold for French because partitive is assigned in the same configurationally determined situations as accusative, namely in causative and small clause constructions.[26]

(16) a   Paul *la / en* fait courir *certains* .
      "Paul makes *her / certain of them* run".

---

[25] If the feminine *cassettes* are partitive there is no past participle agreement in French (i).

     (i)   Jean en a rendu_ plusieurs. "John gave back several of them".

Italian *ne* does require agreement of the past participle, unlike French. It appears that in Italian the past participle can inherit the features although they are not morphologically spelled out, whereas in French the explicit features are necessary to trigger the agreement.

[26] Zagona (p.c.) notes that sentences such as (16c) (her example) provide strong evidence against an inherent analysis of partitive. In this sentence *se faire* acts as an unaccusative and can only assign partitive Case. Animate partitive DPs are more natural in this construction (16 d,e). This fact is probably related to the feature of "control" discussed by Authier & Reed.

b Paul *la / en* considère *certains* intelligent(e)(s).
   "Paul considers *her / certain of them* intelligent".
c IL s'est fait vendre *beaucoup de jupes*.
   "There were a lot of skirts sold".
d IL se fait écraser *de nombreux chiens* dans cette rue.
   "There are numerous dogs that are run over in this street".
e IL se fait avorter *très peu de femmes* au Pérou.
   "There are few women who get abortions in Peru".

Both accusative and partitive DPs can appear in these objective Case configurations.[27] Since partitive is indistinguishable from accusative in these constructions, it must not be a distinct inherent Case. Other standard structural vs. inherent tests indicate that partitive is a structural Case: it has a corresponding clitic *en*, cannot be deleted in conjoined DPs, and doesn't persist in nominalizations.[28]

Another disadvantage of Belletti's treatment of partitive as inherent is that it cannot account for the partitive Case of other nonaccusative constructions. These constructions indicate that partitive is a configurationally checked Case which is not inherently assigned by the verb. First, the distinction between partitive and accusative is neutralized in all contexts where an accusative Case assigner is available. In these instances objective Case is configurationally determined; in minimalist terms, the definite or indefinite (partitive) DP originates in Spec VP_2 and is checked for Case in Agr_{O2}. An inherent

---

[27] Belletti (1988:29) gives examples of ungrammatical partitive (i) vs. grammatical accusative (ii) in small clauses in Italian.

(i) *Studenti ne consideravo [_ intelligenti]. "Students *ne* I considered intelligent".
(ii) Consideravo gli studenti intelligenti. "I considered the students intelligent".

The problem with this contrast does not simply seem to be that of accusative vs. partitive since not all the quantified partitives are ungrammatical (cf. (16)). It may be related to a sort of indefiniteness restriction (cf. (iii)).

(iii) ?Du pain est sur la table. "Some bread is on the table".

[28] See Section 2.4 for a more detailed discussion of these diagnostics. (i) demonstrates the optionality of deletion of true prepositions vs. the obligatoriness of Case prepositions (cf. (22)); partitive *de* cannot be deleted in (i). (ii) illustrates the persistence of true prepositions in nominalizations (cf. (27)) vs. the loss of partitive prepositions (iib); the definite article cannot be deleted (iia) after the genitive *de*, whereas the partitive *de* must be deleted after genitive *de*.

(i) IL y a du pain et *(du)/*le fromage. "There is bread and cheese".
(ii) a On a construit la ville / la construction de *(la) ville.
        "One constructed the city / the construction of the city".
     b On a dégusté du vin / la dégustation de (*du) vin
        "We tasted the wine / the tasting of wine".

treatment of partitive would have to distinguish between the 'accusative partitive' and the 'unaccusative partitive' (both of which are morphologically indistinguishable). Second, constructions other than unaccusatives in which accusative Case is defective show the same pattern of Case marking as unaccusatives: passive and middle voice impersonal constructions allow partitive but not accusative Case.[29] Lasnik (1992:397) notes that "a passive verb loses its ability to assign accusative Case but retains its ability to assign partitive Case" (17)–(18).[30]

(17) a Marc a vendu ces jupes
        "Marc sold these skirts".
     b Ces jupes ont été vendues.
        "These skirts were sold".
     c IL a été vendu beaucoup de jupes.
        "There were many skirts sold".
     d IL en a été vendu beaucoup.
        "There were a lot of them sold".
     e *IL les a été vendues.
        "There were them sold".
(18) a Ces jupes se sont bien vendues.
        "These skirts sold well". [middle voice]
     b IL s' est vendu beaucoup de jupes.
        "There were many skirts sold".
     c IL s'en / *les est [beaucoup] vendu.
        "There were [lots] of them/them sold".

Vendre is an accusative Case assigner whose accusative Case is suspended in passive and middle *se* in (17)–(18). *Vendre* can assign objective Case to

---

[29] The suspension of accusative Case in passive constructions has been generally accepted (Kayne 1975:245). There exist rare exceptions to this rule. Postal (1985:48, 64) cites (i).

  (i) Il le sera dit, que le président est malade.
  "There will be said it, that the president is sick".

[30] Lasnik says it is unclear if English permits partitive Case marking in passives, citing (i).

  (i) *There has been put a book on the table.

He concludes that English differs from Italian in that the former can only assign accusative (and loses this ability in passive), whereas the latter can assign both accusative and partitive. Lasnik fails to note the grammaticality of (ii).

  (ii) There has been a book put on the table.

Yet he actually accounts for it earlier in his article (p. 389) in proposing that *be* assigns partitive Case as do unaccusatives.

definite or partitive in a transitive sentence, yet when accusative Case is suspended (e.g. passive, middle voice) only partitive Case is possible. A uniform treatment of the direct object requires that *les jupes* originate in the same structural position (Spec VP_2) in passive as well as active sentences and that it be checked for Case in the same position (Spec Agr_{O2}). There is no theoretical justification for attributing to a passive verb the ability to assign an inherent partitive Case only under the condition that accusative Case be suspended. Belletti's proposal of distinct inherent partitive Case is not supported.

Finally, some marginal examples of impersonal intransitives containing i[nverted] subjects suggest that partitive is not a Case assigned inherently by certain verbs, but rather a Case that saves a derivation with its built in preposition. Certain linguists have cited intransitive presentationals showing the definiteness effect (19)–(20).[31]

(19) a   Beaucoup de linguistes mangent dans ce restaurant.
        "Lots of linguists eat in this restaurant".
     b   IL mange beaucoup de linguistes dans ce restaurant.
        "There are eating a lot of linguists in this restaurant".
     c   IL en mange beaucoup dans ce restaurant.
        "There are a lot of them eating in this restaurant".
(20) a   IL en travaillait beaucoup chez Renault.
        "There were a lot of them working at the Renault factory".
     b   IL lui en téléphonait de nombreuses à cette époque.
        "There were numerous [women] phoning him then".

(19) and (20) suggest by the *en* diagnostic that the i-subjects of intransitive verbs carry partitive Case. It is impossible that partitive Case is assigned inherently since intransitive verbs assign only nominative.[32] Partitive Case could not be linked with theta role assignment as it should be if it were inherent. If, on the other hand, partitive is a redemptive Case that saves a 'direct object' meeting the definiteness condition, these as well as the earlier examples discussed are accounted for.[33] I-subjects in intransitive

---

[31] Pollock (1978:95) and Legendre (1989:761) furnish examples (19) and (20) respectively, and discussion of this sentence type. These sentences are considered very marginal by many speakers. Chapter 3 and the Appendix address the issue of grammaticality judgments.

[32] Intransitives may exceptionally assign accusative Case (cf. Rothstein 1992 and Chapter 3 of this book). Kayne (1993:12) also points this out: "Unergatives are covert transitives".

[33] This treatment is at odds with Belletti's (1988:22) suggestion that in French "nominative Case is *assigned* to the preverbal subject position (filled by a null expletive element) and

presentational sentences act like the direct objects of (19)–(20) although they are subjects of the intransitive verbs. The i-subject appears to act like a direct object marked by partitive Case.[34] The crucial point is that the partitive preposition suffices as a Case marker in these instances. Partitive is not assigned by the verb, but is checked structurally.

If partitive is not an inherent Case distinct from accusative, then unaccusative verbs cannot be inherent partitive assigners as Belletti claims. Unaccusative verbs such as *arriver* "to arrive" accept an internal argument with partitive Case (the subject position realized with a nominative expletive *IL* in impersonal presentational (21a, b); alternatively, the internal argument moves to the nonthematic subject position, with nominative Case (21c).

(21) a IL est arrivé plusieurs / *les Anglais
         "There arrived several / the Englishmen".
      b IL en est arrivé plusieurs.
         "There arrived several of them".
      c Plusieurs / Les Anglais sont arrivés.
         "Several / The Englishmen arrived".

With unaccusative verbs definite (accusative) DPs are ungrammatical in postverbal position (21a), although definite DPs are acceptable in subject position where they can carry nominative Case (21c). Chapter 3 presents evidence that the partitive DP in these constructions is indeed in the same configurational position as accusative arguments in transitive constructions.

The data presented above in both transitive and nonaccusative constructions indicates that partitive and accusative Case can both appear on direct object DPs. In minimalist terms these DPs originate in Spec VP$_2$ and raise to Spec Agr$_{O2}$ to be checked for Case. In order to understand how the two Cases could be variants, it is necessary to consider the question of nonmatching features. *Nonmatching* contrast with *mismatching* features in that the former are not identical but are compatible, whereas the latter are incompatible and cause a derivation to crash. Partitive and accusative are nonmatched, whereas nominative and accusative are mismatched (Chomsky 1991). The actual mechanism for the matching might be conceived of as in Franks (1995:Chapter 2), with features designated as [+/–] or alternately with

---

realized on the VP adjoined postverbal NP". The evidence indicates that unlike Italian, French inverted subjects carry only partitive Case when there is a nominative expletive.

[34] It would seem that this Case is checked in Agr$_{O2}$, but a thorough investigation is outside the scope of this study.

unspecified values. The feature [+accusative] would entail (perhaps filled in by a general principle) [–nominative, u partitive] where u is an unspecified value. The interpretable feature [+/– definite] may be marked positive with accusative Case. Usually the feature partitive, assigned by the built in preposition *de*, is not significant for Case marking.[35] By general principles, [+partitive] would entail [–definite]. In the case of the nonaccusative constructions examined, the verb raised to Agr_{O2} has accusative suspended, so its features would include [–accusative, u partitive, u definite]. The partitive DP [u accusative, +partitive, –definite] would make a nonmatch, not a mismatch, and in a situation where no other Case were available, partitive could here save the derivation by letting it pass. A definite DP that failed to pass could raise to Agr_S with nominative Case (a last resort). A partitive DP that succeeded in checking its features would procrastinate. "LF movement is 'cheaper' than overt movement [...] The system tries to reach PF 'as fast as possible', minimizing overt operations (Chomsky 1993:30–31). In the example of unaccusative impersonal sentences, the direct object does not raise overtly in the syntax as an economy measure.

In contrast to partitive, accusative is the usual variant of objective Case. Partitive is not then a different Case than accusative, but rather a variant objective Case which can save a direct object when accusative Case is unavailable. A DP checking Case in the Spec of Agr_{O2} can be redeemed by partitive Case if the structural position and the definiteness requirement are met.

2.4 *Structural dative Case*

Empirically, the data presented above indicates that objective (accusative / partitive) is an internal structural Case in French. Several kinds of evidence indicate that dative Case in French is likewise determined structurally (cf. Kayne 1975, Vergnaud 1974, Zaring 1991, Demonte 1992). First, the clitic diagnostic for accusative has a parallel for dative Case (Suñer 1988). Zaring (1991) emphasizes that only direct and indirect objects (as opposed to true prepositional complements) have clitic variants and that nonclitic (tonic) pronouns are ungrammatical with accusative or dative. Dative indirect object

---

[35] Thus partitive 'coexists' with the other Cases *nominative, accusative, dative, oblique*, again suggesting that it is not a unique and separate Case.

    (i) Des femmes (*nominative*) nous ont parlé. "Some women talked to us".

    (ii) Marc a vu des femmes. (*accusative*). "Mark saw some women".

    (iii) Marc a parlé à des femmes (*dative*). "Mark spoke to some women".

    (iv) Marc est sorti avec des femmes (*oblique*). "Mark went out with some women".

status is indicated by the presence of *à* with a full noun phrase or the dative clitic in the pronominal form.[36] The preposition *à*, as *de*, acts as a semantically empty Case marker in many contexts ranging from noun compounding to possessives. It is assumed in this study that the preposition *à* here is simply a Case marker correlate to the morphology of the dative clitic. As argued above, it is the Agr_{O3} node that checks dative Case (Chomsky 1995:fn 76).

Second, Vergnaud (1974) and Kayne (1975) cite two other diagnostics. While true prepositons need not be repeated in conjunctions (22a), Case marking prepositions (22b) must be. The preposition *à* (22b) must be a Case preposition. The second diagnostic is that *tous* stranding is acceptable with dative *à*, but not with true prepositions (22c–d).

(22) a Ils se sont assis sur la table et (sur) les chaises.
      "They sat on the table and (on) the chairs".
   b Ils ont parlé à Marie et au / *le directeur.
      "They spoke to Mary and to / the director".
   c *Ces femmes avec qui j'ai parlé (avec) toutes
      "These women with whom I spoke (with) all"
   d Ces femmes à qui j'ai parlé à toutes
      "These women to whom I spoke to all"

Third, causative constructions demonstrate that dative Case is a function of structural configuration, for the embedded subject appears as a matrix dative in the presence of an embedded object (23b), but is accusative with embedded intransitives (23a).

(23) a Marie a fait travailler Jean.
      "Mary had John work".
   b Marie a fait réparer la voiture à Jean.
      "Mary had John repair the car".

Reed (1991:342) proposes that *faire* enters into a "verbal government chain" which as a unit assigns Case to the arguments of the embedded verb.

---

[36] Kayne (1975) points out the distinction between dative *à* + NP which corresponds to clitic *lui* (i) versus nondative *à* which requires a tonic pronoun (ii).
   (i)   Je [lui] donne le livre à Pauline [*à elle]. "I give the book to Pauline [her]".
   (ii) Je [*lui] pense à Pauline [à elle]. "I think about Pauline [her]".
Sachs (1992:89) proposes the *Lui Principle* using thematic roles to predict cliticization of *à* NP when "the argument is a demoted logical subject or [...] outranked by an agent / source". *Parler* outranks *lui* with an agent subject, whereas *penser* has an experiencer subject.

"Whenever a complex verb is formed, *faire* and the embedded verb are hypothesized to become a true syntactic unit with a single Case frame __ acc __(dat) which as a single constituent assigns Case to the embedded arguments".

A related phenomenon is the variability of accusative / dative cliticization with transitive (24a–b) and unergative (24c–d) constructions discussed by Authier & Reed (1991).

(24) a   Je lui ai fait manger des épinards.
         "I had him (dat) eat the spinach".
     b   Je l'ai fait manger des épinards.
         "I had him (acc) eat the spinach".
     c   Ça lui a fait récriminer de plus belle.
         "That made him (dat) complain even more".
     d   Ça l'a fait récriminer de plus belle.
         "That made him (acc) complain even more".

The determination of Case here is not a function of the selectional properties of the embedded verb or of *faire*. The choice of accusative or dative— correlating with direct or indirect causation is due, they argue, to the semantic feature [+/–Control]. This evidence argues for an analysis of dative as a structural and not inherent Case.[37]

Fourth, there exist verbs which usually take one complement (25a), but may take two; when they have two arguments, the second one becomes dative (25b).

(25) a   Jean paie l'addition / le serveur.
         "John pays the check / the waiter".
     b   Jean paie l'addition au serveur.
         "John pays the check to the waiter".

The Case grid of these verbs is clearly distinct from the theta grid since the same theta role may receive different Cases.

Fifth, adjectives and deverbal nominals indicate that dative Case is not inherent. Dative clitics with *être* + adjective must be theta marked compositionally, not by the verb alone.

---

[37] They point out that ergatives are ungrammatical with dative because these verbs intrinsically lack the feature [Control] and are therefore associated with direct causation.

(26) Il lui est difficile de reconnaître ce problème.
   "It's difficult for him to recognize this problem".

The dative DP does not receive a theta role directly from the verb, and therefore cannot be considered to be inherently Case marked. Furthermore, if dative were inherent, it should persist in nominalizations as in (27).

(27) a Pierre polémique contre la guerre.
        "Peter polemicizes against war".
     b la polémique contre la guerre
        "the polemic against the war"

The impossibility of dative Case in nominalizations (28b) corroborates its structural nature, for only inherent Case persists in these structures (Masullo 1992).[38]

(28) a On [lui] coupe les chevev : à Paul
        "We cut [his] Paul's hair".
     b *la coupe de cheveux à Paul
        "Paul's haircut"

Finally, nonlexical (affected) datives—indirect object clitics not subcategorized by the verb (Authier & Reed 1992, Branchadell 1992)—cannot be assigned Case inherently. Their distribution can be explained by assuming that in these instances dative Case is structural but not inherent. The analysis is supported as well by diachronic evidence. Arteaga (1995) argues that Old French data support a similar structure for the dative in Old French. She shows how this analysis can account for two variants, the double object dative (like the English counterpart) and the verb-second (fronted) dative.

   The empirical evidence clearly supports the proposal that both dative and objective are structural Cases in French. The theoretical analysis argued for in Section 2.2 provides a framework for accommodating the projection of two

---

[38] Masullo (1992:Chapter 2) gives very convincing arguments that dative is a structural Case in Spanish. While many of his arguments do not transfer directly to French, a couple of them can be cited. First, the clitic nature of the dative indicates that as an agreement marker (Suñer 1988) it is "exclusively related to structural Case assignment" (Masullo 1992:70). Second, "dative Case in Spanish always violates Chomsky's Uniformity Condition on inherent Case assignment" (Masullo 1992:71). Chomsky (1986a:194) states the Uniformity Condition: "If α is an inherent Case marker then α Case-marks an NP if and only if α θ-marks the chain headed by the NP".

internal arguments and their necessary linking to two Agr_O nodes, where their two Cases can be checked.

2.5 *Conclusion*

This chapter has argued that given a minimalist approach argument structure and Case are necessarily linked through considerations of economy (shortest distance) and convergence. Furthermore, the number of internal arguments is limited to two as a consequence of the complement limit imposed by the branching conventions of X′ theory (Larson's Single Complement Hypothesis). The approach to Case adopted here assumes that in French the two internal arguments of VP_2 and VP_3 are linked to the Case properties of two Agr_O nodes, Agr_{O2} (objective Case) and Agr_{O3} (dative Case). The binary limitation of internal Case and argument projection is shown to reflect other binary restrictions in the grammar, perhaps contributing to ease of learnability for the language acquirer. The existence of two internal structural Cases, objective and dative in French is borne out by several pieces of evidence. The chapter has also demonstrated that objective Case has two possible realizations, usual accusative or redemptive partitive, a prepositionally marked Case that saves a derivation when accusative is unavailable. Binary internal argument structure describes straightforwardly ditransitive sentences with accusative and dative objects, and is supported by such data. Much more significant support is provided by a variety of superficially unrelated syntactic structures which will be examined in subsequent chapters.

CHAPTER 3

UNACCUSATIVE VERBS AND AFFECTED DATIVES

3.0 *Introduction*

The previous chapter has proposed that internal Case, limited to a maximum of two, may be realized in French as objective (accusative / partitive) or dative Case. It has argued that the Cases, checked in two object agreement nodes, are linked to two argument positions, the Spec of VP_2 and VP_3. The present chapter examines in greater detail two syntactic phenomena that test the Case and linking hypothesis proposed in Chapter 2. These phenomena are unaccusatives, verbs that fail to assign accusative Case, and affected datives, nonarguments that receive dative Case. These two groups furnish an empirical response to the question of dissociability of the Case–argument link: unaccusatives show that a verb can select an argument and yet be Case defective, while affected datives show that structural Case may be assigned to nonarguments. Unaccusative verbs, lexically designated as assigning no accusative Case but allowing partitive as the redemptive objective Case, have no thematic external argument. They furnish a prototype for verbs selecting nonthematic external arguments. Diagnostics used to define membership in this class will be used in subsequent chapters to determine the thematicity of the external argument. Affected datives, clitic pronouns not subcategorized by the verb, support the proposal of structural dative Case made in Chapter 2.

The existence of these two classes of syntactic phenomena is significant because it demonstrates empirically that the link between Case and argument is not unbreakable. More importantly, the dissociability of Case and argument provides a theoretical foundation for syntactic movement. If every argument were predestined to receive Case from its head, there would be no need for movement, at least A-movement. The missing Case and nonthematic external argument provide the syntactic impetus that permits movement, just as the missing tile in a child's matrix puzzle allows movement of the other tiles. Section 3.1 summarizes arguments for a class of unaccusative verbs and furnishes a set of diagnostics for nonthematic external argument constructions.

Section 3.2 presents and extends Burzio's generalization while Section 3.3 investigates French affected datives. The last section responds to the question of an upper limit on the number of internal arguments by showing that for unaccusatives the binary limit holds, for these verbs contrast with true intransitives which *can* take an additional internal argument. This data confirms the limit on internal arguments whether or not Case is available.

3.1 *Case suspension and unaccusative verbs*

This section examines the class of unaccusative verbs (Perlmutter 1989, Herschensohn 1982, Burzio 1986) to elaborate a model of the nonthematic external argument construction. The first three sections motivate a nonthematic external argument; the next section presents evidence for a class of unaccusative verbs.

3.1.1 *Nonthematic external arguments*

The existence of a nonthematic external argument is indicated in French by constructions with impersonal expletives in subject position. These presentational constructions are similar to English *there* sentences, characterized by the presence of expletive *IL* "it, there" in subject position and of a noun phrase in postverbal position. This construction appears in middle voice pronominal (1) and passive (2) as well as lexically determined raising (3) and other impersonals (4).[1]

(1) a   IL se construit beaucoup de bâtiments.
      "There are many buildings constructed".
    b   Beaucoup de bâtiments se construisent.
      "Many buildings are built".
(2) a   IL a été mangé beaucoup de pommes.
      "There were many apples eaten".
    b   Beaucoup de pommes ont été mangées.
      "Many apples were eaten".

---

[1] The acceptability of certain impersonal sentences may vary somewhat according to dialect, but the existence of impersonal passive and middle voice (as well as lexical impersonals) is well documented in traditional grammars. The following grammars cite examples of lexical, middle voice and passive impersonals: Chevalier et al. (1988:325), Grevisse (1993:1124, 1140), Martinon (1927:257), Sandfeld (1929:55, vol. 1). The disagreement about grammaticality is traceable to differences in register since the impersonal sentences are more formal or literary and thus less felicitous in the spoken language. Derived impersonals such as middle and passive are less clearly grammatical to many speakers than are lexical impersonals.

(3) a   IL semble que Jean est malade.
        "It seems that John is sick".
    b   Jean semble être malade.
        "John seems to be sick".
(4) IL est difficile de lire Lacan.
    "It is difficult to read Lacan".

In English the lack of a thematic subject in passive sentences is supported both by the possibility of creating impersonal passives such as (2a) (the expletive *there* filling the subject slot in overt subject English), and of moving the theme to subject position (2b). The expletive subject is semantically empty; the subject position in the *a* sentences is assigned no thematic role by the VP (cf. Chomsky 1981 and references therein). In French the assumption of a nonthematic empty subject position with passives and middle voice *se* accounts for pronominal and passive presentationals (1a),(2a).[2] Since the verbs *construire* and *manger* select direct objects, these DPs are internal arguments. A nonthematic subject in presentational sentences allows the *a* and *b* sentences of (1)–(2) to be related by the unmarked DP movement rule, leftward movement dictated by the c-command restriction on traces.[3]

Presentational sentences are possible with the nonthematic external argument constructions in (1)–(4) and with a group of superficial intransitives (5), not with all intransitives as (6) shows.

(5) a   IL (leur) est arrivé beaucoup d'Américains.
        "There arrived many Americans (to them)".
    b   Beaucoup d'Américains sont arrivés.
        "Many Americans arrived".
    c   IL restait plusieurs enfants dans la salle.
        "There remained several children in the room".

---

[2] Earlier treatments such as Kayne (1975), Kayne (1979) and Guéron (1980) attribute the constructions in (1) and (2) to a rule which derives the a from the b sentences by rightward movement of the subject NP. There is no empirical support for such a movement analysis whereby the object NP moves into the empty subject position and back again, since (1b) and (2b) can be derived simply by leftward NP movement. Stowell (1978), Borer (1980) and Herschensohn (1982) present arguments for base generation of presentation sentences in English, Hebrew and French respectively.
[3] The NP trace can be properly bound after leftward movement of the NP, since the antecedent will c-command it. As Dresher & Hornstein (1979:65) point out, "It is well known that many languages exhibit left–right asymmetries in their syntactic behavior".

     d   Plusieurs enfants restaient dans la salle.
         "Several children remained in the room".
(6) a *IL a dormi beaucoup d'enfants.
         "There slept many children".
     b   Beaucoup d'enfants ont dormi.
         "Many children slept".
     c   *IL sourira trois femmes.
         "There will smile three women".
     d   Trois femmes souriront.
         "Three women will smile".

Work in Romance languages and English (e.g. Herschensohn 1982, Burzio 1986, Hale & Keyser [H&K] 1986, Levin & Rappaport Hovav 1994) has documented the existence of this class of verbs characterized by a structure lacking a thematic external argument. The nonthematic external argument is depicted in derivational representations as $-\theta$ in the Spec VP_1. The term 'subject' will usually be used to refer to the superficial subject position in Spec Agr_S.

Levin & Rappaport Hovav (henceforth L&R, 1994:15–16), in their thorough and insightful study of this class of verbs, clarify the distinction between syntactic and semantic considerations of unaccusativity, particularly with respect to the use of diagnostics. They claim that unaccusativity is a syntactic property with variable semantic correlates. The semantic variability leads to a differentiation among diagnostics.

> All unaccusative verbs, no matter what their semantic class, share certain syntactic properties (the selection of a direct internal argument, the lack of an external argument, and the inability to assign accusative Case). Not all unaccusative verbs are expected to give positive results with respect to all unaccusative diagnostics, because [...] an unaccusative classification is often a necessary, but not a sufficient condition for a verb to test positive with respect to certain unaccusative diagnostics.

Legendre (1989b) reaches the same conclusion in pointing out that distinct tests identify distinct subsets of unaccusatives. Syntactic diagnostics for unaccusatives fall into two classes, tests for nonthematicity of the thematic external argument (corresponding to the position in Spec VP_1) to be examined in Sections 3.1.2–3.1.3, and tests for direct objecthood to be presented in 3.1.4. The first set of diagnostics can be used to determine nonthematic external arguments in constructions other than unaccusatives.

3.1.2 *External argument diagnostics*

Six diagnostics are used to determine the nonthematicity of the external argument, the impersonal presentational, auxiliary selection, indefinite *on*, reciprocal anaphors and two aspects of causative constructions. The ability of unaccusative verbs (and not other intransitives) to permit the impersonal presentational construction is one class of evidence used to distinguish them in French. Presentationals (which show the definiteness restriction described in Chapter 2) do not always elicit clear grammaticality judgments, but nevertheless, there is a strong preference for the grammaticality of unaccusative verbs over other intransitives. This claim is supported by the rich evidence of linguists such as Atkinson (1973), Damourette & Pichon (1930–43), Grevisse (1993) and Martin (1970). Of about two thousand examples of presentationals in the references cited, the overwhelming majority represent a group of thirty verbs used in this construction with great frequency. The group of unaccusatives, which semantically indicate appearance, existence or transition, includes verbs requiring the auxiliary *être* "to be" and other verbs taking *avoir* "to have" as auxiliary, such as *manquer* "to miss". A partial list is provided in (7).[4]

(7) a   *être* auxiliary:
naître "to be born", *mourir* "to die", *venir* "to come" (*devenir, revenir,* etc), *tomber* "to fall", *descendre* "to descend", *aller* "to go", *sortir* "to go out", *arriver* "to arrive", *entrer* "to enter", *rester* "to remain", *passer* "to pass", *apparaître* "to appear".
     b   other:
manquer "to miss", *échapper* "to escape", *pleuvoir* "to rain", *flotter* "to float", *neiger* "to snow".[5]

---

[4] Authier and Reed have pointed out (p.c.) that there is some variability in the definiteness effect in that *manquer* does not as easily admit preposed quantified themes as *arriver*, whereas a preposed definite theme is acceptable.
  (i) Il lui manque beaucoup d'argent. / *Beaucoup d'argent lui manque.
      "He's missing a lot of money".
  (ii) Il aimerait bien construire une maison pour sa famille, mais l'argent lui manque.
      "He would like to build a house for his family but he lacks the money".
It seems that *manquer* takes definites more readily than other unaccusatives.
  (iii) Il lui manque la bonne réponse / l'argent / l'orteil gauche.
      "He's missing the right answer / the money / his left big toe".
These DPs are all qualified, but are nonspecific since they are nonexistent (missing).
[5] While the verbs listed in (9) are by far the most common to the presentation sentence, they are not the only ones. Legendre gives a more exhaustive list which also includes the

In addition to variability in grammaticality judgment, presentational sentences are not entirely trustworthy diagnostics of unaccusativity because exceptionally unergatives or transitives are possible (cf. Chapter 2), although in all cases grammaticality is discourse conditioned. Guéron (1980:673–674) proposes that because presentation sentences obey the definiteness restriction, "the verb must be interpreted as predicating no more than the appearance on the scene of the postposed subject". The predication of the sentence is ultimately subject to questions of focus in its interpretation (Guéron 1980:653).[6]

The locative inversion structure (*over her shoulder appears...*) shares some discourse / semantic restrictions with the presentational sentence. L&R (1994:Chapter 6) point out the inadequacy of using the locative inversion construction as a diagnostic for unaccusativity. They (1994:216) claim that while perhaps a large percentage of the verbs used in this construction are unaccusative, "it is not restricted to verbs independently known to be unaccusative. Rather, we attribute its unaccusative-like distributional properties to the fact that this construction is associated with a particular discourse function". It is assumed in the present study that unaccusative verbs can enter productively into the presentational construction. Verbs with inverted thematic subjects may exceptionally be used in this construction if they are situated with the proper discourse setting; this is a pragmatically controlled exception, not a syntactic regularity.

Another diagnostic for unaccusatives used especially for Italian is auxiliary selection (Perlmutter 1989, Burzio 1986). In all cases of nonthematic external argument verbs the auxiliary *essere* "to be" rather than *avere* "to have" is chosen. Thus there are minimal pairs such as (8) which demonstrate the unaccusative as well as the transitive use of a given verb (Perlmutter 1989:77).

(8) a   Ugo ha affogato il barboncino.
         "Hugo drowned the poodle".

---

transitive–intransitive type. Ruwet (1989) convincingly argues that meteorological verbs are unaccusative.

[6] Martin (1970:381) states, "lorsqu'il ne suggère pas l'idée de survenance ou d'existence, le V_i ne peut en aucune façon se tourner à l'impersonnel". He gives several examples of ungrammatical intransitive presentation sentences, such as (i) and (ii).

(i)   *Il vieillissait visiblement une civilisation. "There ages visibly a civilization".

(ii) *Il maigrissait la plupart des prisonniers.
      "There got thin the majority of prisoners".

b   Il barboncino è affogato.
"The poodle drowned".
c   Hugues a noyé le caniche.
"Hugo drowned the poodle".
d   Le caniche s'est noyé.
"The poodle drowned".

Auxiliary selection in French cannot be used as a diagnostic since it does not correlate consistently with the thematicity of the external argument. Pronominal verbs (8d) always take *être* (which takes *avoir* as auxiliary in French (9a)) but passive (9a) and variable valence verbs (9b,c) take *avoir*.

(9) a   La pomme a été mangée.
"The apple was eaten".
b   On a coulé le bateau.
"Someone sank the boat".
c   Le bateau a coulé.
"The boat sank".

A third argument pointed out by Legendre (1989a:764) (not unrelated to the "arbitrary" subject argument used by Belletti & Rizzi 1988 [B&R]) concerns arbitrary *on* which "appears to be restricted to initial 1s [underlying subjects] (of unergative [true intransitive] and transitive structures). *On* interpretation thus allows us to differentiate unergative from unaccusative verbs". Thus (10a, b) can have two interpretations, whereas unaccusative (10c, d) have only one.

(10) a   On a téléphoné à Pierre.
"Someone / We phoned Peter".
b   On critique beaucoup le nouveau gouvernement.
"Someone / We criticize the new government a lot".
c   On est allé au cinéma.
"*Someone / We went to the movies".
d   On a survécu au tyran.
"*Someone / We survived the tyran".

Judgments on these sentences are subtle, but generally seem to be borne out for unaccusative vs. unergative (cf. Appendix).

Another diagnostic proposed by B&R (1988) is that only true thematic external arguments can bind reciprocal anaphors; derived subjects (such as those of unaccusative *manquer* or *apparaître*) cannot.

(11) a La mère lave son enfant.
       "The mother washes her child".
     b Les enfants se lavent les uns les autres.
       "The children wash each other".
     c La mère manque à son enfant.
       "The child misses her mother".
     d *Les enfants se manquent les uns aux autres.
       "The children miss one another".
     e Les enfants sont apparus à la porte.
       "The children appeared at the door".
     f *Les enfants se sont apparus l'un (à) l'autre.
       "The children appeared to one another".

Unaccusatives prohibit reciprocal anaphors, even if a logical semantic context can be devised.[7] These diagnostics of nonthematic external argument status are complemented by others related to causative constructions.

3.1.3 *Causative constructions*

The lack of external argument with unaccusatives is further supported by two aspects of their behavior in causative constructions. First, a nonthematic external argument accounts for the grammaticality of cliticized datives with this class of verbs as opposed to agentive verbs which disallow datives cliticized to *faire*.[8] Given Reed's (1991) analysis of causatives, it is Case theory that accounts for the Case and word order of *faire*–infinitive constructions. She proposes (Reed 1991:342) that *faire* can assign Case through a complex "verbal government chain", thus predicting cliticization of all pronouns to *faire* rather than the infinitive. In sentences where there is a "mismatch in Case features [...] a simple government chain is formed, *faire* [...] Case marks the lexical embedded subject while the embedded verb

---

[7] Not only is *l'un l'autre* prohibited, but simple reflexive–reciprocal *se* is also (Chapter 5).
  (i)   Marc (*se) monte dans l'arbre. "Marc climbs in the tree".
  (ii) a   L'agent a descendu le criminel. "The agent downed the criminal".
      b   *Les criminels se sont descendus. "The criminals downed each other".
[8] This ungrammaticality was first observed by Kayne (1975:287–298) and attributed to the Specified Subject Condition. Postal (1984:133) argues that such sentences are not ungrammatical because of binding theory.

independently assigns its Case features to the embedded objects". In sentences such as (12) that cannot form a complex verbal government chain, *faire* assigns Case to the embedded subject, while *téléphoner* assigns Case to the embedded dative, precluding cliticization of the dative to *faire*.

(12) a Marie téléphone à ses cousins.
        "Mary phones to her cousins [dative]".
     b Cela a fait téléphoner Marie à ses cousins.
        "That made Mary phone to her cousins".
     c *Cela a fait téléphoner à ses cousins Marie.
        "That made Mary phone to her cousins".
     d *Cela leur a fait téléphoner Marie.
        "That made Mary phone to them".

Reed proposes that two options for movement—XP or X^o—are possible with *faire*, and that word order is a function of Case requirements. In (12b) *faire* assigns Case to *Marie* and *téléphoner* does so to *cousins*. This sentence involves V^o movement (raising of *téléphoner* to AgrP) and AgrP movement to Spec of CP (13 = Reed's example, 1991:349).

(13)

```
                    VP
                   /  \
                  V    CP
                      /   \
                   Spec    C'
                    |      /  \
                  AgrPⱼ   C    IP
                  /  \        /   \
                Agr  VP₁    Spec   I'
                 |   /  \    |    /  \
                Vᵢ  DP  VP₂  I   tⱼ
                       /   \
                      tᵢ   PP
                       |    |
           téléphoner Marie   à ses cousins
```

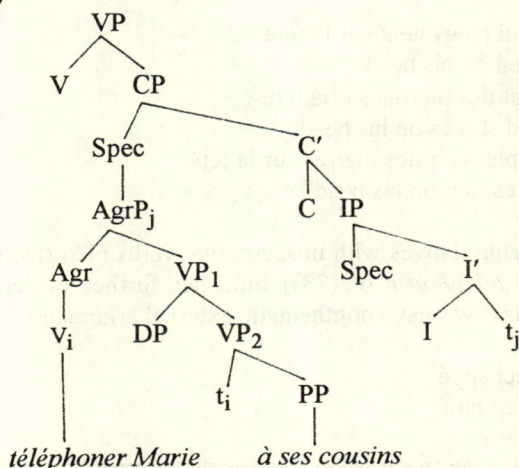

Sentence (12c) without V^o movement would result in an ungrammatical structure because the embedded subject could not receive Case from nonadjacent *faire*. The version with the cliticized dative (12d) is likewise ungrammatical. In (14)–(16) lacking a thematic subject of the infinitive, it is licit for AgrP to move to the Spec of CP position without V^0 movement and for *faire* to constitute a verbal government chain allowing cliticization of the dative.

Case theory is violated by cliticizing the dative to *faire* when it receives Case from the embedded verb, so cliticization of the pronoun *leur* in (13) is prohibited. When there is no embedded thematic subject a verbal government chain can be formed, and cliticization of the dative is possible (14). Ruwet (1972:266) notes this possibility with embedded 'passives'.

(14) a   Je lui ferai porter ce message par Jean.
       "I'll have this message brought to him by John".
    b   Je lui ferai chanter le Messie en entier.
       "I'll have the entire Messiah sung to him".

The grammaticality of (14) is predicted by the analysis of passive alluded to above that assumes a nonthematic external argument. Likewise, no Case violation occurs in causatives when a verb requiring an expletive subject (that is, one which has a nonthematic external argument) in tensed sentences is embedded under *faire* (15).

(15) a   Des pierres lui pleuvaient sur la tête.
       "Stones rained on his head".
    b   IL lui pleuvait des pierres sur la tête.
       "There rained stones on his head".
    c   Je lui faisais pleuvoir des pierres sur la tête.
       "I made stones rain on his head".

The possibility of cliticizing datives with unaccusative verbs (16) (as opposed to intransitives such as *téléphoner* of (23)) furnishes further evidence that they, like *pleuvoir* and passives have nonthematic external arguments.[9]

(16) a   Un cri lui a échappé.
       "A cry escaped him".

---

[9] Unlike English *there*, which can appear with infinitives after exceptional Case marking verbs, French *IL* is the expletive subject of tensed sentences only. In infinitive clauses it never surfaces, and the empty subject position doesn't interfere with dative cliticization. The possibility of cliticizing datives in causative constructions with nonthematic external arguments explains some anomalous facts, given the analysis offered here. Herschensohn (1982:207–208) and Burzio (1986:270–274) discuss examples pointed out by Kayne (1975).

b IL lui a échappé un cri.
   "There escaped from him a cry".
c Le mouvement brusque lui a fait échapper un cri.
   "The abrupt movement made a cry escape him".

The unaccusative hypothesis posits that *un cri* is originally an internal argument, thus not a subject and no obstacle to the placement of the dative pronoun. This analysis also allows a natural explanation of certain inalienable sentences which Kayne (1975:309–327) finds problematic as supposed (but not actual) binding violations. Unexpectedly, grammatical (17d) contrasts with (17b).[10]

(17) a Jean lui marchera sur le bras.
        "John will walk on his arm".
     b *On lui fera marcher Jean sur le bras.
        "We'll make John walk [to him] on his [the] arm".
     c Des pierres lui sont tombées sur la tête.
        "Stones fell on his head".
     d On lui a fait tomber des pierres sur la tête.
        "We made stones fall [to him] on his [the] head".

The grammaticality of (17d) is predicted by the unaccusative account, for *tomber* is one of the verbs listed in (7). The predictability of dative cliticization in causatives is an advantage which falls out from the proposal of a nonthematic external argument.

A second commonly cited (e.g. Postal 1984, Zubizarreta 1985, Burzio 1986, B&R 1988) diagnostic related to causatives is the possibility of omitting thematic external arguments of the embedded verb. Burzio (1986:279) notes that "while verbs can never appear without objects they are subcategorized for, they can appear without subjects in certain constructions". In causative constructions the external argument of the embedded verb may be syntactically absent, much as the agent in passive sentences (18).

(18) a Jean fait réparer la voiture.
        "John has [someone] fix the car / the car fixed".
     b Ces somnifères font dormir tout de suite.
        "These pills make [one] sleep quickly".

---

[10] Given Reed's analysis (17) would require X⁰ as well as X″ movement. With a missing agent (nonthematic external argument) the dative can cliticize to *faire* (17d).

(19) a   *Cet autobus fait arriver rapidement.
         "This bus makes [one] arrive quickly".
     b   *On a fait parvenir à Louise.
         "We had [something] arrive for Louise".

The superficial subjects of unaccusative verbs cannot, however, be omitted
(19), indicating that they are not true thematic external arguments, but
derived. In minimalist terms, the position of Spec VP_1 of unaccusatives must
then be nonthematic. Although Ruwet (1989) and Legendre (1989b) question
the validity of this diagnostic, citing examples of unaccusatives that allow a
missing subject (20), the variability between unaccusatives and transitives
simply underlines the difference between thematic and nonthematic external
argument verbs: the former freely allow missing embedded subjects in
causative constructions; the latter only allow this under mitigated pragmatic
conditions.[11]

(20) a   Une grosse grippe, ça fait rester au lit.
         "A bad flu, that makes [one] stay in bed".
     b   Ces lunettes font paraître plus intelligent.
         "These glasses make [one] seem more intelligent".

A last causative diagnostic proposed by B&R (1988:302) is the
ungrammaticality of derived subjects embedded in causatives. In contrast to
the grammaticality of thematic external arguments realized as either accusative
or dative complements of the superficial verbal complex, passive and some
unaccusative derived subjects are ungrammatical (21a, b).

(21) a   *Jean a fait être mangée la pomme.
         "John had the apple be eaten".
     b   *Cette chanson faisait manquer Paul à Marie.
         "This song made Mary miss Paul".
     c   On fera mourir son chien.
         "We'll have his dog die".
     d   On lui fera tomber Jean dessus.
         "We'll have John fall on it".

---

[11] The addition of discourse softeners, particularly adverbials, also mitigates the
acceptability (Reed & Authier, p.c.)
   (i) Une bonne dose d'arsénic, ça fait mourir en 10 minutes.
   "A good dose of arsenic makes [you] die in 10 minutes".

However, the diagnostic does not seem generally applicable since many unaccusatives (21c, d) are easily embedded under *faire* (cf. Burzio 1986:268–279).

3.1.4 *Direct object diagnostics*

A second line of argumentation for a class of unaccusatives focuses not on the nonthematic external argument, but on the derived subject which moves from direct object position. Legendre (1989b) outlines several diagnostics for underlying "2-hood" or direct object status, four of which include *en* extraction, participial and *croire* constructions. The first argument for the direct object origin of the unaccusative subject is, of course, the correlated sentences such as those in (5) with *arriver* and *rester*, in which the direct object of *a* corresponds to the subject of the *b* sentences.

A second argument in favor of a class of unaccusatives is the availability of *en* extraction with these verbs. The distribution of quantificational (partitive) *en* "some (of it)" indicates that the postverbal DP in the unaccusative sentences is a direct object. Kayne (1975:111–112) notes that quantificational *en* may be extracted only from the direct object position.[12] The grammaticality of *en* with unaccusatives, as opposed to its ungrammaticality with other intransitives, confirms that the postverbal DP is a direct object (22).

(22) IL en restait deux ou trois [gouttes] sur le visage.
  "There remained of it two or three [drops] on the face".

Burzio (1986:Chapter 1) develops parallel arguments with comparable Italian *ne*.

Two other direct object diagnostics indicate that the subject of unaccusatives is derived, that is, moved from direct object position. Past

---

[12] Postal (1986:344) presents additional evidence regarding *en* by pointing out that *en* is linkable to predicate nominals, not simply direct objects.
  (i) C'en est un. "That's one of them".
Belletti (1988) and Lasnik (1992) have observed the similarities of *be* and unaccusatives with respect to Case marking. A discussion of *be* / *être* is outside the scope of this work, but an analysis of *be* relating it to unaccusatives might constitute a compromise between Postal's and Kayne's positions. See also Couquaux (1979) for a discussion of related problems.

participles can be predicated only of direct objects, not true external arguments (23b).[13]

(23) a Le bandit a kidnappé l'enfant.
        "The bandit kidnapped the child".
     b l'enfant kidnappé / *le bandit kidnappé
        "the kidnapped child / the kidnapped bandit"
     c Cette parole m'a échappé.
        "This word escaped me".
     d la parole échappée
        "the escaped word"
     e Les enfants sont partis / arrivés / nés.
        "The children departed / arrived/ were born".
     f les enfants partis / arrivés / nés.
        "the departed / arrived/ born children"

Unaccusative derived subjects group with transitive direct objects in their ability to be modified by past participles (23c–f). A related diagnostic involves *croire* "to believe" which may be followed by a small clause containing an NP (that will be exceptionally Case marked by *croire*) plus an adjective. The adjective may be a past participle modifying a direct object (but not a external argument). Unaccusative subjects (*Paul*) once again pattern with direct objects (*les papillons*), not thematic external arguments (*Pierre*).

(24) a Pierre a attrapé les papillons.
        "Peter caught the butterflies".
     b On croyait les papillons / *Pierre attrapé(s).
        "We believed the butterflies / Peter caught".
     c Pierre a réagi à la question.
        "Peter reacted to the question".
     d *On croyait Pierre réagi à la question.
        "We believed Peter reacted to the question".
     e Paul est parti /mort.
        "Paul left / died".
     f On croyait Paul parti / mort.
        "We believed Paul left / dead".

---

[13] Legendre (1989b) provides a wealth of participial examples including reduced relatives and participial absolutes.

These tests indicate that the subject of nonpresentational unaccusative sentences such as (24e) originates as a direct object. This analysis thus gives further support to the discussion of partitive Case in Chapter 2, since unaccusative presentationals conform to the definiteness restriction.

In minimalist terms, unaccusative sentences have an nonthematic Spec VP_1, a lack of accusative Case, and a DP in Spec VP_2 that is forced to raise to be checked for nominative Case. A typical unaccusative sentence is represented in (25).

(25) a   Ce cri lui échappe. "This cry escapes him".
    b   IL lui échappe un cri. "There escapes him a cry".

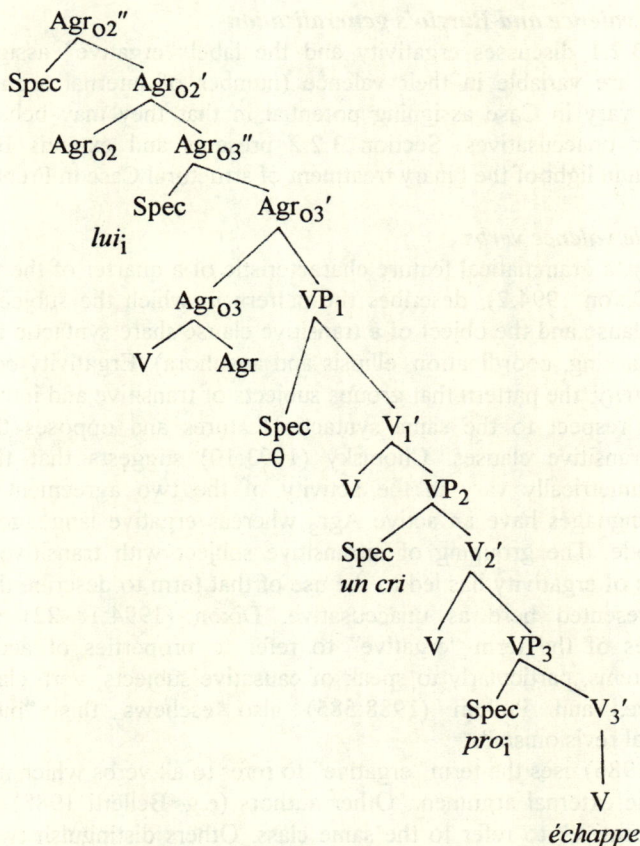

In (25a) the superficial subject raises overtly from Spec VP_2 through Spec Agr_O to Spec Agr_S. It is unable to check off Case in Spec Agr_O because accusative Case is defective and it cannot meet the definiteness condition for partitive. In (25b) the DP in Spec VP_2 meets the structural and definiteness conditions for partitive Case, so can check off objective Case in Spec Agr_{O2}. Expletive *IL* is spelled out at PF. The dative clitic, overtly in the Spec Agr_{O3}, is assigned dative Case. The unaccusative analysis is supported by the evidence presented and also accounts for certain aspects of the causative construction in French. Many of the diagnostics outlined will be used in subsequent chapters to test the thematicity of the external argument of other classes of verbs.

3.2 *Variable valence and Burzio's generalization*

Section 3.2.1 discusses ergativity and the label "ergative" assigned to verbs which are variable in their valence (number of internal arguments). These verbs vary in Case assigning potential in that they may behave like transitives or unaccusatives. Section 3.2.2 presents and extends Burzio's generalization in light of the binary treatment of structural Case in French.

3.2.1 *Variable valence verbs*

Ergativity, a grammatical feature characteristic of a quarter of the world's languages (Dixon 1994:2), describes the pattern in which the subject of an intransitive clause and the object of a transitive clause share syntactic features (e.g. Case marking, coordination, ellipsis and anaphora). Ergativity contrasts with *accusativity*, the pattern that groups subjects of transitive and intransitive clauses with respect to the same syntactic features and opposes them to objects of transitive clauses. Chomsky (1993:10) suggests that the two patterns parametrically vary in the activity of the two agreement nodes: accusative languages have an active Agr_S whereas ergative languages favor the Agr_O node. The grouping of intransitive subject with transitive object characteristic of ergativity has led to the use of that term to describe the class of verbs presented here as unaccusative. Dixon (1994:18–22) roundly criticizes uses of the term "ergative" to refer to properties of accusative language systems, particularly to speak of causative subjects, verb classes or middle voice, and Pullum (1988:585) also eschews this "piece of terminological revisionism".

Burzio (1986) uses the term "ergative" to refer to all verbs which manifest a nonthematic external argument. Other authors (e.g. Belletti 1988) use the term "unaccusative" to refer to the same class. Others distinguish two uses, "unaccusative" to refer to verbs incapable of assigning accusative Case, superficially intransitive and amenable to the presentational construction, and "ergative" to refer to verbs which can have variable argument structure (e.g. "break," "open") (H&K 1986:30). This study will adopt the distinction made by Hale & Keyser, but will use a different terminology in the light of Dixon's criticisms. The verbs discussed in Section 3.1.2 are *unaccusative*, but the verbs which permit variability of the number and distribution of arguments and Case potential can be termed *multivalent*. Unaccusative verbs are lexically designated as being incapable or defective in assigning accusative Case. As Burzio points out, multivalent verbs have a double subcategorization as either transitive or unaccusative. In the latter function their accusative Case is suspended.

In French, multivalent verbs include lexical ones such as *fondre* "to melt" (26a, b), pronominals such as *se briser* "to shatter" (26c, d) and a mixed variety such as *(se) casser* "to break" (26e, f).

(26) a Marc a fondu le beurre.
        "Mark melted the butter".
     b Le beurre a / *s'est fondu.
        "The butter melted".
     c Marc a brisé le verre.
        "Mark shattered the glass".
     d Le verre s'est / *a brisé.
        "The glass shattered".
     e Marc a cassé la branche.
        "Mark broke the branch".
     f La branche a / s'est cassé(e).
        "The branch broke".

The first member of each pair is a typical transitive sentence with an agent subject (or frequently an instrumental nonhuman subject); the second member shows a variability between obligatory and optional pronominal forms (Rothemberg 1974, Labelle 1992b). The categorization of multivalent verbs is complicated by the semantically elusive variability of not only pronominal and nonpronominal forms, but also of lexical and syntactic causatives.[14] Labelle

---

[14] Authier & Reed (p.c.) note the following examples, suggesting that there are two different verbs *couler*, the lexical causative and the intransitive.
    (i) a Le cuirassé a coulé le navire. "The battleship sank the other vessel".
         b Le navire a coulé. "The ship sank".
    (ii) a *Jean a coulé Pierre (en le poussant sous l'eau avec une rame).
            "John sank Peter (by pushing him underwater with an oar)".

(1992b) gives a very perceptive analysis of multivalent verbs, pointing out subtle semantic differences that correlate with the pronominal vs. nonpronominal forms.

Unlike Italian, which shows a clear diagnostic of auxiliary assignment— *avere* "to have" for transitives and unergatives (true intransitives) and *essere* "to be" for multivalents—French cannot use auxiliary selection as a diagnostic for unaccusativity. A large number of strict unaccusatives take *être*, but many do not. All pronominals take *être*, but they are not all comparable. Multivalent verbs such as *fondre* take *avoir* in both transitive and intransitive uses. A treatment of multivalent verbs is outside the scope of this study, since it entails distinguishing the distribution of pronominal and nonpronominal intransitives as well as the relationship of transitive to intransitive forms. Detailed studies of thousands of verbs such as that of Rothemberg indicate that the class of multivalent verbs is fairly broad and lexically productive.

3.2.2 *Extending Burzio's generalization*

As for Case assignment, unaccusatives are never capable of assigning accusative Case, whereas multivalents can assign accusative Case in their transitive use, but have accusative Case suspended in the intransitive construction. Burzio (1986:179) notes the correlation of nonthematic external argument and lack of accusative Case, proposing the following generalization (27).

(27) *Burzio's generalization*
    a $-\theta_S \rightarrow -A$
    b $\theta_S \leftrightarrow A$
    θ_S = thematic subject, A = Accusative Case

(27a) expresses the interdependence of lack of accusative Case and lack of subject theta role characteristic of unaccusative verbs. Burzio (1986:185) extends the generalization to (27b). Bidirectionally (27b) actually makes four claims: it states that a verb which theta marks its subject assigns accusative Case to its object and a verb which doesn't theta mark its subject doesn't assign accusative Case to its object and vice versa. Burzio argues that his generalization is first supported by its empirical accuracy, but that more

---

    b   Jean a coulé (après avoir attendu les secours pendant une heure en nageant).
        "John sank (after waiting for help for an hour while swimming)".
    c   Jean a fait couler Pierre. "John made Peter sink / John drowned Peter".

importantly it is theoretically necessary. Burzio (1986:184) explains the generalization.

> Consider the case of a verb which takes a direct object but does not assign Case to it. The verb will *have to* fail to assign theta role to the subject position, since the only two possibilities for such a direct object to receive Case will be (i) that it be linked to a nonargument subject; (ii) that it move into subject position. Both possibilities require nonthematic subjects.

Goodall (1993:42) presents counterevidence to Burzio's Generalization in passive (nonthematic external argument) constructions "in which case absorption is either not used (as in Kannada and Finnish) or is optional (as in Ukrainian, Nepali and Norwegian)". He presents evidence from several languages that allow accusative Case marking with nonthematic external arguments and concludes "that Case-marking verbs which do not assign a subject theta role do exist". His observations show that accusative Case is not always suspended in passive constructions, but this fact alone is not sufficient to dismiss Burzio's Generalization entirely. Indeed, there is ample data in the languages Burzio originally examines to show that the lack of accusative Case is not the only factor at play. Burzio's motivating logic is that lack of internal Case forces movement of the internal argument to subject position. In English and the Romance languages lack of accusative does not equate to lack of objective Case, for partitive Case is available in nonaccusative structures with expletive subjects.

Burzio's generalization predicts a correlation between internal Case and external theta role. The lack of internal Case may result in movement of the internal argument to subject position. However, the evidence in a variety of languages such as English, German, Italian, Nepali and Ukraninian indicates that internal Case is not always suspended with nonthematic external arguments. Some languages (e.g. Ukrainian and rarely French) allow retention of accusative Case despite lack of external argument theta role. Others (e.g. Italian) allow assignment of partitive Case despite lack of external argument theta role and lack of accusative Case.[15]

Burzio's generalization must be reconsidered in the light of the second chapter's proposal of two structural Cases in French, accusative and dative.

---

[15] The behavior of certain psych verbs which have nonthematic external arguments yet assign accusative Case indicates that Burzio's generalization stated as (27) is inadequate. The extended version, on the other hand predicts this class of verbs. A discussion of Goodall's data is outside the scope of this study, but the Case anomalies he describes might be amenable to analysis as in the French partitive examples.

The unaccusatives delineated in section 3.1. represent a class of verbs lacking one of the structural Cases, accusative. This class corroborates Burzio's generalization in also lacking a thematic external argument. It is reasonable to infer that if one Case, accusative, can be defective or suspended, the other can also. The generalization must then be extended as in (28).

(28) *Burzio's generalization extended*

$\theta_s \leftrightarrow C$

$C = Agr_O$ Case, accusative or dative

(28) predicts that dative Case, like accusative, can be defective or suspended and that consequently the external argument must be nonthematic to permit movement of the Caseless argument to subject position. Burzio's logic is extended thus to predict the existence of a class of *undative* verbs incapable of assigning dative. The next section will present data permitting the testing of (28).

3.3 *Affected datives*

This section looks at a second instance of Case and argument dissociation in French, the nonlexical or affected dative. These dative clitics, not subcategorized by the verb to which they are attached, express the affectedness or interest of an individual related to the discourse. Affected datives include loosely defined categories such as benefactive (29), malefactive (30), (31), inalienable possession (32) and ethical datives (33) (examples from Rooryck 1988, Barnes 1985, Sandfeld 1929).[16]

(29) Je lui ai hébergé ses enfants gratuitement (?*à Paul).
"I housed his children for him. (Paul)"
(30) Les gosses lui ont tué son chat (?*à Hélène).
"The kids killed her cat (on her/on Helene)".
(31) Le gosse lui a attrapé un rhume (?*à Paul).
"The kid caught a cold (unfortunately for him/Paul)".
(32) On lui a cassé la jambe (?*à Paul).
"Someone broke his leg (Paul's)".
(33) Goutez-moi ce kirsch-là!
"Taste this kirsch (for me)!"

---

[16] The opinions (?*) are those given by the linguists cited. Grammaticality judgments are subtle on affected datives and corresponding PP complements (cf. Appendix).

The categories are far from exact—indeed, the difference between malefactive and benefactive is simply one of perspective—and are generally indistinguishable morphologically and syntactically.

Characteristics of affected datives have been observed by traditional and generative linguists. Kayne (1975) notes that these datives do not correspond to lexical prepositional phrases with *à*, unlike lexical datives (34) which are subcategorized by the verb. The near ungrammaticality of the full noun phrases in parentheses in sentences (29)–(33) indicates that the verbs in these examples do not subcategorize for the dative PPs.

(34) On lui a envoyé une lettre (à Hélène).
     "Someone sent a letter to her, to Helene".

Leclère (1976, 1978) discusses differences between lexical and nonlexical verb classes, and Barnes (1981, 1985) points out that there are lexical, semantic and discourse restrictions on the verbs that allow affected datives. Rooryck (1988) proposes syntactic diagnostics for affected datives. Like intrinsic clitics such as *y*, *en* in *y avoir*, *s'en aller*, affected datives do not correspond to a lexical argument and therefore require an account distinct from that of subcategorized datives.

The morphological identity of nonlexical and lexical datives, and the semantic diversity of their interpretation have obscured the syntactic cohesion of this group. Section 3.3.1 gives an overview of the distribution of affected datives and 3.3.2 argues that they are not equivalent to lexical datives, but are nevertheless dependent on lexical designation by the verb and can thus be used as diagnostics of the dative potential of a verb.

3.3.1 *Distribution of affected datives*

Chapter 2 has shown that dative is a structural Case marked either by *à* or the dative clitic. Verbs selecting lexical datives often indicate transfer or communication (*donner, offrir, demander, téléphoner* "to give, offer, ask, phone"). These verbs subcategorize for a direct object and a second internal argument of the verb realized as the dative. In contrast, the distribution of affected datives is constrained by semantic characteristics of the verb and discourse conditions as well. Some apparent semantic restrictions are discussed by Barnes (1985:173) who points out that the dative clitics usually possess characteristics of animacy and affectedness (35). Leclère (1976) suggests that the generally nonstative verbs associated with affected datives imply intentional action by the subject (36).[17]

(35) a Elle lui a coupé les cheveux.
      "She cut his hair".
    b *Elle lui regarde la tête.
      "She looks at his head".
(36) a Paul lui a fait une bronchite.
      "Paul had a cold to her".
    b *Paul lui a eu une bronchite.
      "Paul had a cold to her".

Affected datives are register sensitive since they are characteristic of informal spoken language. The more subtle grammaticality judgments vary from individual to individual as the survey in the Appendix indicates, but judgments are straightforward on agentive transitive sentences. Although one can construct ungrammatical sentences with affected datives by altering semantic and discourse conditions, one can likewise construct grammatical sentences with the majority of transitive verbs (by manipulating the discourse context), even if they do not subcategorize for a dative. Despite the suggested prohibition against affected datives with stative verbs, even unlikely candidates such as stative *voir, croire* can enter into this construction (37) (Rooryck 1988:106, Ruwet 1982:172).

(37) a Je lui ai vu une jupe bizarre.
      "I saw a strange skirt on her".
    b Je lui croyais une maîtresse dans chaque port.
      "I believed him to have a mistress in every port".

Unaccusative verbs such as *tomber, sortir* "to fall, go out" can be constructed with affected datives as long as they are followed by an adverbial complement (38a), but intransitives with no verbal complement are ungrammatical (38b).

---

[17] Affected datives are not subcategorized, but they are conditioned by the lexical properties of the verb and the discourse setting. Leclère points out that "la troisième personne ne peut pas apparaître dans bien des cas où le datif éthique deuxième personne est très naturel".(1976:45) Barnes (1985) thoroughly reviews semantic characteristics of affected datives (animacy, affectedness) and their verb (volition, stativity). On the notion of affectedness see Cheng & Ritter (1988).

(38) a Le plafond lui est tombé dessus.
    "The ceiling fell down on him".
  b *Le plafond lui est tombé.
  c *On peut lui compter dessus.
    "One can count on him".

Strongly favored are the prepositions *sur, dans* "on, in" and their pro-forms *dessus, dedans*, but affected datives are allowed only with concrete uses of these prepositions (38c). Unergatives constructed with a PP may possibly have a affected dative when they denote intentional action (e.g. *gribouiller* "to scribble", *pisser* "to piss"), but degrade in grammaticality when they don't (39).[18]

(39) a Les gosses lui ont gribouillé sur tous les murs.
    "The kids scribbled on all the walls to her".
  b Le chiot lui a pissé dans ses laitues.
    "The puppy pissed in her lettuces to her".
  c *Les invités leur ont dormi dans toutes les chambres.
    "The guests slept in all the bedrooms to them".

Although discourse conditions can often be altered to create acceptable environments for most classes of verbs, one group is markedly ungrammatical with affected datives. Psychological experiencer verbs such as *amuser* (whose direct object is the experiencer) resist most strongly the presence of a affected dative (40).[19]

(40) a *Les marionnettes lui ont amusé ses enfants.
    "The puppets entertained her children for her".
  b *La vidéo lui a ennuyé ses collègues embêtants.
    "The video bored her obnoxious colleagues for her".

---

[18] Examples (39a, b) are from Barnes (1985:161, 164). Roberge (p.c.) has pointed out that in some dialects of Québécois French any intransitive is acceptable with a affected dative if there is an explicit or implicit complement. He furnishes the following examples.
  (I) On lui a dormi ça. "Someone slept him that".
  (ii) On lui a mangé. [object implied] "Someone ate on him".
[19] Grammaticality judgments vary somewhat with affected datives, but the majority of continental and Québécois French speakers consulted found these psych verbs to be substantially less acceptable than standard transitive verbs. An animate subject makes the sentence more acceptable than an inanimate one.

c   *On leur a humilié l'ingrat paresseux.
    "We humiliated the lazy ingrate for them".
d   *Le nouveau patron lui a intéressé les employés.
    "The new boss interested the employees for him".
e   *Le plat peu appétissant leur a dégoûté les clients.
    "The unappetizing plate disgusted the clients for them".

In contrast, subject experiencer psych verb are marginally acceptable despite their stative character.

(41) a   ?On leur déteste cette attitude pompeuse.
         "We detest their pompous attitude".
     b   ?Mon grand-père, on lui aimait bien son béret noir.
         "My grandfather, we really loved his black beret".
     c   ?La bourgeoise bien habillée lui a déploré ce manteau usé.
         "The well dressed lady deplored his worn out coat".

Because the examples in (40) appear semantically and pragmatically acceptable their unacceptability must be due to syntactic reasons. The class represented in (40) will be termed *undative* since it has defective dative Case: verbs such as *ennuyer* take neither lexical nor affected datives. Chapter 4 explores this class of verbs and bears out the predictions made by Burzio's extended generalization concerning such a class.

3.3.2 *Affected datives as nonarguments*

Three kinds of evidence support the treatment of affected datives as nonarguments: they are not subcategorized by the verb; they cannot undergo *qu* extraction; they cannot appear in nonclitic positions in pronominal form (Herschensohn 1992, Branchadell 1992, Authier & Reed 1993).

First, affected datives correspond to no full nominal argument of the verb. Lexical dative verbs such as *envoyer* in (34) show a complementary distribution of dative clitics and prepositional phrases with *à*. Kayne (1975) has used this distribution to support the movement of these clitics from a PP complement position. One might claim that the affected dative clitic corresponds to the marginally acceptable lexical PP with *à* of sentences (29)–(33); however, the questionable acceptability of the prepositional phrase with *à* does not support a derivation of the dative clitic from a PP, but rather suggests that the PP is a marginal semantic variant.[20] The possibility of paraphrasing an affected dative by a PP with prepositions other than *à* indicates a nonsystematic or fortuitous correspondence between lexical PPs and affected datives. As with other optional prepositional phrases (usually of an adverbial nature), some prepositions are more acceptable than others in adjunct PPs. The assumption of nonsystematic correspondence between *à* PPs and affected datives accounts for the variable acceptability of *à* and the possibility of paraphrasing with other prepositions such as *pour* "for".

The second kind of evidence indicating the unusual status of French affected datives is their syntactic immobility. Unlike lexical datives, they disallow *qu* extraction in questions and relatives (Authier & Reed 1992:301). Sentence (34) with a subcategorized dative may be questioned or relativized.

(42) a   *A qui* a-t-il envoyé la lettre?
         "To whom did he send the letter?"
     b   le type *à qui* il a envoyé la lettre
         "the guy to whom he sent the letter"

Subcategorized accusative clitics show the same pattern of *qu* movement. Affected datives, on the other hand, may not be *qu* extracted.

(43) a   *A qui a-t-il tué son/le chat?
         "To whom did he kill her/the cat?"
     b   *la dame à qui on a tué son/le chat
         "the woman to whom someone killed her/the cat"

If the affected datives were true arguments of the verb, they should be extractable in *qu* constructions as lexical datives and accusatives are.

The third kind of evidence against the argument status of affected datives is that they disallow constructions with stressed pronouns. Kayne (1975:Chapter 2) points out the complementary distribution of clitic pronouns with tonic pronouns in cleft and the *ne...que* constructions in arguing for a movement analysis of clitics. Stressed pronouns are acceptable with verbs which subcategorize lexical datives in these constructions. Sentence (34) with

---

[20] In Olsson's (1984) statistical study the number of instances of clitics far outweighs the full PPs. Rooryck (1988:98) points out "la variation d'acceptabilité des datifs non lexicaux lexicalisés montre que ce datif de forme clitique n'a pas de rapport univoque avec une forme non clitique, lexicalisée".

a subcategorized dative may be realized with a clefted stressed pronoun or the *ne...que* construction (44).

(44) a C'est *à elle* qu'il a envoyé la lettre.
        "It's to her he sent the letter".
     b Il n'a envoyé la lettre qu'*à elle*.
        "He sent the letter only to her".

Affected datives do not allow extraction in the cleft construction or realization as a tonic pronoun in the *ne...que* construction (45). These arguments indicate that affected datives are intrinsically clitic as *y, en* and certain reflexives (Kayne 1975:386).

(45) a *C'est *à elle* qu'il a tué son chat.
        "It's to her that he killed her cat".
     b *Il n'a tué son/le chat qu'*à elle*.
        "He killed her/the cat only to her".

    Branchadell's (1992) dissertation gives a thorough overview of affected datives in Romance. His persuasive reasoning that these datives are Case marked in the same manner as lexical datives is adopted here.[21] His proposal that affected datives are theta marked by V′ is similar to that of Authier & Reed (1993:307) who claim that these datives are not VP internal and not selected by any element in the sentence, but rather are licensed by the highest VP segment. "Affected datives are theta bearing affixes which are a reflection of the external theta grid of the highest VP projection at D-structure". These aspects of their analysis are adopted here. It is assumed that affected datives are base generated in Spec Agr_{O3} and that their interpretation is effected as Authier & Reed suggest.
    In minimalist terms the affected dative clitic is base generated in the Spec Agr_{O3} position where it must be checked for dative Case, but it does not correspond to a *pro* in VP_3. This proposal is supported by two aspects of affected datives: first, there is no syntactic evidence that the affected dative is raised from a lower VP position; and second, the semantic interpretation, as Authier & Reed and Branchandell point out, relates to the entire sentence. Hence their c-commanding position accounts for their semantic interpretation.

---

[21] His view that dative Case is inherent is not adopted in the light of the arguments given in Chapter 2 and in Masullo (1992). Masullo convincingly treats Spanish affected datives as examples of incorporation. The Spanish data is quite different from the French.

The verb, while not necessarily a lexical dative Case assigner, must permit an unspecified value for dative Case. Undative verbs are predicted to have a negative value for dative Case which would result in a mismatch with an affected dative; the derivation would crash when a verb such as *amuser* raised to Agr_{O3}. The presence of an affected dative would also preclude a second dative originating in Spec VP_3 because it would be unable to check off its dative Case and the derivation would crash (46); a typical affected dative construction is portrayed in (47).

(46) a *Je lui ai donné son pull aux enfants.
          "I gave her pullover to the children for her".
     b   *Elle lui téléphonera à ses parents.
          "She'll call her parents for him".

(47) Le gosse lui a tué son chat. "The kid killed her cat to her".

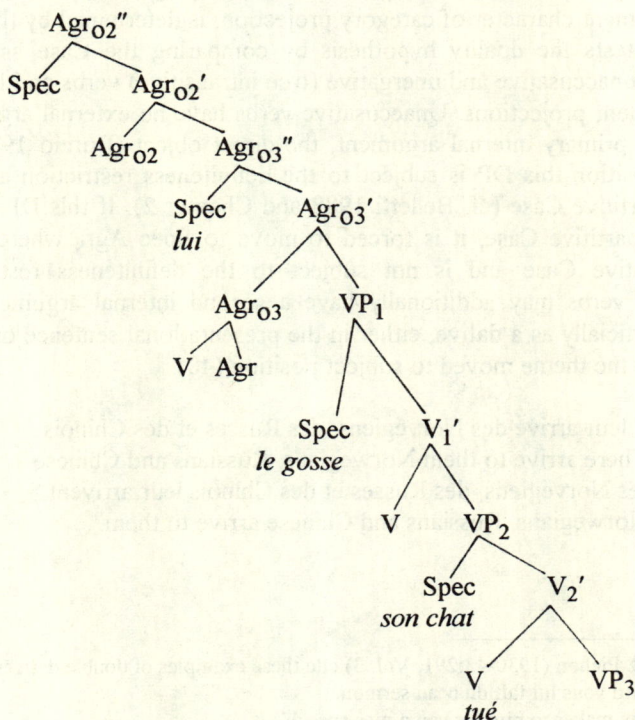

The verb raises overtly as does the external argument *le gosse* to Spec Agr_S. French affected datives do not constitute selected arguments of the verb as do lexical datives; rather they must be base generated in clitic position. Some rare examples of double datives are possible with first and second person clitics (morphologically unspecified for dative); these may include a lexical with an affected dative.[22] The linking of dative Case with Spec VP_3 is indirect for affected datives, since they do not originate in that position, but are base generated in clitic position. The distribution of affected datives is not only a function of the syntactic limitations described above, but will be shown to be a function of the Case assigning potential of the verb. They permit the testing of dative Case assignment and the validity of Burzio's generalization.

3.4 *Case assignment and binary internal argument structure*

Chapter 2 has argued that Case and argument position are linked by the pairing of potential agreement and VP nodes postulated of the Larsonian shell. It has furthermore put forth the hypothesis that a binary limit, forced by the single complement character of category projection, is determined by this link. This section tests the duality hypothesis by comparing the Case assigning properties of unaccusative and unergative (true intransitive) verbs and looking at their argument projections. Unaccusative verbs have no external argument, but have one primary internal argument, the direct object (Burzio 1986). In postverbal position this DP is subject to the definiteness restriction and can only carry partitive Case (cf. Belletti 1988 and Chapter 2). If this DP cannot be saved by partitive Case, it is forced to move to Spec Agr_S where it can carry nominative Case and is not subject to the definiteness restriction. Unaccusative verbs may additionally have a second internal argument that appears superficially as a dative, either in the presentational sentence or in the sentence with the theme moved to subject position (48).

(48) a IL leur arrive des Norvégiens, des Russes et des Chinois.
         "There arrive to them Norwegians, Russians and Chinese".
     b Des Norvégiens, des Russes et des Chinois leur arrivent.
        "Norwegians, Russians and Chinese arrive to them".

---

[22] Damourette & Pichon (1930-43:291, Vol. 3) cite these examples of double datives.
   (i) Le renard vous lui fait un beau sermon.
        "The fox makes to him for you a nice speech".
   (ii) Elle te vous le retourne. "She turns it around to you [pl] for you [sg]".

While the lack of external argument with unaccusatives is supported by substantial evidence, it is conceivable that these verbs could take additional internal arguments. The question tests the validity of the duality hypothesis. In fact, unlike true intransitives which can under limited circumstances take an additional internal argument, unaccusatives cannot. True intransitives such as "run", "dream", "smile" can accept a very limited number of internal arguments which semantically mimic the verb or are closely linked to the verb. These cognate objects have been studied in French as well as English (Rothstein 1992, L&R 1994, Ruwet 1989) (49).

(49) a   Marc a couru (les cent mètres).
          "Mark ran (the hundred meters)".
     b   Marc a pleuré (toutes les larmes de ses yeux).
          "Mark cried (all the tears of his eyes)".
     c   Marc a toussé (un peu de fumée).
          "Mark coughed (a little smoke)".

The ability of unergatives exceptionally to assign accusative Case has been noted in their designation as covert transitives (Burzio 1986, Kayne 1993). Unaccusatives, however, do not permit such an additional argument although as superficial intransitives (50b–e) they resemble the unergatives of (49) (cf. Ruwet 1989:334).

(50) a   Après l'explosion, IL leur pleuvait des briques dessus.
          "After the explosion, there were bricks raining on them".
     b   Des briques leur pleuvaient dessus [sur les passants].
          "Bricks rained on them [the passersby]".
     c   L'exposition de blanc neigeait de toutes les cases.
          "The display of white snowed from all the cases".
     d   Marc est resté à Rome.
          "Mark stayed in Rome".
     e   Le livre lui est tombé dessus.
          "The book fell on him".

In (50a, b, e) there are two internal arguments, the dative linking Spec VP$_3$ and Spec Agr$_{O3}$ and the first internal argument, originating in Spec VP$_2$ and checked for Case in Spec Agr$_{O2}$. If the DP meets the definiteness requirement it can procrastinate (50a), or it may raise to Agr$_S$ with nominative Case (50b–e). Superficially an intransitive verb such as unaccusative *rester* (50d) looks like intransitive unergative *tousser*. Only the unergative can take a cognate object, however, precisely because it can, as a covert transitive, assign accusative Case, and because it has an available argument position in Spec VP$_2$. Unaccusatives, on the other hand, can't assign accusative Case, don't have an available argument position in Spec VP$_2$, and therefore cannot have an additional internal argument (51).

(51) a   *Après l'explosion, des briques pleuvaient les passants.
         "After the explosion, bricks rained [on] the passers-by".
     b   *Marc a / est resté un séjour agréable à Rome.
         "Mark stayed a pleasant stay in Rome".
     c   *Marc a / est parti une sortie rapide.
         "Mark departed a quick exit".
     d   *Marc lui a / est tombé une chute terrible.
         "Mark fell a terrible fall to him".
     e   Marc lui est tombé dessus.
         "Mark fell on him".

The binary limit on the number of internal arguments provides an explanation for the difference between unaccusatives and unergatives: the latter can, under unusual circumstances accept an additional argument, a lexical exception but not a violation of the binary limit. In fact, unergatives can even take two internal arguments, as Ruwet (1989:335) notes (52).

(52) a   Luc lui a vomi tout son repas dessus.
         "Luc vomited his whole meal on her".
     b   Cet abruti m'a craché un énorme glaviot dans l'oeil.
         "This creep spit a huge spittle in my eye".

Unaccusatives, however, already have two potential internal arguments, the DPs in Spec VP$_2$ and Spec VP$_3$. The addition of another argument would constitute three internal arguments. If three internal arguments were permitted with these unaccusatives, all the sentences in (51) should be acceptable. But they are not, and their ungrammaticality is not simply due to the unavailability of a sufficient number of Cases, but to an intrinsic limit on the number of arguments as the next paragraph will show.

This claim can be tested by looking at the role of partitive Case. Given the possibility of assigning partitive Case to the direct object, dative to the indirect and nominative to the subject (an option exploited in the impersonal constructions), a sentence such as (51d) should be possible.

(51)d   *Marc lui est tombé une chute terrible.

A conceivable derivation with partitive rather than accusative Case marking of the cognate object of the unaccusative could for sentence (51d) assume that *lui* is in the Spec Agr_{O3}, *une chute* originates in Spec VP_3, raises to be checked for objective Case in Spec Agr_{O2}, and that *Marc*, marked with nominative Case, raises directly from Spec VP_2 to Spec Agr_S without passing through Spec Agr_{O2}. This derivation violates the minimal distance principle and ignores the specificity of the link between agreement and VP nodes. The derivation crashes as the ungrammaticality of (51d) shows, even though there appear to be enough Cases for the three arguments. The impossibility of this derivation confirms the specificity of the agreement–VP links and the requirement that direct objects pass through Agr_{O2} on their way to Spec Agr_S. It also confirms the dual limit on internal arguments independently of the twofold nature of internal Case. The limit described with respect to unaccusatives will be borne out with respect to other verb classes in subsequent chapters.

   Similar observations concerning unaccusative verbs are made by Rothstein (1992) and L&R (1994) who point out that true intransitives in English can be constructed with direct objects in resultative constructions (53a, b). The same verbs are ungrammatical when used in simple transitive sentences (53c, d).

(53)a   They laughed John off the stage.
    b   They ran their shoes threadbare.
    c   *They laughed John.
    d   *They ran the shoes.

Resultatives can also be constructed with unergatives taking fake reflexives (54) (L&R 1994:35).

(54)a   Dora shouted *(herself) hoarse.
    b   The mistress grumbled *(herself) calm.
    c   The officers laughed *(themselves) helpless.

However, Rothstein claims (1992:127), "resultative constructions will be impossible with unaccusative verbs, which do not assign Case".

(55)a   *The window swung itself open.
    b   *The river froze itself solid.
    c   *The cart rolled the rubber off its wheels.

The two studies underline the inability of unaccusatives to assign accusative Case as opposed to unergatives which can assign accusative in cognate object constructions.

3.5 *Conclusion*

In this chapter the binary hypothesis of Case and argument structure has been examined in the light of two constructions, unaccusative verbs and affected datives. Unaccusative verbs, incapable of assigning accusative Case, still may have two (but no more) internal arguments. The inability of these verbs to accept a third internal argument bears out binary internal argument structure. On the other hand, transitive verbs which take only one internal argument are able to add an additional nonargument, the affected dative. They are ungrammatical with a class of psych verbs termed undatives.

Unaccusative verbs such as *arriver* constitute a class characterized by a nonthematic external argument and the inability to assign accusative Case. For this reason the direct object of unaccusative verbs is usually forced to move to subject position to carry nominative Case. Unaccusative verbs contrast with true intransitives with regard to argument structure: unergatives, which take one external argument, can in certain circumstances be constructed with an internal argument; however, unaccusatives which select two internal arguments, cannot take an additional argument. The evidence presented in this chapter furnishes a set of diagnostics for nonthematic external arguments that will be used in the following chapters. Affected datives also constitute diagnostics because they will be used to test the dative assigning capacity of different classes of verbs.

These two syntactic constructions amply illustrate the dissociability of the Case–argument link. Unaccusatives take up to two internal arguments but have one internal Case, accusative, suspended. In the absence of redemption by partitive Case, the unaccusative direct object is forced to raise to nominative Spec Agr$_S$, confirming Burzio's generalization. An extension of Burzio's generalization proposed in this chapter predicts a link between structural dative as well as structural accusative and the nonthematic external argument.

CHAPTER 4

CASE DEFECTIVE PSYCH VERBS

4.0 *Introduction*

Chapter 3 has examined affected datives, nonarguments that carry structural Case, and unaccusative verbs that select two potential internal arguments but have only one internal Case to assign. Chapter 4 uses these two constructions to investigate the behavior of psychological experiencer (psych) verbs. It is argued that two subclasses of psych verbs have nonthematic external arguments, one group that assigns dative but not accusative Case, and another that assigns accusative but not dative Case. The second group thus constitutes a class of undatives parallel to the unaccusatives presented in Chapter 3. The undatives bear out proposals concerning Case made in previous chapters and support the binary approach to argument structure, in that they accept only two internal arguments.

The chapter is organized as follows: Section 4.1. presents data on psychological experiencer verbs and discusses previous treatments. Section 4.2 evaluates problems related to the thematic structure of the different varieties of psych verbs, considering the treatments of Grimshaw (1992) and Pesetsky (1995) in the light of a minimalist approach. Section 4.3 argues that undative psych verbs select a nonthematic external argument and that the second (nonaccusative) argument raises to superficial subject position. The last section reevaluates Burzio's generalization and the binary hypothesis in terms of psych verbs.

4.1 *Psychological experiencer verbs*
4.1.1 *Three classes of psych verbs*

Belletti & Rizzi (1988, henceforth B&R) distinguish three classes of psych verbs in Italian, represented by parallel examples in French (1)–(3).

(1) a Gianni teme questo.
     "John fears this".

    b   Pierre déteste les mouches.
        "Peter hates flies".
    c   Pierre voit les mouches.
        "Peter sees the flies".
(2) a   Questo preoccupa Gianni.
        "This preoccupies John".
    b   Les mouches dégoûtent Pierre.
        "Flies disgust Peter".
(3) a   Questo piace a Gianni.
        "This pleases [to] John.
    b   Les mouches répugnent à Pierre.
        "Flies repulse [to] Peter".

It was noted in Chapter 3 that verbs of the *amuser* class do not accept affected datives, and they were hence dubbed "undatives". Adopting this terminology, the three classes of psych verbs are designated as *transitive* (1), *undative* (2), and *unaccusative* (3). Psych verbs manifest five characteristics that distinguish them from typical agentive verbs and that have been investigated by linguists: theta role distribution, interpretation and valence variability, subject (non)thematicity, Case suspension and backward anaphora.

The three classes show different configurations of apparent thematic roles. This chapter adopts the labels "experiencer, theme" for presentational purposes, although the appropriateness of such labeling has been questioned (cf. Chapter 2). Transitive psych verbs such as *adorer, craindre, détester* "to adore, fear, detest" have as superficial subject the experiencer, and as direct object the theme (4). These verbs behave syntactically like other typical transitives which have a subject agent / experiencer and direct object theme.

(4) Les païens adorent les idoles.
    "The pagans adore the idols".
    experiencer   *theme*

The subject of transitive *adorer* type verbs is the experiencer; syntactic evidence and previous analyses all support a derivation in which *les païens* originates as a thematic external argument. Ruwet (1972:189) furnishes a partial list including *admirer, adorer, aimer, apprécier, déplorer, détester, estimer, mépriser, redouter, regretter, supporter* "to admire, adore, love, appreciate, deplore, detest, estimate, scorn, dread, regret, tolerate".

The *amuser* class (represented by *amuse, disgust, frighten, preoccupy*) has a distribution of theta roles that appears to be the opposite of the transitive class: the undative class has a subject theme and direct object experiencer (5a, c). Furthermore, this class has pronominal variants such as *s'amuser* "to have fun". Ruwet (1972:189) provides a partial list including *agacer, dégoûter, effrayer, ennuyer, étonner, gêner, horrifier, humilier, impressionner, intéresser, préoccuper, surprendre, terrifier* "to irritate, disgust, frighten, bore, startle, bother, horrify, humiliate, impress, interest, preoccupy, surprise, terrify". With the pronominal variants (5b, d) the experiencer is the subject and the theme is often the object of a preposition (5d). The *se*, while referentially identical to the subject, is not easily identified with a thematic role.

(5) a   Les marionnettes amusent les enfants.
    "The marionnettes amuse the children".
    theme   experiencer
  b   Les enfants s'amusent.
    "The children have fun".
    experiencer
  c   Ce projet intéresse Jean.
    "This project interests John".
    theme   experiencer
  d   Jean s'intéresse à ce projet / Marie / elle.
    "John is interested in this project / Mary / her".
    experiencer   theme

The PP in (5d) is not a dative as the tonic pronoun indicates; *à Marie* in pronominal form cannot cliticize as *lui*.

The third group, unaccusative psych verbs such as *manquer, plaire*, have a superficial structure whose thematic experiencer is a dative and whose theme is often the subject (6).

(6) a   IL lui manque plusieurs livres.
    "There are several books missing to her".
    theme   experiencer
  b   Les livres volés manquent à Marie.
    "The stolen books are missing [to] Mary".
    theme   experiencer

The dative experiencer is a sine qua non for an experiencer reading, and the sentence is usually not impersonal since the theme is often specific (6b). Sentence (6a) implies more of a concrete reading (the books are gone) as opposed to a sense of emotional loss in (6b). Unaccusative psych verbs include the verbs described in Chapter 3 used in a figurative rather than literal interpretation. While the undative *amuser* class of psych verbs has the emotive meaning as its primary one, the class of unaccusative psych verbs has both an emotive and concrete interpretation. It includes *aller (bien), appartenir, arriver, déplaire, importer, manquer, dis/ap/paraître, plaire, répugner, rester, suffire, tomber, sur/re/par/venir,* "to go, belong, arrive, displease, concern, miss, dis/appear, please, repulse, remain, suffice, fall happen/come". These verbs allow impersonal constructions with postverbal theme (with potential partitive *en*), or may have themes in subject position as in (3), (6). Many of these verbs take *être* as an auxiliary; however auxiliary selection is not as consistent a diagnostic for unaccusativity in French as in Italian.[1]

Linguists such as Lakoff (1970) and Postal (1971) have observed that psych verbs of the first and second variety often mirror each other in the distribution of their semantic arguments in that some verbs seem to be thematic reversals of the other (e.g. *dislike / disgust*). In certain cases a single verb seems to have a variable valence, such as *grieve* (Pesetsky 1995:18).

(7) a   Sue grieved over / at the court decision.
    b   The court decision grieved Sue.

The variability of valence and or theta role distribution poses a problem for the linking of thematic and argument structure, particularly for a proposal such as the UTAH. The misalignment has thus been a topic of interest to linguists for some time.

A third area of distinction for psych verbs is the potential nonthematicity of the external argument. Since none of the arguments in the psych sentences is a true agent, all arguments have theta roles deemed lower than agent on the thematic hierarchy. The nonthematicity of unaccusative verbs is well accepted as is the thematicity of the transitive verbs' external argument. The undative verbs constitute the area of greatest investigation, and the question of subject nonthematicity is related to the question of Case suspension, corollary to Burzio's generalization. The last question is equivalent to asking whether undatives are different or the same as unaccusatives.

---

[1] Most of the unaccusatives do not permit pronominal variants, although *se suffire, se plaire* "to suffice, please oneself" are exceptions that are examples of inherent se. B&R point out the existence of pronominal variants for Italian *preoccupare*, but they do not deal with the pronominal form of these psych verbs. Chapter 5 deals with psych pronominals.

The fifth issue, backward anaphora, involves a marginal construction that has plagued linguists for years. In principle *amuse / please* psych verbs allow anaphors contained within the subject to be bound by the indirect or direct object (8a) in violation of c-command restrictions, and in opposition to typical transitives (8b).

(8) a   These rumors about himself please / worry John.
    b   These rumors about himself falsely represent John.

In fact, although this issue has been a preoccupation of linguists for years, grammaticality judgments on these sentences are quite subtle. Both French and English speakers interviewed in this study were unable to distinguish consistently between psych verbs and transitive verbs in these constructions.

4.1.2 *Previous treatments*

Ruwet (1972:181–251), in his thorough examination of French psych verbs, convincingly argues against a transformational linking (proposed by Postal 1971) of the *détester / dégoûter* pairs. He also points out that the crossing of thematic roles is only apparent, for the selectional restrictions on the different classes are not quite the same. As for backwards anaphora, he says that generally French does not furnish adequate data, and that there are certain clear counterexamples to backward binding. He opts for Jackendoff's thematic hierarchy over a syntactic explanation for this phenomenon.

Bouchard (1992:28) reiterates Ruwet's observation that there is only an apparent crossing of theta roles, and "an attempt to assign thematic roles uniformly at Deep structure is not substantiated". His article, a perceptive investigation of psych extensions of concrete verbs such as *frapper* "to strike", emphasizes the productivity of psych constructions, verbal and periphrastic. He shares the skepticism of Ruwet and the present study in pointing out that backward binding is not limited to psych expressions alone.

Legendre (1989a), working in a relational grammar framework, takes a syntactic approach that ignores nonthematicity, Case suspension and backward binding. She proposes the following derivation for *manquer* verbs: the final 3 (indirect object) derives from an initial 1 (subject), while the final 1 derives from an initial 2 (direct object). Herschensohn (1992c) agrees with Legendre's 2 to 1 promotion, but rejects the 1 to 3 inversion, arguing that adverbial binding is not an adequate test for subjecthood.

B&R (1988:334) note the tripartition of traditional theta role distribution by which psych verbs challenge the UTAH. They claim that in (2) and (3) "both theme and experiencer are VP-internal at D-structure" and propose the following structure for *preoccupare* (*amuser*) and *piacere* (*manquer*) type verbs (9).

(9) B&R's proposal

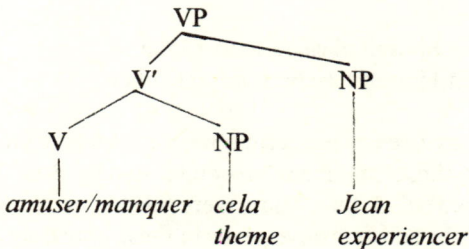

```
                    VP
                  /‾‾‾‾‾‾‾‾‾‾‾
              V'              NP
            /‾‾‾              |
        V        NP          |
        |        |           |
  amuser/manquer  cela      Jean
                  theme    experiencer
```

They argue that unaccusative and undative psych verbs have a nonthematic external argument and that the theme moves to subject position. They do not address the issue of Case suspension. Their syntactic treatment of psych anomalies carries into their handling of backward anaphora.

Grimshaw (1992) argues that semantic considerations, not syntactic structure alone, account for the variety of thematic distribution with psych verbs. Subscribing to Baker's UTAH and accepting the traditional theta labels of theme and experiencer, she claims that the mapping of thematic to syntactic structure is a function of two dimensions, the thematic and the aspectual. The aspectual dimension is "a projection of the event structure of the predicates" (ibid.:26). She maintains that the enrichment of argument theory with the aspectual dimension permits an account of apparent discrepancies in theta / argument alignment in *fear* / *frighten* pairs. The distribution for *fear* follows directly from the thematic hierarchy (the experiencer becomes the subject). The syntactic reversal of *frighten* is attributed to a misalignment of the thematic and aspectual dimensions. She holds that undatives are not like unaccusatives and do not have nonthematic external arguments. She doesn't discuss backward binding.

Pesetsky (1995), like Grimshaw, takes semantics into account in proposing a refinement in theta role designation and a more complex morphosemantic structure of psych verbs. He chooses to replace the term theme with *causer* (as *projet* in (5c)) or *target / subject matter of emotion* (*projet* in (5d)).

(5) c   Ce projet intéresse Jean.
    d   Jean s'intéresse à ce projet.

Pesetsky thus formalizes the distinction noted by Ruwet, but pushes the discussion in a "neo-Lakovian" (Lakoff 1970) direction, accounting for the difference between (5c, d) by proposing that object experiencer (5c) verbs carry a zero *caus* morpheme that adds a causative dimension to the base lexical content of the verb. Pesetsky accepts B&R's treatment of backward anaphora, but rejects their nonthematic treatment of undatives.

4.2 *Semantic considerations of psych verbs*

The studies presented in the preceding section deal with two aspects of psych verbs, semantic considerations of thematic role mapping (including aspect and mode) to be dealt with in this section, and syntactic considerations of structure (including subject thematicity and argument positioning) to be dealt with in Section 4.3. B&R focus on the overt syntax to account for psych anomalies, while Grimshaw and Pesetsky investigate complex semantic notions that lead to syntactic reversals such as the *fear / frighten* pair. Section 4.2.1 considers thematic roles and lexical features and Section 4.2.2 reconsiders backward anaphora.

4.2.1 *Another psychological dimension*

Both Grimshaw and Pesetsky find the B&R treatment of psych verbs incomplete from a semantic perspective because the latter do not account for an added dimension that renders simple theta roles inadequate to the psychological task. For Grimshaw the added dimension is aspectual, and for Pesetsky it includes an enrichment of theta roles and verbal morphology. Grimshaw (1992:41) claims that the external argument / subject of *fear* is aspectually and thematically the most prominent argument whereas the subject of *frighten* has maximal aspectual but not thematic prominence and is *not* an external argument. Although she does not relabel theta roles, her distinction hinges on the notion of causation because for *frighten* the theme is a cause, but for *fear* it is not. The aspectual dimension she proposes is an elaboration on Dowty (1979), but she provides (1992:24–25) "no independent evidence" that the analysis will work for psych verbs.

Pesetsky's finer grained semantic treatment attributes the difference between *fear and frighten* to two factors, the heterogeneity of theta roles with the two verbs, and the presence of a causative (zero) morpheme with *frighten*. Hence, if ghosts (*causer* theta role) frighten John (*experiencer*), they cause him to be frightened, but if John (*experiencer*) fears ghosts (*target / subject*

matter theta role), ghosts are the topic or focus of his fears, not the cause.[2]
Fear is a simplex verb whereas *frighten* is a complex verb containing the *caus*
morpheme. Pesetsky motivates the zero morpheme with evidence such as the
fact that nominalizations of psych verbs have the simple, not causative
meaning. *John's fright* can only refer to his own fear, and *the ghosts' fright* is
ungrammatical with the reading that ghosts frighten someone.[3]

Postulating that theta role assignment is a function of predication, H&K
(1993b:93–94) provide a framework for accommodating both Grimshaw's
and Pesetsky's observations.

> The syntactic projection of lexical categories and arguments conforms to the
> principles of Unambiguous Projection (Kayne 1984) and Full Interpretation
> (Chomsky 1986a) [...] There is no process of "thematic role assignment", apart
> from Predication; and there are no "thematic roles", apart from the lexical relations
> expressed in unambiguous, fully interpreted projections of the elementary lexical
> categories.

Theta roles reflect semantic primitives such as the notion of causation that can
contribute to verbal complexity. The lexico-semantic insights of Grimshaw
and Pesetsky are not dependent on the existence of theta roles, so her
conservatism (1992:20) in rejecting Pesetsky's relabeling, or his relabeling are
really not crucial to their analyses. What is important is the more basic
semantic content that affects the lexical entry. H&K (1993b:85ff.) discuss
causative / inchoative pairs, examples of verbal complexity, in terms quite
compatible with Pesetsky's work. Grimshaw's proposal of an aspectual
dimension to lexical conceptual structure is supported on independent and
quite distinct grounds.[4] For example, Zagona (1988, 1992, 1994) uses
aspectual features in a very precise and syntactically constrained manner to
predict differences in tense interpretation. The H&K model provides the
means for constructing the presyntactic lexical derivation, for mapping
arguments into syntactic positions, and for providing the basis for systematic
differences in interpretation of psych verbs.

---

[2] Pesetsky distinguishes the two theta roles *target* and *subject matter*, but does not furnish
diagnostics for differentiating them. He later (1995:63) shows they are conjoinable,
suggesting that they are nondistinct.
[3] Pesetsky extends his proposal to a wide range of phenomena including double object
constructions and causative / inchoative verbs.
[4] Grimshaw (1992:25) claims that the aspectual analysis of psych verbs is "stipulated", so it
is not the best candidate for supporting her proposed aspectual dimension.

4.2.2 *Psych binding anomalies*

It has long been noted (Lakoff 1970, Postal 1971, Jackendoff 1972, Ruwet 1972) that reflexive anaphors appear to violate c-command restrictions with psych verbs as in (10a) where the experiencer in object position binds an anaphor within the subject. In principle nonpsych verbs disallow binding violations (10b), although judgments are quite subtle.

(10) a　Les photos de lui-même amusent Paul.
　　　　"The photos of himself amuse Paul".
　　 b　?Les photos de lui-même représentent Paul parfaitement.
　　　　"The photos of himself represent Paul perfectly".

The acceptability of (10a), despite the binding violation has generally been accounted for by appealing to a thematic hierarchy (Jackendoff (1972:43ff.): Jackendoff's basic idea is that the notion of prominence, not simply that of configuration, is relevant for the assignment of an antecedent to an anaphor. This involves a thematic hierarchy by which an experiencer is more prominent than for example, a theme.

B&R (1989:313), in seeking a structural account of the binding anomaly, suggest that Principle A of the binding theory should be modified to apply either at D or S-structure, claiming that this slight reformulation allows an explanation of the psych binding anomaly. Pesetsky (1995:42ff.) essentially adopts their position. In the configuration they propose (11) the antecedent *Paul* can correctly c-command the anaphor *lui-même* at D-structure, so B&R are led to choose this arrangement over one in which *Paul* is generated in direct object position.

(11) [$_{VP}$[$_{V'}$ amuser [$_{DP}$ photos de lui-même]][$_{DP}$ Paul]]

This reasoning also allows them to claim that "there must be strict principles constraining the projection of theta-structures onto D-structures" (ibid.:293–294) and that "even in the problematic area of psych verbs the theory constraining the syntactic projection of theta-grids has an important regularity to capture". According to B&R the structure proposed not only accounts for the binding anomalies, but also furnishes an identical D-structure / theta role correspondence for two of the three classes of psych verbs. Although these two claims appear theoretically desirable, B&R are obliged to make two ad hoc theoretical modifications to make their system work, the reinterpretation of Principle A, and the proposal that accusative Case can be either inherent or structural (ibid.:331–333).

The marginality of the backward anaphors and the ad hoc nature of B&R's modifications strongly suggest that the binding anomalies should be dealt with in pragmatic terms, not syntactic.[5] In the minimalist framework binding theory holds at the LF interface, so B&R's proposal is inapplicable. The anaphors in question are always in subjectless maximal projections (*photos of himself*, not **Mary's photos of himself*), and with psych verbs are in thematic subjectless sentences. It is not unreasonable that these orphan anaphors seek an antecedent pragmatically rather than structurally. As B&R note, there seems to be no difference in backward binding options for unaccusatives or undatives, so internal arguments seem equally prominent in this respect. Bouchard (1992:39–42) provides convincing evidence that backward reflexivization is not due to a special syntactic structure for psych verbs. After a quarter century Ruwet's (1972:219) words may be most appropriate: "Il s'agirait alors simplement d'un de ces nombreux problèmes qui restent inexpliqués, quelque soit le cadre théorique dans lequel on se place". The following sections turn to the overt syntax to discuss argument structure, subject thematicity, and Case of *amuser* undatives.

4.3 *Syntactic considerations of psych verbs*

While the mapping of semantic roles onto syntactic positions can be accommodated by the H&K model, there remain questions concerning syntactic movement with psych verbs. The direction taken here, which has been virtually ignored in previous studies, is that of Case assignment and suspension, the crucial feature determining movement possibilities for these verbs. Two areas will be examined: the thematicity of the subject in Section 4.3.1 and the structural distribution of arguments (a reevaluation of B&R's structure in (9)) in Section 4.3.2.

4.3.1 *Diagnostics for nonthematic external arguments*

This section argues that *amuser*, like *manquer*, selects a nonthematic external argument.[6] In addition to the syntactic diagnostics outlined in Chapter 3, an additional morphological argument will be given. Auxiliary selection is not considered since all *amuser* type verbs take *avoir*.

---

[5] Chomsky (1993:37–43) discusses anaphoric binding ambiguities in sentences with reconstruction effects.

[6] Pesetsky (1995:38) claims to have "sufficiently refuted" the athematic proposal, but mainly argues against the idea that the subject theme originates as a direct object, not against nonthematicity (cf. Chapter 3).

The first argument concerns the impersonal construction requiring a nonthematic external argument position filled by expletive *IL*. The impersonal construction is ungrammatical with transitive (12a) and unergative (12b) constructions, both of which have thematic external arguments. The impersonal construction is grammatical with unaccusatives (12d), and passive (12e).

(12) a *IL [impers] adore plusieurs idoles.
         "There adore several idols".
     b *IL a dormi trois garçons.
         "There slept three boys".
     c *IL amuse plusieurs enfants.
         "There amuse several children".
     d IL manque plusieurs livres.
         "There are several books missing".
     e IL a été mangé plusieurs pommes.
         "There were eaten several apples".

Burzio (1986:137) points out that the IL impersonal construction is possible with only nonthematic external argument verbs. The impersonal test indicates that the external argument of unaccusative (12d) is nonthematic as is the external argument of passive constructions (12e). Simplex sentences with undatives are usually ungrammatical (12c), but presentational sentences *can* be constructed with a CP complement (Grevisse 1993:1153) (13).[7]

(13) a IL m'ennuie de partager avec les filles.
         "It bothers me to share with the girls".
     b IL m'étonne que M. Mauriac vous représente un idéologue.
         "It startles me that M. Mauriac represents you as an ideologue".

Because CPs are usually not Case marked (the Case Resistance Principle of Stowell 1981), the lack of a second internal Case with undatives is not consequential for CP complements.

Second, arbitrary *on* is only permissable as a deep subject as in (14a). *On* is ungrammatical with *manquer / amuser* (14 b,c) with the reading of

---

[7] Grimshaw (1992:33) claims that the impossibility of *IL* with *amuser* argues against the nonthematic external argument status of these verbs. The ungrammaticality is predictable because these verbs obligatorily subcategorize an experiencer and theme, but cannot assign Case to the theme argument because they lack dative Case.

"someone". Legendre points out that the "we" reading is often acceptable when the arbitrary reading is not.

(14) a Dans ce pays lointain, on adore les idoles.
        "In this faraway land, we / someone adores idols".
     b Depuis qu'il est seul, on lui manque beaucoup.
        "Since he's been alone, he misses us / *someone".
     c On a bien amusé les enfants hier soir.
        "We / ?*Someone really amused the children last night".

Grammaticality judgments on the arbitrary interpretation are subtle, although both Legendre and B&R use this interpretation as a diagnostic for nonthematic external arguments. According to some informants a change in context may allow an arbitrary interpretation with a nonthematic external argument verb .

(15) a On ne manque jamais de respect à sa mère.
        "One never lacks respect for her mother".
     b On amuse les enfants si on ne veut pas qu'ils soient déagréables.
        "One amuses children so they are not disagreeable".

However, the interpretation of (15) is the generic one that B&R (1988:300, fn 6) put aside. The desired interpretation is neither the generic, nor the "corporate" use described by5 (1995:39ff.).[8] Legendre (1989a:763–766) develops the *on* argument for French for both *manquer* and *préoccuper*, claiming that the arbitrary interpretation appears to be restricted to thematic external arguments of unergative and transitive verbs. The sentences are acceptable with the reading that *on* = "we".[9]

---

[8] Pesetsky's (1995:40) interesting observations on the corporate *they*, "prototypically governments, bosses, criminals, or shopkeepers", do not capture the *arb* interpretation that is desired here. His claim that agentivity is the key factor (i) seems to be on the right track, but doesn't give perfect results as (ii) shows.
    (i) a They punched me at the supermarket.
         b *They received a punch in the nose at the supermarket.
    (ii)   They received a $5000 bribe for turning a blind eye.
[9] Informants interviewed in this study agreed on the grammaticality of the *arb* interpretation with thematic external argument verbs, but opinions were mixed with unaccusatives and undatives (cf. Appendix). The sentences tested for this phenomenon did not cover a range of lexical items and were not screened against the generic interpretation.

Third, only thematic external arguments can bind reflexives (16a, b), but the subject of *manquer / amuser* cannot (16c, d).[10]

(16) a Les enfants se lavent les uns les autres.
        "The children wash each other.
     b Les païens s'adorent les uns les autres.
        "The pagans adore one another".
     c *Les enfants se manquent les uns les autres.
        "The children miss each other".
     d *Les enfants s'amusent/se préoccupent les uns les autres.
        "The children amuse/preoccupy one another".

Fourth, thematic, but not derived subjects may be omitted when embedded under causative *faire*. In French, true transitive (17a, b) and intransitive (unergative) (17c) verbs may be embedded in causative constructions without an external argument as in (17a). On the other hand, *manquer / amuser*, like unaccusative *arriver* (18a), disallow this construction (18b, c). They superficially resemble the true transitives (*X amuse les enfants*) or the unergatives (*X arrive*), but the superficial subject represented by *X* cannot be absent whereas the superficial subject of *adorer* or *dormir* can be. If unaccusatives and undatives had a thematic external argument (18b, c) should be allowable, but these sentences are ungrammatical.

(17) a Le prêtre faisait adorer les idoles.
        "The priest made [someone] adore the idols".
     b Il a fait réparer ses chaussures.
        "He had [someone] repair his shoes".
     c Ces somnifères font dormir rapidement.
        "These pills make [someone] sleep quickly".
(18) a *Cet autobus fait arriver rapidement.
        "This bus makes [someone] arrive quickly".
     b *Cette chanson faisait manquer à quelqu'un.
        "This song makes [someone] miss someone".
     c *Cette blague faisait amuser les enfants.
        "This joke made [someone] amuse the children".

The fifth diagnostic, considered unreliable for nonpsych unaccusatives (19d), seems quite consistent for undatives. B&R (1988:302) claim

---

[10] One reader finds *amuser* acceptable with a reciprocal reading.

"structures containing a derived subject cannot be embedded under the causative construction in Italian". French psych verbs, both unaccusative and undative resist this construction (19).

> (19) a   Marc a fait réparer la voiture au mécanicien.
> "Mark had the mechanic repair the car".
> b   *Cette librairie faisait manquer les livres à Marie.
> "This bookstore made Marie miss the books".
> c   *Cette blague faisait amuser les enfants aux marionnettes.
> "This joke made the marionnettes amuse the children".
> d   On fera mourir son chien.
> "We'll have his dog die".

While *les livres* and *les marionnettes* may be superficial subjects in the simplex sentences embedded in (19), they cannot be thematic external arguments by this diagnosis.

A last syntactic diagnostic is dative cliticization with *faire* causatives (specified subject effects) as in (20) (cf. Chapter 3).

> (20) *Cela leur a fait téléphoner Marie [à ses parents].
> "That made her phone them [her parents]".

Datives may not be cliticized to *faire* in the presence of a thematic subject of the embedded verb. Given the ungrammaticality of any datives with undatives, and of (19c) in particular, causative dative cliticization would be predicted to be ungrammatical with *amuser*. The undative verbs are aggressively accusative in that they do not appear easily without a direct object. Since this causative diagnostic requires the embedded verb to have an apparent subject and indirect object, and no direct object, it is not easy to create such a sentence.[11] One can logically conceive such a sentence with an affected dative, but it is equally ungrammatical in the causative as well as the simplex sentence (21).

---

[11] The presence of an embedded direct object and indirect object creates two datives (the indirect object and the agent of the embedded verb) but only the dative of the complex verb can cliticize to *faire*, not the dative of the embedded verb (Ruwet 1972).

> (i)   Marc lui a fait apporter des pommes à Paul.
> "Mark had her bring apples to Paul". / *Mark had Paul bring her apples".

(21) a   Ce bruit est agaçant.
         "This noise is irritating".
      b   Ce bruit agace énormément.
         "This noise irritates terribly".
      c   *On lui a fait agacer énormément ce bruit.
         "We had this noise irritate terribly to him".
      d   On lui a fait tomber des pierres dessus.
         "We had stones fall on him".

(21c) should be grammatical on the model of the unaccusative (21d) if *ce bruit* is not a thematic external argument, but the undative character of *agacer* disallows dative Case assignment by *faire*. Using Reed's analysis, the ungrammaticality would be due to a mismatch in Case features between *agacer* and *faire* precluding the formation of a verbal chain (cf. Section 3.1.3 and Reed 1991:342). Causative data confirm the undative Case characteristics of *amuser / agacer* type verbs.

A last diagnostic discussed by Pesetsky (1995:79–80), but not for the same purpose, is possession with deverbal nominals. He points out that inchoative / causative verbs like *grow* allow only the direct object as a possessor, not the causative subject (22), unlike typical transitives (23).

(22) a   Tomatoes grow. / Bill grows tomatoes.
      b   the growth of tomatoes / *Bill's growth of tomatoes
(23) a   The enemy destroyed the city.
      b   the city's destruction / the enemy's destruction of the city

Verbs like *grow* constitute the multivalent class that Burzio terms ergative and argues to have a nonthematic external argument in inchoative use. A closer look reveals that possessor distribution with deverbal nominals can serve as a diagnostic for subject thematicity: only thematic external arguments and direct objects can serve as possessors with transitive (24) and unergative (25) verbs. With multivalence or nonthematic external argument verbs only the direct object can be the possessor(26)–(28).

(24) a   L'ennemi a détruit la ville.
         "The enemy destroyed the city".
      b   la destruction de la ville / de l'ennemi
         "the destruction of the city / of the enemy"
(25) a   Marc a réagi.
         "Mark reacted".

     b   la réaction de Marc
         "the reaction of Mark"

(26) a   IL est arrivé plusieurs étudiants; ils sont arrivés.
         "There arrived several students; they arrived".

     b   l'arrivée des étudiants
         "the arrival of the students"

(27) a   Le chef a gelé le jus; le jus a gelé.
         "The chef froze the juice; the juice froze".

     b   la gelée du jus / *du chef
         "the jelly of the juice / of the chef"

(28) a   Les marionnettes amusent les enfants.
         "The marionnettes amuse the children".

     b   l'amusement des enfants / *des marionnettes
         "the amusement of the children / of the marionnettes"

This morphological diagnostic indicates that *amuser* selects a nonthematic external argument.[12] The diagnostics all point to the nonthematic status of the external argument selected by undative verbs, but beg the definition of "nonthematic subject" in minimalist terms, a point addressed in Section 4.4.

4.3.2 *Psych internal argument structure*

B&R (1988:293–294) assume that the theme of *manquer / amuser*, which eventually becomes the subject, is an underlying direct object as in (9): they designate it as the NP of V' and state that the "verb directly theta-marks the theme, and the constituent Verb + theme compositionally theta-marks the experiencer". The structure they propose raises the question of whether unaccusatives and undatives are indeed the same class with a superficial Case difference, or whether they are substantially different. This section looks at their differences, supporting structure (9) for unaccusatives, but rejecting it for *amuser* undatives.

The D-structure of (9) proposes that the experiencer of *manquer* verbs is the second internal argument (experiencer) of the verb, a sister of V', which manifests dative Case at S-structure and that the first internal argument (theme) is the direct object. The acceptability of *en* with psych unaccusatives

---

[12] Other examples of undatives show the same pattern: *P ennuie M, l'ennui de M / *de P; P surprend M, la surprise de M / *de P; P préoccupe M, la préoccupation de M / *de P* "P bores / surpises / preoccupies M, the boredom / surprise / preoccupation of M / P".

supports the direct object status of their postverbal theme (29) (examples from Legendre 1989a:761).[13]

(29) a   IL lui en plairait beaucoup [de femmes].
       "There would please him a lot of them [of women".
   b   IL lui en manquera trois [de couleurs].
       "There will be missing to him three [colors]".

The ability of unaccusative verbs to assign dative Case to both lexical and affected datives is well documented so the structure proposed in (9) appears reasonable in terms of both Case assignment and dominance relations for the experiencer dative and theme direct object of *manquer*.[14] The same structure does not appear uncontroversial, however, for the internal arguments of *amuser*.

In apparent contradiction to B&R's proposals, several syntactic tests for direct objecthood render questionable their claim that the theme of *amuser* is the underlying direct object.[15] While the theme *les marionnettes* of *amuser* fails direct object diagnostics, the experiencer *les enfants* meets the diagnostics of direct objecthood for French, partitive *en*, accusative clitics, *qu* morphology, passive, participial control and *croire* constructions (cf. Section 3.1.4). In (30) these constructions are possible with *les enfants*, indicating that this experiencer is indeed the direct object (italicized in (30)).

(30) a   Les marionnettes amusent *les enfants*.
       "The marionnettes amuse the children".
   b   Les marionnettes *en* ont amusé *plusieurs*.
       "The marionnettes amused a several of them".
   c   Les marionnettes *les* amusent.
       "The marionnettes amuse them".
   d   *les enfants que* / *qui les marionnettes amusent
       "the children whom / who the marionnettes amuse"

---

[13] Grimshaw (1992:30) excludes *amuse* psych verbs from the unaccusative class because they fail *ne* cliticization and auxiliary selection diagnostics in Italian.

[14] Both Grimshaw and Pesetsky implicitly approve such a structure in their acceptance of a traditional understanding of unaccusatives (nonthematic external argument, direct object movement) and their rejection of B&R's treatment of *amuse* verbs as unaccusatives.

[15] B&R point out island properties of the experiencer of *amuser* to argue that is not a D-structure direct object. They admit, however, that judgments on these sentences are quite subtle. Speakers of French questioned gave a variety of grammaticality judgments which showed no consistent pattern related to the two classes.

    e *Les enfants* sont amusés [par les marionnettes].
      "The children are amused [by the marionnettes]".
    f *les enfants* amusés
      "the amused children"
    g On croyait *les enfants* amusés.
      "We believed the children [to be] amused".

On the other hand, the theme, *les marionnettes* (italicized in (31–35)), claimed by B&R to be the deep direct object, fails all the direct object diagnostics. It has been argued that *en*, like Italian *ne*, "is derived from base-generated, direct object positions only" (Burzio 1986:137). However, *en* is not extractable from the theme of *amuser* even though the impersonal construction is available under limited conditions (31).

(31)a *IL *en* a amusé les enfants [*beaucoup de marionnettes*].
      "There were amused children [many marionnettes]".
   b IL m'a étonné *que Paul soit parti*.
      "It startled me that Paul left".
   c C'était *un départ* qui m'a étonné.
      "It was a departure that startled me".
   d *IL *m'en* a étonné un [*de départs*].
      "It startled me one of them [departures]"

    The theme of *amuser* (the cause of amusement) cannot be cliticized as a direct object either, although it is acceptable as a subject clitic (32b) and carries only subject, not direct object *qu* morphology (32c).

(32)a *[IL] *les* amuse les enfants.
      "There amuses them the children".
   b *Les marionnettes / elles* amusent les enfants.
      "The marionnettes / they amuse the children".
   c *les marionnettes* *que / *qui* amusent les enfants
      "the marionnettes whom / who amuse the children"

A passivized theme (the cause of amusement) is impossible with *amuser* (33).[16]

---

[16] Pesetsky (1995:21–37) argues convincingly against B&R's claim that psych passives are adjectival.

(33) *Les marionnettes sont amusées.
"The marionnettes are amused".

Participial control (with the interpretation that the puppets are the cause of amusement) cannot obtain with the theme of amuser, except with present participles which show subject control (34).

(34) les marionnettes *amusées / amusantes
"the amused / amusing marionnettes"

The croire construction also indicates only the experiencer, not the theme as the direct object (35).

(35) *On croyait les marionnettes amusées.
"We believed the marionnettes amused".

The lack of substantiation for the accusative direct object status of the theme of these psych verbs puts into question the underlying structure proposed by B&R for undatives. In order to account for the superficial accusative Case of amuser experiencers, B&R (1988:332–333) propose that "the morphological entity Accusative Case can be a manifestation of both syntactic classes: structural Case and inherent Case". The arguments adduced in Chapter 2 clearly support a treatment of accusative as a structural Case, not a mixed structural / inherent approach. The derived subject character of the theme will be addressed in the next section.

The syntactic characteristics of amuser psych verbs—the derived subject properties of the theme and the direct object behavior of the experiencer—can be accounted for simply by exchanging the place of the two complements in B&R's proposal. Given the structure in (36) for amuser, the theme may move to subject position with nominative Case, while the experiencer has accusative Case.[17]

---

[17] The undative nature of these psych verbs that can assign only accusative, but not dative Case is explored in Section 4.4.

(36) Alternative proposal

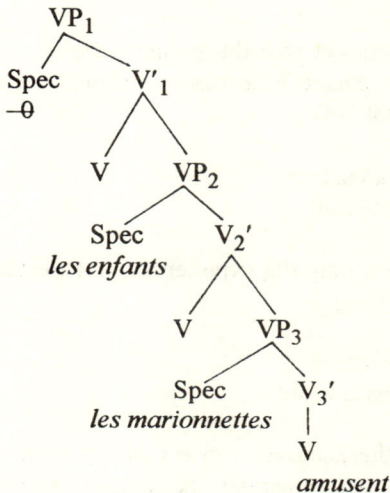

```
        VP₁
       /    \
    Spec    V'₁
     -θ    /    \
          V     VP₂
               /    \
            Spec    V₂'
          les enfants /  \
                     V    VP₃
                        /     \
                     Spec     V₃'
                les marionnettes |
                                 V
                              amusent
```

The clearly accusative features of agreement on the past participle and direct object clitic are proof that the verb is assigning accusative Case to the experiencer, *les enfants*. On the other hand, given the undative hypothesis, *les marionnettes* could not be checked for Case by Agr_{O3}, and the sentence in which the theme did not move to subject position would therefore be ungrammatical.

4.4 *Case suspension and subject nonthematicity*

The syntactic evidence favors (36) over (9) as the configuration for *amuser*, and thus disfavors B&R's reinterpretation of Principle A to account for anaphoric anomalies. It also supports the Case proposal of Chapter 2 that accusative and dative Case are structural over their suggestion that accusative may be inherent or structural. The syntactic pattern of psych verbs is then a function of the syntactic requirements of available argument positions and Case assignment. Section 4.4.1 delineates the derivation of psych verbs, 4.4.2 discusses Burzio's generalization and the duality hypothesis, and 4.4.3 reexamines the nonthematic external argument.

4.4.1 *Derivation of undative and unaccusative psych verbs*

Unaccusative psych verbs (*manquer*) have a nonthematic external argument and defective accusative Case; undative psych verbs have a nonthematic external argument and defective dative Case. Accusative Case targets the Spec of VP_2 while dative Case targets the Spec of VP_3. Unaccusatives allow the experiencer in Spec VP_3 to receive dative Case; the theme in Spec VP_2 raises to Spec Agr_s with nominative Case. Undatives allow the experiencer in Spec VP_2 to receive accusative Case; the theme in Spec VP_3 raises to Spec Agr_s with nominative Case. The behavior of these verbs supports the duality hypothesis, for the maximum number of internal Cases and arguments is two. Nonthematic psych verbs lack an external argument and one Case (as Burzio's generalization predicts). The class of *manquer* verbs has dative but lacks accusative Case, while the *amuser* class has accusative but lacks dative; both also lack a thematic external argument. If the two classes of nonthematic psych verbs were not Case defective, they would not require movement of the theme to subject position.

Case assignment with undatives underlines the specificity of Case to structural configuration. The objective Cases, accusative and partitive, are linked to Spec VP_2. Dative is linked to Spec VP_3. When accusative Case is suspended the partitive may come into play in impersonal constructions. When dative Case is suspended there is no redemptive Case to save the DP in Spec VP_3. The Spec of VP_3 must be Case marked dative, or it is forced to move to get Case. The three classes of psych verbs discussed in this chapter manifest three distinct underlying structural configurations of theta roles, transitive (37), undative (38), and unaccusative (39).

In transitive (37) the experiencer occupies the Spec VP_1 and the theme occupies the Spec VP_2. In (38) and (39) the Spec VP_1 is empty and nonthematic. In (38) the experiencer is in Spec VP_2 and the theme in Spec VP_3; in (39) the opposite distribution of theta roles finds the theme in Spec VP_2 and the experiencer in Spec VP_3. In both sentences the theme is Caseless and forced to move, while the experiencer receives accusative or dative Case. In (38) the experiencer in Spec VP_2 raises (overtly as a clitic or covertly as a lexical DP) as usual to Spec Agr_{O2}. The theme in Spec VP_3 eventually raises to Spec Agr_s with nominative Case, but passes through Spec Agr_{O3}. The exigencies of Case assignment force movement of the internal arguments.

(37) *Transitive* Les païens adorent les idoles.
               "The pagans adore the idols".

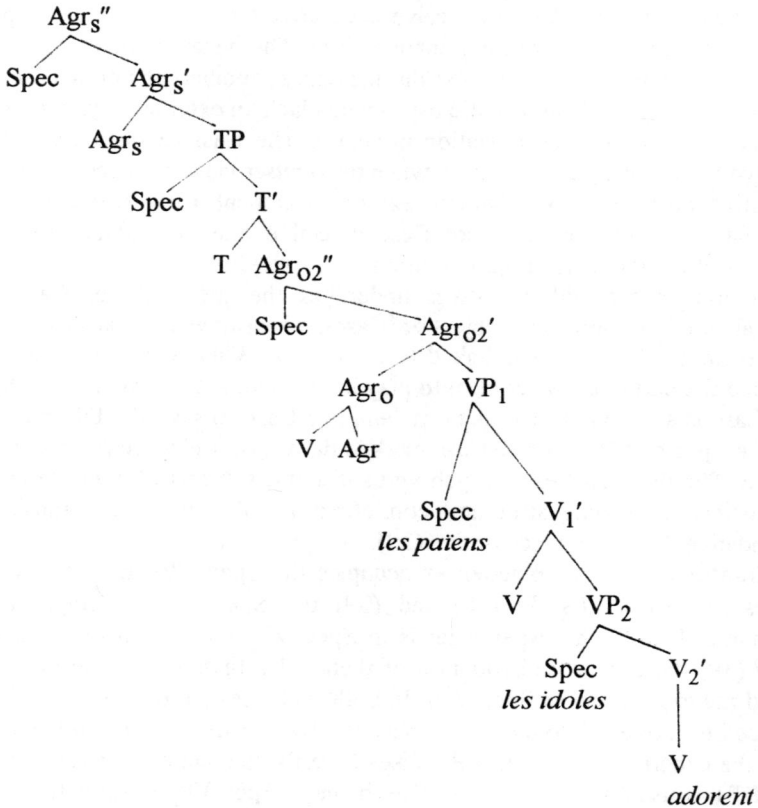

In (37) the DP in Spec VP_1 raises to Agr_s with nominative Case. In (38) and (39) the Spec VP_1 is nonthematic and cannot furnish a superficial subject. The DP in either VP_2 (39) or VP_3 (38) raises to Spec Agr_s'' with nominative Case.

(38) *Undative*   La blague amuse les enfants.
                   "The joke amuses the children".

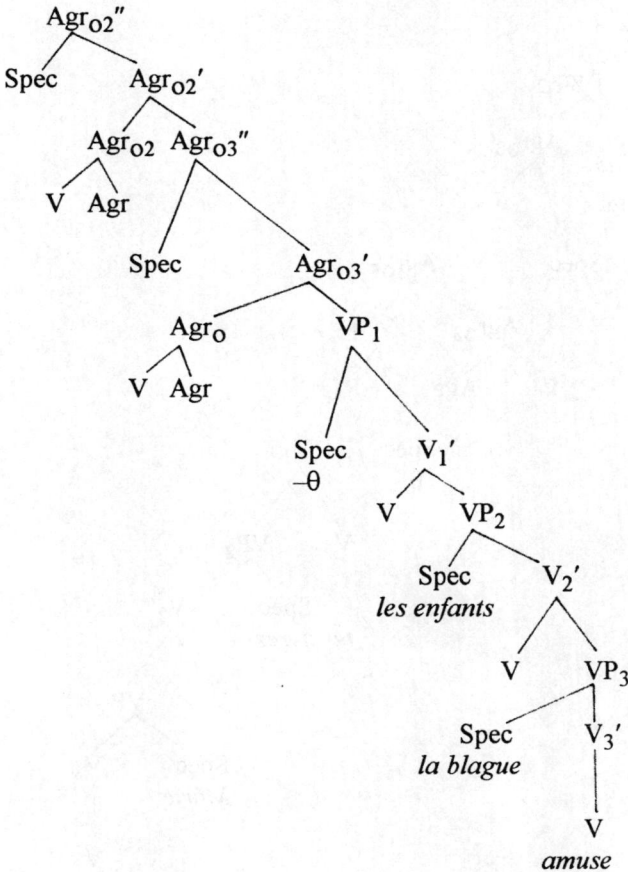

```
        Agr_o2"
       /     \
   Spec      Agr_o2'
            /      \
        Agr_o2    Agr_o3"
        /  \     /
       V  Agr   /
              Spec      Agr_o3'
                       /      \
                   Agr_o      VP_1
                   /  \      /    \
                  V  Agr  Spec    V_1'
                         -θ      /    \
                                V    VP_2
                                    /    \
                                 Spec    V_2'
                              les enfants /   \
                                         V    VP_3
                                            /    \
                                         Spec    V_3'
                                      la blague   |
                                                  V
                                                amuse
```

(39) *Unaccusative*   Les livres manquent à Marie.
                    "Mary is missing the books".

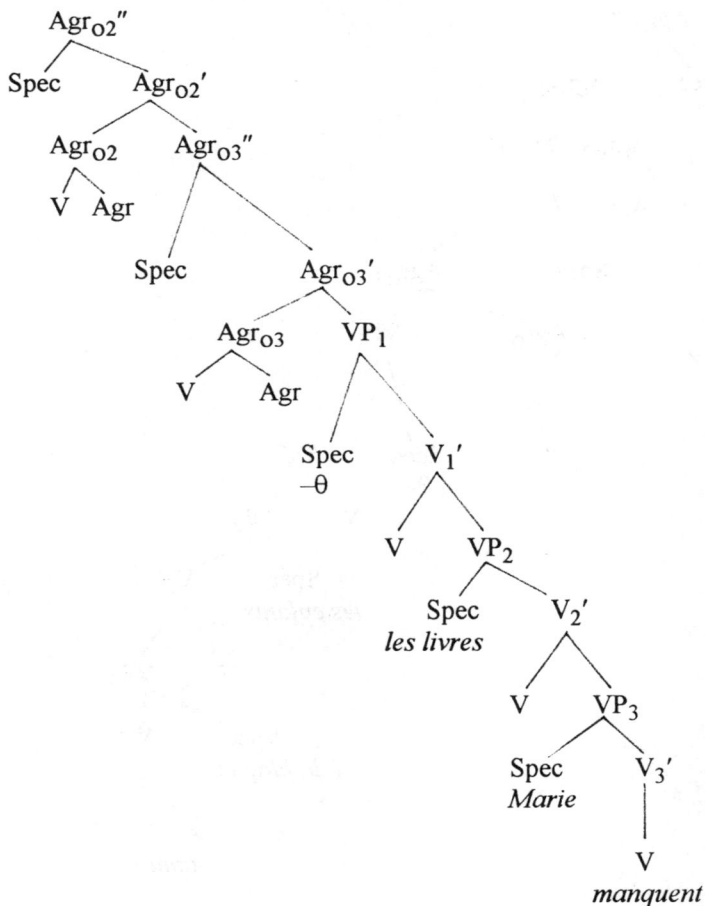

4.4.2 *Burzio's generalization and binary complements*

The data presented in 4.3 indicates that undatives, like unaccusatives, have a nonthematic external argument, but that unlike unaccusatives they do not have a direct object that raises from Spec VP_2 to Agr_s with nominative Case. Like unaccusatives, they are Case defective, but the defective Case is not accusative, it is dative. Given the existence of two structural Cases in French, this defect is precisely what Burzio's extended generalization predicts. Both classes of psych verbs have a nonthematic external argument and both have one defective Case. For unaccusatives the DP in Spec VP_2 lacks accusative Case, so must raise with nominative for the derivation to converge. For undatives the DP in Spec VP_3 lacks dative Case so it must raise with nominative Case for the derivation to converge. The lack of dative Case with undatives is confirmed by their ungrammaticality with lexical and nonlexical datives and their Case incompatibility with *faire* in causative constructions.

The base position of the theme of unaccusatives in Spec VP_2 is confirmed by direct object diagnostics that underline the specificity of the agreement node–VP tier link. The base position of the theme of undatives cannot be Spec VP_2 (Section 4.3.2), nor Spec VP_1 (Section 4.3.1), so must be Spec VP_3, although there are no indirect object diagnostics to add independent evidence. The interplay of Case assignment and argument structure *does*, however, provide independent support for the undative configuration proposed and for the duality hypothesis. In addition to the ungrammaticality of affected datives, two constructions, the presentational and the overload sentence, furnish evidence for the dual limit on arguments.

The presentational construction, available for sentences with nonthematic external arguments, contains arguments that do not raise overtly, and thus it indicates the base positions of those arguments. Unaccusatives have an escape hatch from their defective accusative Case by being able to access redemptive partitive; this Case allows fairly productive use of the impersonal presentational (within the confines of indefiniteness and discourse, see Chapter 3). Undatives have no redemptive Case so they require the internal argument to raise. The only escape clause is the rare impersonal construction with an accusative object (experiencer) and a non Case marked CP (*IL m'étonne que...*). The lack of dative Case and the obligatory nature of the accusative with undative verbs means that their only option for nonmovement of the theme in VP_3 would be if it did not need to receive Case. This is exactly what happens with clausal complements that are not Case marked (Stowell's Case Resistance Principle). While DP complements are ungrammatical (40d), CP complements are all right as in (13) and (40c).

(40) a Qu'ils partent m'étonne.
      "That they're leaving startles me".
   b Leur départ m'étonne.
      "Their departure startles me".
   c IL m'étonne qu'ils partent.
      "It startles me that they're leaving".

    d *IL m'étonne un / leur départ.
       "It startles me a / their departure".

Sentences such as (40) show that undatives possess a second internal argument slot (in VP$_3$); they just can't use it most of the time because they can't assign dative Case (the Case targeted to VP$_3$). Even when one structural Case is suspended, there are at least two internal argument slots, confirming the duality proposed.

    Overload sentences show that there are *no more* than two internal positions. Pesetsky argues that psych verbs involve three, not two theta roles, experiencer, causer, and target / subject matter of emotion. He points out that all three cannot be present at once.[18]

    (41) a Ce bar dégoûte Marie.
          "This bar disgusts Mary".
       b Marie se dégoûte de la bière.
          "Mary is disgusted by beer".
       c *Ce bar dégoûte Marie de la bière.
          "This bar disgusts Mary of beer".

In (41) the verb *dégoûter* thematically selects three roles, *Marie* as experiencer, *ce bar* as causer, and *la bière* as subject matter of emotion. The ungrammaticality of (41c) cannot be due to a thematic overload, or to a Case overload since the preposition *de* could Case mark *la bière*. The ungrammaticality is due to the lack of an extra argument position: Spec VP$_1$ is nonthematic, Spec VP$_2$ is filled by *Marie* and Spec VP$_3$ is filled by *ce bar*. If an unlimited number of additional arguments could be added as long as they were Case marked inherently, (41c) should be acceptable; but it is not. Only two selected internal arguments are allowed according to the argument limit. This limit and the lack of dative Case predict the ungrammaticality of affected datives, presentational sentences, and overload constructions with undative psych verbs.

---

[18] Pesetsky (1995:60) gives of number of examples of this sentence type. He proposes (ibid.:198–200) the Target / Subject Matter Restriction to account for this ungrammaticality. The restriction is an instance of Travis's (1984:131) Head Movement Constraint. According to Pesetsky the zero morpheme *caus* is embedded under *amuse*, and its arguments must raise to attach to the verb. If there are intervening heads in the form of prepositions that mark the target / subject matter, the head movement of *caus* is blocked.

4.4.3 *Nonthematic external arguments*

Studies treating nonthematic external arguments in a principles and parameters framework (e.g. Burzio 1986, B&R 1988) assume a VP external subject position (Spec IP) that is the landing site for NPs seeking nominative Case. Under minimalist assumptions, the thematic external argument of transitive constructions has a VP internal (Spec VP$_1$) position and is already Case marked with nominative. It simply must raise to have its Case checked in Spec Agr$_S$; this movement also results in checking off the strong nominative feature of Tense and leads to the Extended Projection Principle effect. When the external argument is nonthematic, as with unaccusative verbs and passive, the direct object may carry nominative Case and raise to Spec Agr$_S$. The present study has portrayed the nonthematic external argument as an unfilled node, an apparent superfluity in that no constituent starts out in that position. There are three interrelated indications that the derivation takes the nonthematic Spec VP$_1$ into account. First, selectional restrictions distinguish verbs with nonthematic external arguments (e.g. unaccusative and raising) from those with thematic external arguments, the latter taking an agentive or experiencer external argument and the former taking only internal arguments. Second, the arguments are not randomly distributed with Case checking as the only guarantee of their viability. To the contrary, the arguments selected by and assigned Case by the verb show a clear specificity of VP tier to Case checking agreement node (cf. Chapter 3): for example, objective NPs can't originate in Spec VP$_3$. Finally, the crossing pattern of raising requires passage of internal arguments through intermediate nodes, so for example, the direct object raises through Spec Agr$_{O2}$ even if it is nominative Case marked. For undatives, the crossing pattern of the derivation requires that the DP in Spec VP$_3$ raise through Spec Agr$_{O3}$ on its way to Spec Agr$_S$.

Grimshaw and Pesetsky explicitly reject the grouping of *amuse* verbs with unaccusatives, yet try to capture the syntactic and semantic qualities that distinguish undatives from true transitives through their added dimensions.[19] The analysis put forth in this chapter proposes that *amuse* undatives are like unaccusatives in having defective Case and nonthematic external argument (by Burzio's generalization), and like transitives in assigning accusative Case. It is assumed that general principles determine the original mapping of the

---

[19] For Grimshaw *amuse* verbs take a "thematic subject" but no external argument as a consequence of their aspectual misalignment. For Pesetsky (1995:224) also the subject of *amuse* verbs is thematic, but the affixation of the causative morpheme "eliminates the external argument of the predicate to which it attaches". It is difficult to see how their treatments are different from that of a nonthematic external argument.

arguments into the argument positions, taking into account finer morpho-semantic considerations (such as those raised by Pesetsky and Grimshaw). The analysis proposed here adequately accounts for the data and supports an independently motivated hypothesis concerning Case suspension and argument duality.

4.5 *Conclusion*

This chapter has reexamined the syntax of French psych verbs, arguing for a derivation that is distinct from yet draws on those of B&R, Grimshaw and Pesetsky. The analysis demonstrates the importance of Case assignment in determining syntactic representation since movement of internal arguments is determined by the availability of dative or accusative Case. The psych verbs examined could conceivably constitute a distinct verbal class with one to one syntactic expressions for each of the thematic roles required. It has been shown, however, that the thematic roles are accommodated by the same structural configurations and verb classes, transitive and unaccusative, as nonpsych verbs. The syntax of psych verbs is similar to that of other verbs, and as such is determined in large part by predicate argument structure and Case assignment. The greater importance to syntactic derivation of structural phenomena over semantic notions such as "psychological" underlines the fact that a very limited number of syntactic roles defined by Case theory and predicate argument structure are able to translate a variety of thematic roles.

Psych verbs also support the binary hypothesis of Case and argument projection and the extension of Burzio's generalization. Undative psych verbs, as unaccusatives, have a nonthematic external argument and one suspended internal structural Case. They nevertheless can have up to two internal arguments (but no more). The argument missing internal Case can raise to superficial subject position with nominative Case. The impossibility of more than two intenal arguments is borne out by the overload sentences, to be looked at again in Chapter 5 in its examination of psych pronominals.

CHAPTER 5

CASE SUSPENDING PRONOMINALS

5.0 *Introduction*

This chapter studies another instance of Caseless arguments, the DPs that become superficial subjects of absorber pronominal verbs (intrinsic, neutral, middle voice, and psych). These verbs conform to Burzio's generalization in having no thematic external argument and no accusative Case. It is argued that *se* lexically absorbs accusative Case and one argument, creating constructions with a nonthematic Spec VP_1, a lexical configuration that forces movement of the remaining internal argument to Spec Agr_S with nominative Case. Psych pronominals pose a special problem because their nonpronominal corresponding verbs are undative, that is, already Case and thematic defective. It is shown that psych *se*, like other absorber *se*, absorbs accusative Case and one thematic argument. The restriction of Burzio's generalization and the binary limit on Case and argument structure predict the distribution of arguments, their syntactic movement, and the ungrammaticality of an additional internal argument.

The chapter draws on Herschensohn (1994) to situate a treatment of French psych pronominals such as *s'amuser* "to have fun" in a uniform analysis of *se*, much in the spirit of Manzini (1986), Otero (1986) and Wehrli (1986). The first section discusses the distribution of French *se* and the dilemma of pronominal psych verbs. The second section proposes an analysis for *se* by which psych *se* absorbs accusative Case, one internal argument and one theta role.[1] The third section situates a treatment of *se* in a minimalist framework, using Emonds's (1991) approach to distinguish lexical absorber *se* from syntactic identificational *se*. It also revisits the difference between pronominal and plain (nonpronominal) psych verbs, pointing out similarities and differences in their derivations. Section 5.4 discusses clitic sequencing with respect to binary argument structure, showing that clitic cooccurrence restrictions echo the binary limit on arguments.

---

[1] As in Chapter 4, theta roles are used for presentational purposes to label and keep track of arguments.

5.1 *Distribution of* se
5.1.1 *Identificational and absorber* se

Se is an anaphor bound by a lexical or clitic subject in French. Otero (1986) distinguishes two functional classes of *se* in French, Identificational [*Id*] and Absorber [*Abs*], the former being referential (reflexive–reciprocal (1)) and the latter nonreferential (intrinsic, neutral, middle voice, psych (2)). Referential *se* can be accusative (1a, b) or dative (1c, d).

(1) *Id se*
    a   Marc se/le [+accusative] lave.
        "Mark washes himself/him".
    b   Marc et Marie se/les lavent.
        "Mark and Mary wash each other/them".
    c   Marc se / lui [+dative] brosse les cheveux.
        "Mark brushes his own / her hair".
    d   Marc et Marie se / leur écrivent des lettres.
        "Mark and Mary write letters to each other".
(2) *Abs se*
    a   Marc s'évanouit. (*intrinsic*)
        "Mark faints".
    b   La glace se brise. (*neutral*)
        "The mirror breaks".
    c   Le pain se mange. (*middle*)
        "Bread is eaten".
    d   Les enfants s'amusent. (*psych*)
        "The children have fun".

Some examples of intrinsic *se* (Grevisse 1993:1135) are *se désister, s'évader, s'évanouir, se repentir, se souvenir* , "to desist, escape, faint, repent, remember". Some examples of neutral *se* (cf. Ruwet 1972:89) are *se dissiper, se briser, s'agglomérer, s'espacer, se réunir*, "to dissipate, break, agglomerate, go to outer space, meet".[2] Middle *se* is fairly productive with

---

[2] Ruwet (1972:94) describes the difference between middle and neutral: "les constructions que j'appelle moyennes ont 'un sens passif', ce qui veut dire qu'elles sont perçues comme impliquant la présence d'un agent, non exprimé, et différent du sujet superficiel, tandis que la présence d'un tel agent n'est pas perçue dans le cas des neutres".

agentive transitive verbs taking inanimate objects (see Section 5.3.1). Psych *se* is found with the undative class of verbs described in Chapter 4.

The *Id* and *Abs* classes show a number of syntactic distinctions, such as the impossibility of the *ne...que* construction with *Abs disperser* as compared to *Id regarder* (3)–(4) (Ruwet 1972:93).

    (3) a   Pierre se regarde.
           Pierre looks at himself".
       b   Pierre ne regarde que lui-même.
          "Pierre looks only at himself".
    (4) a   Les manifestants se dispersent.
          "The demonstrators dispersed themselves".
       b   *Les manifestants ne dispersent qu'eux-mêmes.
          "The demonstrators dispersed only themselves".

Furthermore, *Abs se* verbs show a systematic semantic variation from the nonpronominal form. The semantic distinctions which characterize *Abs se* are not uniform for all of the subclasses (i.e. middle, neutral, etc.), but what is significant is that *Id se* does not show a semantic variation between the *se* and non *se* form of the verb, whereas *Abs se* does. This semantic alternation has been extensively discussed by linguists such as Ruwet (1972), Zribi-Hertz (1982), Cinque (1988), Labelle (1992b).[3]

It has been shown that certain cases of *Abs se* correlate with the absence of the external argument / theta role and the suspension of accusative Case assignment as in the passive construction. Belletti (1982b) (as Chomsky 1981) offers the classic proposal linking middle *se* to passive. She proposes that in the middle voice construction, which she terms another case of passive, "*si* is assigned the theta role otherwise assigned by VP to the subject NP; *si* absorbs objective Case otherwise assigned by V to its direct object NP" (Belletti (1982b:5). Burzio (1986:38) extends this kind of analysis to neutral and

---

[3] Labelle (1992b) examines differences among transitive, intransitive and reflexive forms of change of state verbs. She points out (ibid.:4) that contrasting with the intransitive *rougir* "to redden" the reflexive construction *se rougir* "to redden" "is the only one possible for entities having inherent characteristics which are insufficient for bringing about the process". The intransitive (i) contrasts for this reason with reflexive (ii).

    (i)   Jeanne (*se) rougit. "Jeanne blushes".
    (ii) Il vit le mouchoir *(se) rougir soudain.
         "He saw the handkerchief suddenly redden".

Zribi-Hertz (1982:348–349) examines in detail the *se-moyen* construction, pointing out a number of semantic properties.

intrinsic *si / se* in treating these two classes as ergatives. He assumes *si* is in these cases "a morphological reflex of the 'loss' of subject theta role which marks the derivation of ergative entries from transitive ones: a lexical process". The lack of subject theta role is correlated with the inability to assign accusative Case by Burzio's generalization. Bouchard, Jaeggli, Otero and others have adopted the general outlines of these analyses.[4]

5.1.2 *The psych pronominal dilemma*

Psych pronominals pose a dilemma with respect to their derivation and relation to other *se*. While intrinsic, neutral and middle voice *se* appear to conform to Cinque's (1988:566) statement that they "perform the same function: that of dethematizing the [NP, IP] position and suspending the assignment of structural accusative Case", psych *se* does not. It has been argued in chapter 4 that psych verbs such as *préoccuper* or *amuser* select a nonthematic external argument and that an internal argument raises from Spec VP_3 to Spec Agr_S (5a).

(5) a Ce bar dégoûte Marie.
       "This bar disgusts Mary".
    b Marie se dégoûte de la bière.
       "Mary is disgusted with beer".
    c *Ce bar dégoûte Marie de la bière.
       "This bar disgusts Mary with beer".

Psych verbs are already lexically specified to have a nonthematic external argument, so the Spec VP_1 cannot be further dethematized (Belletti & Rizzi 1988:308). They are lexically specified as Case defective, lacking the ability to assign dative Case. Psych *se* cannot be classified with *Id se* because it is not directly referential as is *Id se*, and it differs from middle *se* because psych verbs have no external argument / theta role to be absorbed. The assumption of earlier treatments that *Abs se* dethematizes the subject and suspends accusative Case is straightforward for middle *se*, but cannot account for psych *se* which already has a lexically dethematized subject. Finally, psych *se* verbs are productively constructed with either a prepositional argument, the subject

---

[4] Bouchard (1984:69) extends this type of analysis even to account for *Id* reflexives. "So (i) would be derived in our analysis from the D-structure (ii) [numbers adjusted] by *move alpha,* with a S-structure as in (iii).

(i) Jean se rase.
(ii) [NP e] se rase Jean.
(iii) Jean$_i$ se rase t$_i$".

matter of emotion (the beer in (5b)) or a causer (the bar in (5a)), but a sentence containing both theta roles is ungrammatical (5c). These overload examples (cf. Section 4.4) contribute to the dilemma, but will also provide the solution to it. An investigation of the absorption features of psych verbs and defective dative Case will resolve all of these questions.

5.2 *Absorption properties of* se

Section 5.2 will investigate three phenomena related to *Abs se*: absorption of accusative Case, dethematization of one argument position, and argument absorption. It will be shown that these three aspects of *Abs se* are related yet distinct. Section 5.2.1 shows that in absorption accusative Case is suspended whereas partitive Case is not, further support for the proposed Case revision of Chapter 2; it also considers Case absorption with Case defective verbs. Section 5.2.2 investigates dethematization with *Abs se*. Section 5.2.3 presents evidence for internal argument absorption with psych pronominals.

5.2.1 *Case absorption*

The accepted view presented above of *Abs se* absorbing one Case, one argument and one theta role supports the theory of Case proposed in Chapter 2, but raises questions with regard to Case defective verbs, unaccusatives and undatives. Chapter 2 argues that French verbs, transitive and intransitive, are capable of assigning two structural Cases, objective and dative. The two Cases are independently motivated as structural by noninherent assignment of Case to unselected arguments (e.g. exceptional Case marking, causative constructions and affected datives). Structural Case is checked in two object agreement nodes (Agr_{O2} and Agr_{O3}) that are specifically linked to two VP nodes (VP_2 and VP_3) in a three tiered Larsonian shell. Evidence from French shows that while the Case of Agr_{O2} is accusative, a redemptive Case, partitive, is available in situations where accusative is unavailable. The proposal supports the essentials of Belletti's (1988) discussion of partitive, but demonstrates that partitive is not an inherent Case (lexically determined and assigned in conjunction with theta marking), but a Case that is structurally checked in Spec Agr_{O2}. The built in preposition *de* acts as the Case marker (Giusti 1991b).

Previous studies of pronominal constructions (Chomsky 1981, Belletti 1982b, Burzio 1986, Otero 1986, Cinque 1988) have proposed that *Abs se* absorbs objective Case (along with one argument and one theta role); these studies do not address the difference between accusative and partitive objective Case. Empirical evidence shows that the objective Case suspended is accusative and that the suspension of accusative Case is linked to lack of thematic subject as Burzio's generalization predicts. Both traditional grammars and generative treatments confirm that it is accusative Case that is absorbed by *se*, leaving the direct object with no accusative Case. The direct object may raise to subject position or it may remain is situ if saved by partitive Case.[5] The behavior of pronominals documents Burzio's generalization in that loss of accusative (shown by the ungrammaticality of (6b)) forces movement (6c) or a possible save by partitive Case (6a).[6]

(6) a   IL se pense bien plus de choses qu'IL ne s'en dit.
         "There are many more things thought than said".
    b   *IL se pense ces choses.
         "There are thought these things".
    c   Ces choses se pensent mais ne se disent pas.
         "These things are thought but not said".

Abs se constructions allow the direct object to be checked for partitive Case in Spec Agr_{O2} or to raise with nominative Case.

Dative Case is not suspended in middle constructions, although clitic cooccurence restrictions prohibit dative clitics (7d).

(7) a   L'aumône se donne aux pauvres.
         "The offering is given to the poor".
    b   La porte s'ouvre aux passants.
         "The door opens to passersby".
    c   Ce genre de livre se vend aux bonnes soeurs.
         "This kind of book sells to nuns".
    d   *Ce genre de livre se leur vend.
         "This kind of book sells to them".

The data presented in this section verifies that is only accusative Case that can be absorbed by *Abs se*, so this is another characteristic distinguishing it from *Id se* which can be either accusative or dative (1). Although *Abs se* is

---

[5]   Grevisse (1993:1139–1140) provides examples of both types, movement and presentational.
      (i)   Ses tableaux se vendirent bien. "His paintings sold well".
      (ii) IL se brule par an 20.000 livres de cire.
            "There is more than 20,000 pounds of wax burned per year".
[6]   The proposal that partitive is inherent (Belletti 1988) is unmotivated since it would require that the pronominal form of the verb assign partitive whereas the plain form assigns accusative, an arbitrary stipulation that finds no independent motivation.

phonetically equivalent to *Id se*, it is not semantically, syntactically or morphologically the same. Just as passive morphology can only absorb accusative Case (and not dative), *Abs se* only absorbs accusative. This fact is crucial to an understanding of its role with Case defective verbs.

If *Abs se* must have accusative Case to absorb, its ungrammaticality is predicted in nonaccusative constructions. Indeed, *se* is ungrammatical with verbs which do not assign accusative, that is, intransitive *(courir)*, unaccusative *(arriver)*, and raising *(sembler)* verbs, and *se* is ungrammatical in constructions where a verb's accusative assigning potential has been lost, namely passive (8).[7]

(8) a *Marc se court.
        "Marc runs".
    b *Marc s'arrive.
        "Marc arrives".
    c Marc lui / *se semble courir nulle part.
        "Marc seems to him / himself to be running nowhere".
    d *Les pommes s'ont / se sont été mangées.
        "The apples were eaten".

Although *Id se* can correspond to a dative argument (1c), *Abs se* cannot absorb dative Case even if the verb is a lexical dative assigner (8c).[8] Apparent cases of intrinsic dative *se* such as *s'imaginer qqch* "to imagine s.t. [to oneself]" are actually instances where the verbs assign both accusative and dative Case and cannot be constructed with dative alone. They are not instances of intrinsic *se* as (2a).[9]

Another difference between *Abs* and *Id se* is their behavior with respect to past participle agreement and the path that they follow in their respective derivations. The past participle rule formulated in Chapters 1 & 2 is applicable to a chain with links in Spec Agr_{o2} and Spec VP_2. *Id se* raises to either Agr_{o2} or Agr_{o3}, depending on whether it is Case marked accusative or dative.

---

[7] Exceptionally, unergatives such as *courir* can assign accusative to cognate objects (cf. Chapter 3), but they are nevertheless incapable of being constructed with *se*.

[8] Unaccusative verbs are only rarely able to have pronominal variants (e.g. *se plaire* "to be pleased"). Verbs such as *sembler* which assign dative but not accusative would seem to be candidates for a dative *se*, yet cannot be constructed with it.

[9] Examples of these kinds of datives are shown below.
    (i) Elle se l'imagine. "She imagines it [to herself]".
    (ii) Il se les est tous tapés. "He grabbed them all for himself".
    (iii) Jean se la coule douce. "John takes it easy".

Dative *se* does not trigger past participle agreement, but accusative *se*, like all accusative clitics, does. *Abs se* absorbs accusative Case, that is, removes it from the computation, but this *se* does *not* pass through Spec Agr_{O2}; rather, it is part of the verb's morphology. Only the raising of the argument from Spec VP_2 through Spec Agr_{O2} triggers past participle agreement. *Abs se* cannot occupy Spec Agr_{O2} because the direct object must pass through that node as the agreement indicates. This is the evidence for the difference in paths between the two *se*. The sentences in (9) exemplify agreement with direct object clitic in Spec Agr_{O2} (9a, c) and with subject raised from Spec VP_2 through Spec Agr_{O2} to Spec Agr_S (9e).

(9) a   Elle *s'* [acc] est lavé *e*.
          "She washed herself".
     b   Elle s' [dat] est lavé les mains.
          "She washed her hands".
     c   Elle se [dat] *les* [acc] est lavé *es*.
          "She washed them".
     d   IL s'est vendu plusieurs jupes.
          There were several skirts sold".
     e   *Les jupes* se sont bien vendu *es*.
          "The skirts sold well".

Sentences (9a, c) have *Id se* and *les* accusative clitics; dative *se* (9b) doesn't trigger agreement. There is no agreement with *Abs se* in (9d). The only Case that *Abs se* can absorb is accusative Case in middle, neutral, psych and intrinsic *se* constructions. The requirement of accusative absorption explains the difference between unaccusative and undative Case defective verbs: the former cannot have *se* and the latter can. The lack of accusative Case is predicted to correspond to a lack of thematic subject according to Burzio's generalization. The next section bears out this prediction.

5.2.2 *Dethematization*

The standard diagnoses (cf. Chapter 3) bear out the nonthematic status of the external argument of *Abs se* verbs.[10] First, intrinsic, neutral and middle

---

[10] Auxiliary selection is not a reliable diagnostic in French because all cases of *Abs se* and *Id se* take *être*. Possession of deverbal nominals is inapplicable, since it is only the plain version of the verb that can be nominalized (cf. Chapter 4). Dative placement with causatives is also inapplicable as a diagnostic due to clitic cooccurrence restrictions.

verbs are grammatical with the presentational construction with expletive *IL* in subject position (10).

(10) a IL s'est évanoui plusieurs personnes.
        "There fainted several people".
     b IL s'est brisé deux verres.
        "There were two glasses broken".
     c IL se mange beaucoup de pain en France.
        "There is a lot of bread eaten in France".

Second, *on* is ungrammatical to varying degrees (cf. Appendix) with the arbitrary reading, an interpretation available only for thematic external arguments (11).[11]

(11) a On s'est évanoui en apprenant cette nouvelle.
        "We / *Someone fainted on learning such news".
     b On s'est dispersé.
        "We / *Someone dispersed".
     c On s'est amusé au Parc Astérix.
        "We / ?Someone had fun at Asterix Park".

Third, reciprocal anaphors, possible only with thematic and not derived subjects, are impossible with *Abs se* (cf. Ruwet 1972:94).

(12) a *Elles se sont évanouies l'une l'autre.
        "They fainted one another".
     b *Les deux équipes se sont réunies l'une l'autre.
        "The two teams got each other together".
     c *Les vestons se lavent les uns les autres.
        "The jackets wash each other".
     d *Les enfants s'amuseront les uns les autres.
        "The children will have each other have fun".

---

[11] It is nearly impossible to create a middle sentence with a human subject with an arbitrary interpretation because the middle voice is by definition usually predicated of an inanimate patient. Ruwet (1972:97) cites (ia).
(i) a Les enfants, ça se lave en 10 minutes.
       "Children, they can be washed in 10 minutes".
    b On se lave en 10 minutes. "Someone washes himself in 10 minutes".
       / *Someone can be washed in 10 minutes".

Fourth, thematic subjects embedded under *faire* may be absent. The superficial subjects of *Abs se* sentences (as those in (2)) *cannot* be missing. The impossibility of eliminating this argument in causative constructions indicates that the subject of *Abs se* constructions is derived (13).[12]

(13) a *Cette nouvelle choquante fait s'évanouir.
         "This news makes [someone] faint".
     b *Le vent a fait se briser.
         "The wind made [something] shatter".
     c *L'appétit fait se manger.
         "Appetite has [something] be eaten".
     d *Cette blague fait s'amuser.
         "This joke makes [someone] have fun".

The last, rather unreliable diagnostic (cf. Chapters 3 & 4), the ungrammaticality of derived subjects under *faire*, shows a mix of grammaticality for the different varieties.

(14) a Cette nouvelle choquante fait s'évanouir Marie.
         "This shocking news makes Mary faint".
     b ?Le vent a fait se briser ces verres.
         "The wind makes the glasses break".
     c *L'appétit fait se manger le pain.
         "Appetite makes bread be eaten".
     d *Ces marionnettes font s'amuser les enfants.
         "These marionnettes have the children have fun".

The diagnostics for nonthematicity indicate that the external argument of *Abs se* verbs is nonthematic. For neutral and middle *se* this position is *de*thematized since these verbs alternate with thematic subject versions.[13] Psych verbs pose the now familiar dilemma: since they are already Case defective and hence have nonthematic external arguments, how can they be further dethematized? Section 5.2.1 has shown that *se* absorbs accusative Case. It cannot further dethematize the subject position of psych verbs

---

[12] Traditional grammars indicate that intrinsic se may or may not be present embedded under *faire*.

[13] Certain kinds of syntactic behavior indicates that the roles are not totally absorbed or suspended. For example, Ruwet (1972) and Vinet (1988) point out that certain agent oriented adverbials are possible with middle *se*. An exploration of these differences is outside the scope of this study.

(B&R:308), so it must dethematize another argument position. This position cannot be Spec VP$_2$ since the experiencer must be in the same position in plain and pronominal psych sentences (viz. in Spec VP$_2$). The only candidate is Spec VP$_3$. The overload sentences (5c) presented in Chapter 4 provide corroborating evidence for the dethematization of this position.

(5) a   Ce bar dégoûte Marie.
        "This bar disgusts Mary".
    b   Marie se dégoûte de la bière.
        "Mary is disgusted with beer".
    c   *Ce bar dégoûte Marie de la bière.
        "This bar disgusts Mary with beer".

The overload conundrum posed by Pesetsky asks why (5c) is ungrammatical when it is clear that undative psych verbs select three distinct thematic roles.[14] The answer put forth in Chapter 4 was that there are only two internal argument positions available since the external argument position is nonthematic (correlating with defective dative Case per Burzio's generalization). The binary limit conspires with Burzio's generalization to exclude one of the three theta roles selected by psych undatives. Unlike unaccusatives, which have no accusative Case to give up to *se*, undatives assign accusative Case, and therefore can be constructed with *Abs se*. This *se* absorbs accusative Case, one theta role and one argument. The lack of accusative Case forces the experiencer to move to subject position. *Se* needs to absorb a theta role, but psych verbs have no external theta role to absorb, so instead it is the causer theta role that must be absorbed in pronominal psych sentences. Pesetsky (1995:55–63) discusses extensively the necessity of positing the three internal theta roles for psych undatives, experiencer, causer and target / subject matter of emotion. He justifies the three roles by showing how they entail different truth conditions. The existence of three internal theta roles with undative psych verbs provides the key to understanding how they can dethematize when they already have a nonthematic external argument.

In the pronominal psych sentence (5b), the causer theta role has disappeared, and Spec VP$_3$ is instead filled by the subject matter role. What has happened is that the causer role and its potential argument have been absorbed, just as the agent role and its argument are absorbed from Spec VP$_1$ with other varieties of *Abs se*. The absorption clears the path for the alternative psych theta role, subject matter of emotion. With psych verbs *Abs*

---

[14] Section 5.2.3 returns to this issue.

se affects the position of the second internal argument through dethematicization, opening it up to another thematic relation and it affects the verb by changing it into an intransitive. Psych pronominals are unaccusative undatives, doubly unthematic and doubly [structural] Case deprived. The only structural Case available to them is nominative, although they regularly select a prepositional argument that is inherently Case marked (the subject matter).

5.2.3 *Internal argument absorption*

Id se replicates the behavior of other transitive verbs with respect to argument structure and Case assignment.[15] Reflexive and reciprocal *se* represents one of the verb's internal arguments / theta roles and carries usually accusative and sometimes dative Case. *Id se* is in complementary distribution with subcategorized full NPs in internal argument positions (1) and is thus similar to other object clitic pronouns. *Abs se* also correlates with one of the verb's arguments: it appears in lexical contexts whose *se*-less variants consistently have one additional argument / theta role (15).

(15) a   Paul nettoie ces lunettes.
         "Paul cleans these glasses".
     b   Ces lunettes se nettoient facilement.
         "These glasses clean easily".
     c   Les policiers ont dispersé la foule.
         "The police dispersed the crowd".
     d   La foule s'est dispersée.
         "The crowd dispersed".
     e   Le froid ennuie Marie.
         "The cold bothers Mary".
     f   Marie s'ennuie.
         "Mary is bored".

This relationship of *se* to *se*-less variants constitutes the data on which Belletti's original proposal is based: the middle *se* variant shows passive like lack of subject theta role and objective Case. Cinque (1988:528) has described this correlation by the feature [+arg(ument)], a trait that characterizes those instances of *se / si* that act as arguments and carry a theta role. Spanish and Italian permit [−arg] *se / si* in impersonal uses, but French allows only [+arg]

---

[15] Wehrli argues that all cases of se are argument absorbers. It is assumed here that all cases are [+arg], but there is a distinction between *Abs se* which does indeed absorb an argument lexically and *Id se* which is linked to an argument syntactically.

se in both *Id* and *Abs* uses, as the data in (1) and (7)–(8) indicate.[16] Implicit in earlier treatments is the assumption that the argument absorbed in the neutral and middle constructions is the external argument, since the subject is dethematized.

Psych *se* also absorbs accusative Case and one argument; however, this *se* clearly cannot correspond to the external argument of the verb, since psych verbs by definition have nonthematic external arguments. *Se* must rather constitute one of the internal arguments. Zubizarreta (1985) and others have noted the optionality of the external argument in passive and middle constructions. Conversely, the direct object is generally nonexpendable. With psych verbs it is the second internal argument, less essential than the direct object, which is absorbable by *se*. It has generally been assumed that *Abs se* absorbs objective Case, absorbs the external argument and dethematizes the subject. Psych *se* forces a reevaluation of this assumption, and an uncoupling of the three phenomena. *Se* always absorbs accusative Case, but the absorption of theta role and argument for psych *se* is unlike that for other varieties of *Abs se* since it is the second internal argument and its causer role that are absorbed. Because *se* has absorbed accusative Case, the argument in Spec VP_2 cannot be assigned accusative and can only be checked for nominative by raising to Spec Agr_S. The availability of the VP_3 node for absorption is indicated by the presence of selected prepositional arguments with intrinsics, middles and psych pronominals.[17] Examples of intrinsics are: *se moquer de, se souvenir de, s'efforcer à, se repentir de* "to make fun of, remember, force oneself, repent". Middle sentences may allow dative (7), but psych pronominals lack both accusative and dative Case.

The proposal that psych *se* absorbs the argument and theta role causer of VP_3 raises the question of why another argument / theta role can take its place, whereas such replacement is impossible in Spec VP_1 when it is dethematized. The answer is that the only Case available to Spec VP_1 is nominative, since the external argument must raise to Agr_S to be checked for

---

[16] The [–arg] *se / si* can appear with all classes of verbs, unaccusative as well as transitive.
  (i) Se vende pan aqui. "Bread is sold here".
  (ii) Se llega a las once. "One arrives at 11 o'clock".
Cinque (1988:558–566) argues that middle si is [–arg]. A discussion of Italian is outside the scope of this work. The arguments given in this chapter indicate that middle *se* in French is [+arg].
[17] In principle, dative Case should be available for intrinsic and neutral pronominals, but they do not take lexical datives, so it is virtually impossible to test their ability to assign dative. Clitic cooccurrence restrictions prohibit affected datives, although nonpronominal versions of the neutral verbs admit them (cf. Section 5.4).

Case; it cannot be Case marked by a preposition because it could not be Case checked in situ nor in Agr$_S$. On the other hand, a selected argument in Spec VP$_3$ (viz. the subject matter) *can* be Case marked by a preposition.

This proposal also calls for a reappraisal of Pesetsky's treatment of theta roles. This study has adopted his delineation of thematic relations selected by psych verbs and his recognition of the morpho-semantic variation between plain and pronominal psych verbs. A thorough investigation of the variation between object experiencer *amuser* and subject experiencer *s'amuser* is outside the scope of this study, but a few remarks are in order to indicate lines of possible future research. First, the relationship of the two versions is not unlike causative / inchoative pairs, so that any treatment should be able to account for the morphology of causation and the role of *se* (Labelle 1992b). Second, while theta roles per se may be redundant, they have proven useful in identifying arguments and in distinguishing absorption properties. Furthermore, the theta hierarchy, despite its shortcomings, seems to have some function in determining argument distribution, anaphoric relations and cliticization (cf. Sachs 1992). Future research should attempt to clarify these points.

The dethematization and suspension of one argument are distinct, just as suspension of accusative Case is distinct from dethematization. In all instances of *Abs se* the direct object cannot be assigned Case, and its Caselessness forces movement to subject position.

5.3 *Syntactic and lexical levels of grammatical functions*

This section proposes that the difference between *Abs* and *Id se* can be characterized as lexical vs. syntactic respectively. The first section discusses morphosyntactic theory and lexical insertion. Section 5.3.2 fleshes out the treatment of the two types of construction within a minimalist framework. Section 5.3.3 discusses the differences between pronominal and plain psych verbs.

5.3.1 *Morphosyntactic theory*

The distinguishing qualities of *Abs se*—semantic modification and suspension of Case and one argument—confirm its lexical character. *Id se*, subcategorized as an internal argument, entails no semantic alteration and is thematically related to the verb as other transitive arguments. On the other hand, *Abs se*, which modifies the meaning of the verb, is lexically determined. The difference between *Id* and *Abs se* can thus be analyzed in terms of the level at which *se* is related to its verb, that is, the syntax or the lexicon, an approach reflecting the spirit of Emonds's treatment of morphosyntax. He proposes (Emonds 1991:129–130) that morphemes which induce a semantic feature are inserted at D-structure, while all others (those which induce no semantic modification) are inserted at S-structure. The two processes are described: "deep structure insertion is restricted to inserting elements associated with (either conditioned by or inducing) the presence of a purely semantic (non-syntactic) feature. [...] When no semantic features are associated with insertion, s-structure is always the level of insertion".

Applying this approach to *se*, his distinction accounts for both change in interpretation associated with *Abs se* compared to *Id se* and theta role absorption. The differences in interpretation are subtle for the four classes of *Abs se*, none of which has a clearly identifiable theta role for *se* (cf. fn 1, 2). Intrinsic *se* is often an inchoative marker, although there exist inchoative verbs without *se*. Intrinsic pronominals do not appear in syntactic variants of plain verbs with thematic subjects, but the superficial subject of the pronominals behaves like an internal argument in not showing agentive qualities. Burzio suggests that intrinsic pronominal subjects originate VP internally. Campos & Kempchinsky (1991) also lend support to this treatment. Neutral *se* of change of state verbs such as *se casser, s'aggrandir* is argued by Labelle (1992b:394–397) to have absorbed the subject theta role so that "the entity undergoing the change is linguistically presented as a passive participant". Middle *se* sentences are characterized by a generic reading involving an atelic verb, an arbitrary agent, and usually a nonhuman object.[18] Psych *se* has absorbed the causer role; the remaining argument, the superficial subject, is an experiencer. In all cases of *Abs se* the subject of the sentence is a kind of patient.[19]

---

[18] Ruwet (1972) points out the ungrammaticality of agents and punctual aspect with middles.

    (i) a   *Cela se dit par le peuple. "That is said by the people".

         b   *Ce livre s'est vendu hier à une bonne soeur.

            "This book was sold yesterday to a nun".

However, he notes that an instrumental agent may be acceptable (iia) and traditional grammars cite middles with punctual aspect (iib).

    (ii) a   L'éducation du coeur se fait par les mères.

            "The education of the heart is done by mothers".

         b   Ses tableaux se vendirent bien. "His paintings sold well".

[19] A lexical treatment of middle *se* is at odds with several other analyses (Ruwet 1972, Manzini 1986, Cinque 1988) that propose that derivation of middle *se* is syntactic. One of the main motivations for treating middle *se* syntactically and not lexically is that it implies an agent, whereas neutral *se* implies no agent. An exploration of this issue is outside the scope of this work, but the agent related arguments do not appear sufficient to retain the syntactic account of middle *se*.

All instances of *Abs se* are characterized by a nonthematic external argument in the Spec of VP_1 and a *se* that is [+arg, +acc]; the superficial subject originates in the Spec of VP_2, moves through the Spec of Agr_{O2} and raises to superficial subject position, leaving agreement on the past participle. Under this analysis, the Spec of VP_1 is nonthematic and the [+acc] verb has lost its accusative assigning qualities, one selected theta role and one argument, all of which have been absorbed by *se*, now attached to the verb. The basic meaning of the verb has been modified in a manner similar to that described by Emonds. The only Case available to the DP in Spec VP_2 is nominative, so it must raise to Spec Agr_S to check off that Case or the derivation crashes. Past participle agreement indicates that all four classes of *Abs se* entail movement from Spec VP_2 through Spec Agr_O to Spec Agr_S, since agreement obtains between the raised subject and the past participle in these cases. *Abs se* is then determined at the lexical level, absorbing both an argument and accusative Case. The *Abs se* structures thus look very much like the unaccusative and undative verbs with nonthematic Spec of VP_1. This analysis reflects Burzio's insight concerning the character of intrinsic and neutral reflexives, but relates that idea to psych pronominals as well.

5.3.2 *Derivation of* Id *and* Abs se

This and the next section review the underlying structure and the absorption characteristics of each class of *Abs se* and the derivation of these as compared to psych verbs. A typical transitive sentence is depicted in (16). This sentence has a thematic external argument in VP_1, and two internal arguments in VP_2 and VP_3. Each VP tier carries an argument that is linked by Case checking to an agreement node. The clitics (including dative *se*) license coindexed *pro* in argument position. The distinction between *Id* and *Abs se* is represented structurally in the presence vs. absence of an argument *pro* in the syntax.

(16) *Transitive*
   Marc offre la glace aux enfants. Marc la leur offre.
   "Mark offers the ice cream to the children. He offers it to them."
   Marc s'offre la glace.
   "He offers it to himself".

(16)

Agr_{O2}''
- Spec la_i
- Agr_{O2}'
  - Agr_{O2}
    - V Agr
  - Agr_{O3}''
    - Spec se_k / $leur_j$
    - Agr_{O3}'
      - Agr_{O3}
        - V Agr
      - VP_1
        - Spec $Marc_k$
        - V_1'
          - V
          - VP_2
            - Spec $la\ glace$/pro_i
            - V_2'
              - V
              - VP_3
                - Spec $les\ enfants$/pro_j/$_k$
                - V_3'
                  - V *offre*

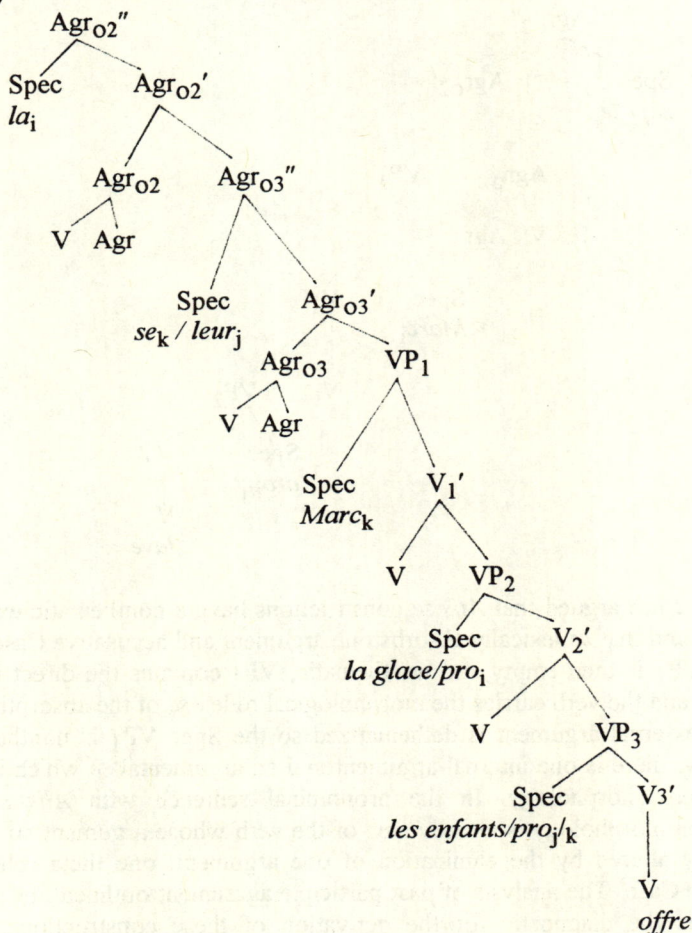

Illustrations of the verb phrase of pronominal sentence types are shown in the representative trees below. *Id se* verbs (17) behave as typical transitive verbs: the Spec of VP_1 raises to subject position with nominative Case and the verb raises. The Spec of VP_2 contains a *pro* licensed by the clitic *se*, like the clitics in (16).

(17) *Id se pronominal*
$Marc_i$ se_i lave. $Marc_i$ le_j lave. "Mark washes himself/him".

(17)

$$
\begin{array}{l}
\text{Agr}_{O2}'' \\
\quad\diagdown \\
\text{Spec} \quad \text{Agr}_{O2}' \\
se_i\,/\,le_j \\
\qquad \text{Agr}_O \quad \text{VP}_1 \\
\qquad \text{V Agr} \\
\qquad\qquad \text{Spec} \quad V_1' \\
\qquad\qquad Marc_i \\
\qquad\qquad\qquad \text{V} \quad \text{VP}_2 \\
\qquad\qquad\qquad\qquad \text{Spec} \quad V_2' \\
\qquad\qquad\qquad\qquad pro_{i/j} \\
\qquad\qquad\qquad\qquad\qquad \text{V} \\
\qquad\qquad\qquad\qquad\qquad lave
\end{array}
$$

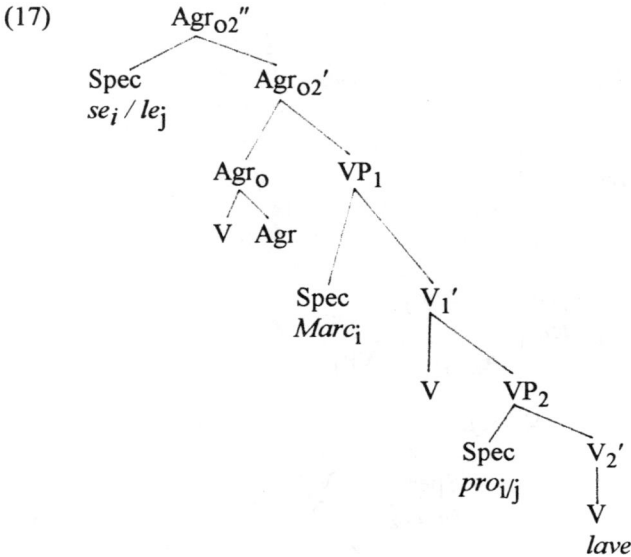

Section 5.2 has argued that *Abs se* constructions have a nonthematic external argument and that *se* lexically absorbs one argument and accusative Case. The Spec of VP$_1$ is then empty and nonthematic, VP$_2$ contains the direct object argument and the verb carries the morphological reflex *se* of the absorption. In (18) the external argument is dethematized so the Spec VP$_1$ is nonthematic and empty, there is one internal argument and an argumental *se* which is part of the verb morphology. In the pronominal sentence with *Abs se* the pronominal morphology is already part of the verb whose argument structure is lexically altered by the elimination of one argument, one theta role, and accusative Case. The analysis of past participle agreement outlined in Chapter 2 provides the diagnostic for the derivation of these constructions. That analysis proposes that past participle agreement, as Case assignment, is an instance of Spec–head agreement between Agr$_O$ and its specifier. When there is overt movement of the direct object (the Spec of VP$_2$) to or through the Agr$_{O2}$ node, this agreement obtains.

(18)*Abs se pronominal*
   Marc s'évanouit. La glace se brise."Mark faints. The mirror breaks".
   Le pain se mange. Les enfants s'amusent.
   "The bread is eaten. The children have fun".

(18)

$$Agr_{O2}''$$

Spec Agr_{O2}'

Agr_{O2} VP_1

V   Agr

Spec V_1'
$-\theta$

V VP_2

Spec V_2'
Marc / la glace / le pain / les enfants

V VP_3

V

s'évanouit / se brise / se mange / s'amusent

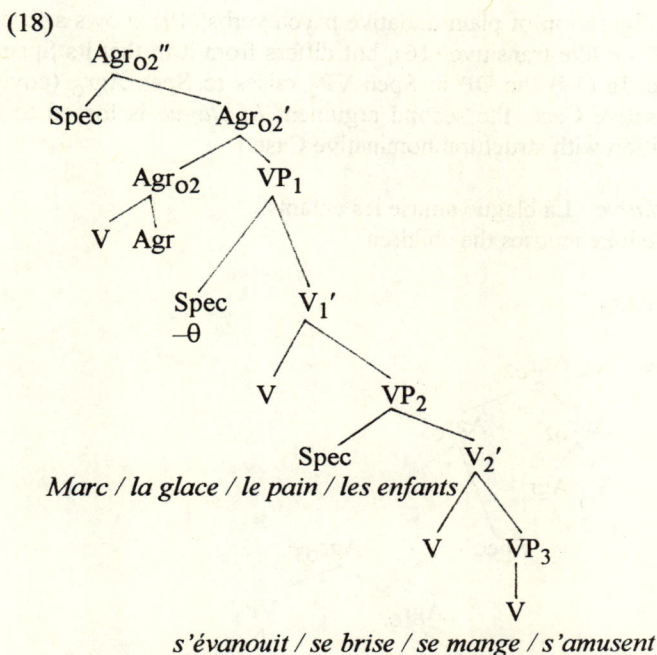

5.3.3 Pronominal and plain psych verbs

This section reviews the derivation of undatives and compares it to the derivation of pronominal psych verbs. For unaccusative and *Abs se* verbs the superficial subject originates in the Spec of VP_2, moves through the Spec of Agr_{O2} and raises to superficial subject position, leaving agreement on the past participle. The analysis proposed in this and the previous chapter assumes (as B&R, Grimshaw, Drijkoningen and others) the traditional treatment of transitive and unaccusative psych verbs, but it proposes that the *frighten / amuser* group is characterized by defective dative Case and, through the extended Burzio's generalization, by a nonthematic external argument. Unlike unaccusatives whose DP in Spec VP_2 moves to Agr_{O2} before raising to Spec Agr_S, undative internal arguments raise from the Spec of VP_3 to Spec of Agr_{O3} before raising to Spec of Agr_S. This treatment also predicts systematic differences between plain (*amuser*) and pronominal (*s'amuser*) psych verbs, the former undative and the latter both undative and unaccusative.

The configuration of plain undative psych verbs (19) shows a three tiered structure of VP like transitive (16), but differs from it in that its Spec VP_1 is nonthematic. In (19) the DP in Spec VP_2 raises to Spec Agr_o (covertly) to check accusative Case; the second argument *la blague* is forced to raise to subject position with structural nominative Case.

(19) *Undative*   La blague amuse les enfants.
     "The joke amuses the children".

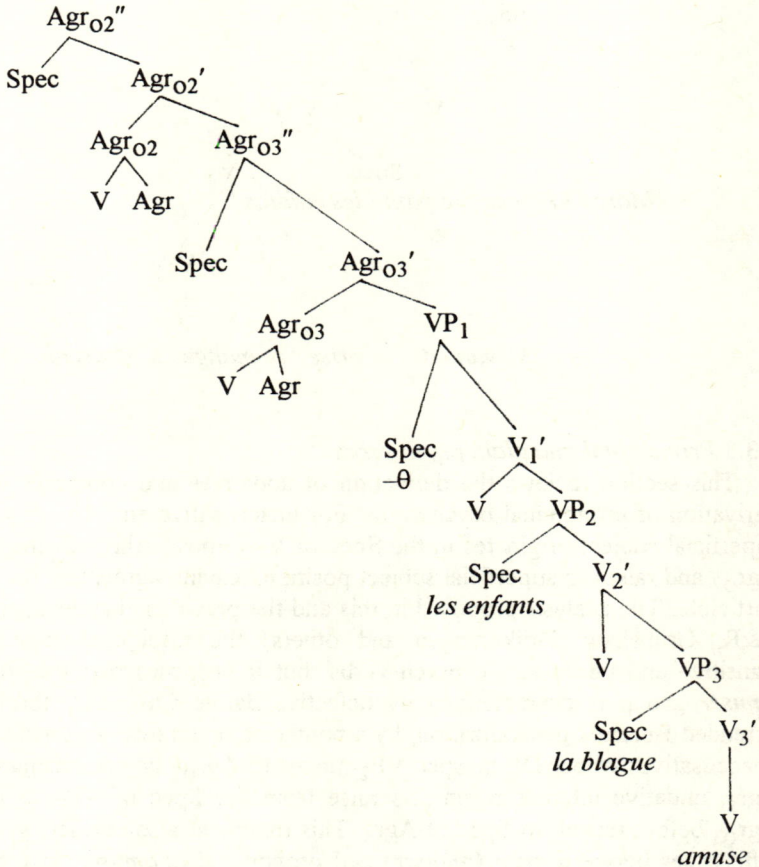

Two kinds of syntactic evidence show that the DP *la blague* does not raise by moving through Spec Agr_{O2} as unaccusatives, but rather by passing through the Spec Agr_{O3}. On theoretical grounds this movement is to be preferred because it is the shortest distance (Chomsky 1992:21), resulting in the crossing (not nesting) pattern described in Chapter 1. Second, on empirical grounds, there is no evidence that the theme of undatives passes through Spec Agr_{O2}. Unlike the direct object of unaccusative verbs, the second internal argument of psych undatives does not pass through the Spec of Agr_{O2} node and trigger past participle agreement. In undative constructions the arguments raise from Spec VP_3 to Spec Agr_{O3} and then to Spec Agr_S, without passing through Spec Agr_{O2} and triggering past participle agreement.

In terms of feature checking, undative verbs fail to mark the Spec of VP_3 with dative, so the DP that raises to Spec Agr_{O3} must be marked [+nominative] to raise further to Spec of Agr_S. Otherwise the derivation crashes. In the pronominal psych version both internal Cases are missing, dative because the verb is Case defective, and accusative because it has been suspended in the *Abs se* construction. Only the DP in Spec VP_2 can raise through Agr_{O2} to Agr_S with nominative Case. If it doesn't raise (20a) or if the DP in VP_3 isn't Case marked by a preposition (20b), the derivation crashes. The derivation also crashes if the DP in VP_3 raises with nominative because the direct object is still missing accusative (20c) and the target must be Case marked by a preposition.[20]

(20) a *S'intéresse Jean [no Case] à ce problème.
        "Is interested John in this problem"
     b *Jean s'intéresse ce problème [no Case].
        "John is interested this problem".
     c *Ce problème s'intéresse Jean [no Case].

A final difference between plain and pronominal psych verbs is that the former can take two internal arguments that will be Case marked structurally (nominative and accusative), but the latter can take only one due to the suspension of both internal Cases. In the plain version (21a) the experiencer is the direct object receiving accusative Case and the theme / causer moves to subject position because dative Case is suspended.

---

[20] In this last scenario redemptive partitive is not available (i), due perhaps to the presence of a thematic argument, not an expletive, in subject position.
   (i) *Ce problème s'intéresse plusieurs / des enfants.
        "This problem is interested several students".

(21) a   Les mathématiques préoccupent Jean.
         "Mathematics preoccupies John".
      b   Jean se préoccupe de ce problème.
         "John is preoccupied by this problem".

In the pronominal version (21b) *se* absorbs the second internal argument and causer theta role, opening the position for the theme / subject matter theta role that is prepositionally Case marked.

5.4 Clitic cooccurrence and the binary hypothesis

Pronominal constructions support the approach to Case and argument structure proposed: the availability of two internal argument positions in *Abs se* constructions in spite of the suspension of accusative Case supports the dual character of internal argument structure. They also confirm the extension of Burzio's generalization. The behavior of clitics offers further indication that duality is an important feature of language. This section looks first at clitics and then reexamines the binary hypothesis.

The ungrammaticality of dative clitics with pronominal constructions raises the issue of restrictions on clitic number and cooccurrence. For example, affected and lexical dative clitics are always ungrammatical with *se* (22b, d), although they are grammatical with nonpronominal equivalents (22c).

(22) a   On lui a cassé son jouet.
         "Someone broke his toy to him".
      b   *Son jouet se lui est cassé.
         "His toy broke to him".
      c   Son jouet lui a cassé entre les mains.
         "His toy broke to him right in his hands".
      d   On lui a mangé son pain.
         "Someone ate his bread to him".
      d   *Son pain se lui est mangé.
         "His bread got eaten to him".

Grevisse (1993:1005) formulates the cooccurrence restriction: "les pronoms conjoints *me, te, se, nous, vous* ne peuvent pas se trouver juxtaposés deux à deux, ni se joindre aux pronoms *lui, leur*". The prohibition appears to be fairly arbitrary and specific to French, since it doesn't hold for other Romance languages such as Spanish.[21] Spanish allows affected datives with *se* (23a) and also allows three clitic sequences (23b).

(23) a Se le rompió [el juguete] al niño.
     "[The toy] broke to the boy".
   b Se me lo rompió.
     "Someone broke it to me".

A more significant restriction, which echos the binary limit on arguments, is the strong preference for a limit of two nonsubject pronouns. Although sequences of three clitics are attested, pronouns are generally restricted in French to no more than two. They thus manifest a kind of binary harmony which can be seen to be a function of the dual character of the Agr_O node. Emonds (1975, 1978) establishes the need for two clitic nodes under the verb node in order to describe clitic ordering within his structure preserving framework. His analysis provides a clear description of clitics in French and supports the claim that languages permit only structure preserving, root and local transformations. He follows Kayne (1975) in proposing that clitics such as those in *s'évanouir, y avoir* and *s'en aller* are intrinsically clitic and have no possible sources in full NPs. Herschensohn (1980:203–206) revises Emonds's rule to reflect better the fact that there is a two clitic limit in French, a fact explained by the structure preserving constraint given the necessity of two intrinsic clitic nodes as a language specific expansion of the X-bar schema. Emonds's and Herschensohn's proposals make the interesting claim of a two clitic limit established as a function of the X-bar expansion of the VP in French. The need for two clitic nodes is justified by intrinsic reflexives and intrinsic *y* and *en*.

The justification of two clitic nodes imposes a theoretical limitation on the number of clitics. This proposal can be recast in terms of the minimalist program, using the binary nature of Agr_O as the theoretical limitation of two clitics. Agr_O has two sites for clitics in Spec Agr_{O2} and Spec Agr_{O3}, and thus usually permits only two occupants. In principle Agr_O may check no more than two Cases. These Cases specifically correlate with two arguments for standard transitive verbs: accusative Case is assigned to the argument originating in the Spec of VP_2 while dative Case is assigned to the argument originating in the Spec of VP_3. The behavior of unaccusative, psych and pronominal verbs indicates, however, that there are instances of Case

---

[21] Other Romance languages have their own restrictions; for example, Spanish prohibits *le lo*, replacing it with *se lo*.

suspension when one internal Case is defective, yet the number of internal arguments can still be two, one of which moves to subject position with nominative Case. The number of internal arguments cannot, however, exceed two. Likewise, Agr_O can receive in principle two possible object clitics, accusative and dative, corresponding to the specs of VP_2 and VP_3 respectively.

Not all clitics in French correspond to the accusative and dative complements of the verb. The prepositional clitics *y* and *en* may even represent adjuncts not subcategorized by the verb. Nonlexical datives are likewise not selected by the verb. A complete treatment of clitics is outside the scope of this study, but a few observations indicate a direction for a possible analysis. The preference for two clitics can be explained by assuming that the clitic positions used by accusative and dative clitics can alternatively be occupied by the prepositional clitics *y* and *en*. They are inherently Case marked, so, like partitive NPs in Spec VP_2, they can pass Case checking in Agr_O. Partitive *en* (from VP_2) could be checked in Agr_{O2}, as has been argued in Chapter 2. Prepositional *y* could be checked in Agr_{O3}. In any case, clitic ordering must be subject to a filter at PF. The double Agr_O puts a limit on the number of clitics that is not directly related to Case assignment, since adjunct clitics are inherently Case marked.

The preference for the binary clitic limit is demonstrated by the fact that two clitics are favored even though it is in fact possible to envisage inputs with three or four clitics (including arguments and adjuncts) that could all be cliticized (24)–(25).

(24) a   Il m'y donnera des stylos.
      "He'll give me some pens there".
   b   Il m'en donnera au bureau.
      "He'll give some to me in the office".
   c   ?Il m'y en donnera.
      "He'll give some to me there".
   d   *Il me lui y en donnera.
      "He'll give some to me there for him".
(25) a   Je t'ai demandé ce service à la maison.
      "I asked this service [of] you at home.'
   b   Je te l'ai demandé à la maison.
      "I asked it of you at home".
   c   Je t'y ai demandé ce service.
      "I asked this service of you there".

d ?Je te l'y ai demandé.
"I asked it of you there".
e *Je te le lui y ai demandé.
"I asked it of you there for him".

The sequences of more than two clitics are syntactically less acceptable (although they are semantically fine), and degrade progressively with the addition of more clitics.[22]

Sachs (1992:187–188) presents counterexamples to the two clitic limit, but informants interviewed by the present study (cf. Appendix) essentially rejected sequences with three or four clitics. What is significant is not the complete ungrammaticality of three clitic sequences, but rather their conspicuous absence when they are semantically quite possible. French differs from Spanish on this point because the latter readily allows three clitic sequences (23b). The difference appears to be related to the null subject parameter which can be seen to provide an extra clitic slot (that of the subject). The difference also seems to be related to the fact that in Spanish *se* can absorb nominative Case as well as accusative. Dobrovie-Sorin (1995) elucidates differences between nominative and accusative *se* / *si* in Romance. Exceptional three clitic sequences in French are probably cases of adjunction to the Agr_O nodes.[23]

The two clitic preference in French can be seen as a manifestation of the dual limit on Case and argument positions because it reflects the double agreement nodes linked to the two internal argument positions in the Larsonian VP shell. The limit is also confirmed by pronominal *Abs se* constructions which can accept two internal arguments even though Case is suspended. Overload sentences with psych pronominals, while thematically

---

[22] In the case particularly of affected datives a sequence of greater than two clitics is found (for example, Postal 1983:374).

(i) Pierre me la lui a fait envoyer. "Peter had me send it to her".

Sachs (1992) gives a thorough overview of clitic sequences and argues that cooccurrence restrictions are predictable from the thematic hierarchy.

[23] The examples provided by Grevisse (1993:988) not only exceed the limit, but blatantly violate cooccurrence restrictions. He points out that "la langue familière emploie d'une manière explétive le pronom de la première ou deuxième personne pour exprimer l'intérêt que le locuteur prend à l'action".

(i)   Je te vous les prends. "I take them to you you [sg., pl.]".
(ii) Je te vous lui ai craché. "I spit to you to him".
(iii) Je vais te me le coller au bloc.
     "I'm going to stick him to the block to you to me".

possible, are ungrammatical because they have too many arguments for too few Cases.

(26) a *Marie se dégoûte un bar [no Case] de la bière.
        "Mary is disgusted a bar with beer".
     b Jean s'intéresse les mathématiques [no Case] au problème.
        "John is interested math in the problem".

Partitive cannot save the derivation in (26a) because *un bar* constitutes one argument too many. Even if it carried partitive Case, it could not check off the partitive because Agr_{O2} is the passage node for *Marie*. Intrinsic and neutral *se* can't be used to test the hypothesis because they cannot be constructed with any more arguments. Middle *se*, on the other hand, can be used to test the possibility of more than two internal arguments. For middles, the direct object is forced to raise with nominative Case, but the internal argument(s) may remain in situ if they can avoid the Case filter with partitive (27a) or a CP that doesn't need Case (27b), if accusative is necessary, the derivation crashes (27c).

(27) a IL se dit des choses flatteuses aux étrangers.
        "There are flattering things said to strangers".
     b IL se dit aux promeneurs que les pelouses sont interdites.
        "It is said to the strollers that the lawn is off limits".
     c *IL se dit cette chose flatteuse aux étrangers.
        "There is said this flattering thing to strangers".

(27) demonstrates that two internal argument positions are available even if internal Case isn't. Since affected datives are impossible with *se*, they cannot be used to test the binary cap on internal arguments. It is, however, possible to test the limit with selected PP arguments. A possible candidate is *dire* "to speak" constructed with its selected PP with *de* "about".

(28) a Ces choses scandaleuses se disent facilement au public.
        "These scandalous things are easily said to the public".
     b Ces choses scandaleuses se disent facilement des stars.
        "These scandalous things are easily said about stars".
     c ?Ces choses scandaleuses se disent facilement des stars au public.
        "These scandalous things are easily said about stars to the public".
     d ?IL se dit des choses scandaleuses des stars au public.
        "There are scandalous things said about stars to the public".

The marginality of (28 c, d) is not due to semantic reasons since it is not illogical to say scandalous things about movie stars to the public. The marginality of (28c, d) can be attributed to the limit on the number of internal arguments. *Abs se* and clitic cooccurrence show a marked preference for a limit of two even when more than two thematic arguments are possible. Both of these constructions also show that the limit is not as stringent when PP complements are involved.

5.5 *Conclusion*

The analysis proposed accounts for both the thematic argument / accusative Case absorption and the change in interpretation associated with *Abs se* compared to *Id se* which syntactically resembles nonpronominal counterparts. The syntactic nature of *Id se* results in syntax and semantic interpretation that are straightforwardly parallel to nonpronominal sentences. The lexical character of *Abs se* involves absorption of an internal argument and accusative Case and entails a change in interpretation of the verb from a transitive to a neutral. The proposed analysis of French pronominals gives a unified account of *Id* and *Abs se* by treating differences between them as a function of level of lexical insertion. Psych pronominals are similar to other *Abs se* in that they absorb one of the verb's thematic arguments and modify the meaning of the verb. The fact that all French *se* are [+arg] accounts for their syntax and for differences between French and other Romance languages.

CHAPTER 6

INALIENABLE UNDATIVES

6.0 *Introduction*

In French possession may be indicated by the presence of a possessive determiner modifying the possessed noun. Inalienable possessions—that is, body parts and other closely related possessions (e.g. family or objects)—are often modified by the definite article rather than the possessive determiner. These definite article inalienable DPs are selected by verbs which superficially show two patterns of argument distribution: the possessor is either a dative object or the superficial subject. This chapter argues that the second class of these inalienable verbs has a nonthematic external argument and a syntactic behavior similar to that of psych undatives, and that this class of verbs offers further support for the analyses proposed in earlier chapters.

The first section describes French inalienable constructions, adopting Vergnaud and Zubizarreta's (1992) proposal and strengthening their distinction between inalienable definite determiners as locally bound and possessive determiners as locally free. The second section develops an analysis of trivalent verbs that can be accusative, unaccusative or undative. Section 6.3 discusses the significance of these constructions for the binary hypothesis.

6.1 *Inalienable constructions*
6.1.1 *Possessive determiners, alienable and inalienable*

In English, inalienable body parts (2)–(5) are usually determined by a possessive determiner as are alienable possessions (1). French uses the possessive determiner for alienable and inalienable possessions (1)–(2), but most frequently uses the definite determiner when the body part is a selected argument of the verb (3)–(5).

    (1) Jean a lavé son verre.
        "John washed his glass".
    (2) Jean₁ a lavé ses₁ mains.
        "John washed his hands".

(3) a   Pierre lui$_i$ a lavé [les mains]$_j$.
       "Peter washed her hands".
    b   Jean s$_i$' est lavé [les mains]$_i$.
       "John washed his own hands".

The possessor in French is usually indicated by an indirect object pronoun, either reflexive (3b) or nonreflexive as *lui* (3a). Sometimes the subject is the possessor (4).

(4) Pierre$_i$ a levé la$_i$ main.
   "Peter raised his hand".

In certain locative expressions (e.g. *hit on the head, kiss on the cheek*), the possessive determiner in English may be suppressed in favor of the definite article. On the other hand, French most commonly uses the definite article with body parts, so possessive suppression appears to be usual in French, but unusual in English.

The apparent complementarity of alienable and inalienable possession in French has led to traditional explanations such as this one offered by Grevisse (1993:910): "On remplace l'adjectif possessif par l'article défini quand le rapport d'appartenance est assez nettement indiqué". The dichotomy is not, however, as strict as Grevisse suggests, because the use of the possessive determiner with a body part is permitted in a broad range of circumstances. For example, the possessive is required when the body part is modified by an adjective or other complement (5) (Hatcher 1944:459).

(5) Il a levé sa/*la belle main blanche.
   "He raised his beautiful white hand".

The possessive is used to emphasize possession, to indicate the alienability of a body part (e.g. false teeth or artificial limbs) or as a stylistic variant. Finally, the possessive is preferred with a number of verbs such as *voir* "to see" as in (6).

(6) Pierre a vu sa / *la main dans la glace.
   "Peter has seen his/the hand in the mirror".

The data indicate that possessive determiners act as nominal subjects, as Milner (1982), Aoun (1985) and others have observed: Aoun (1985:35) claims "in French the Specifier of the NP counts as the most prominent element (= subject) with respect to the elements occurring in this NP". The possessive DP is opaque because the possessive determiner is referential and the subject of the DP. Unlike possessive DPs which have an accessible subject in the possessive determiner, inalienable DPs with definite determiners have no accessible subject. Lacking an internal referential subject, the inalienable body part must take its reference from another argument, usually the indirect object. As Guéron (1986:50) notes, "the body-part NP has no potential reference; that is, it is not an R-expression".[1] Herschensohn (1992a:379) observes that the inalienable definite determiner, which is referentially transparent, has an interpretation akin to the generic article of sentences such as (7).

(7) Le pouce rend l'homme capable d'employer des outils.
"The thumb renders man capable of using tools".

The interpretation of the determiner is partially a function of the semantic qualities of the noun modified. In the case of body parts, one necessary aspect of their interpretation is that of belonging to a body. The nonreferential definite article has an interpretation similar to other arbitrary elements discussed by Cinque (1988).

6.1.2 Predicational analysis of inalienable constructions

Vergnaud & Zubizarreta (1992) (henceforth V&Z) provide a thorough and well conceived analysis of definite inalienables, arguing that these noun phrases, like generics, are not denotational and must gain denotation through predication. They spell out details of an analysis which responds to observations made in the previous section. They are primarily concerned with accounting for distributive effects and the type / token readings that characterize inalienables, but in doing so furnish a well argued account of definite and possessive inalienables.

They begin with an examination of distributive effects (8) and the type / token readings that characterize inalienables (9)–(10). In (8) and (9) a syntactically singular inalienable DP effects a distributive interpretation by association with a plural possessor; in (8) the interpretation licenses a syntactically plural pronoun *ils*.

---

[1] Guéron (1986:50) observes that the inalienable's "inability to contain a descriptive adjective suggests that under [inalienable] construal, the body-part NP has no potential reference; that is, it is not an R-expression". The possessive determiner by contrast does create a referring expression according to Guéron. Body parts which are modified by possessive determiners are R-expressions which behave syntactically like any other referring DP. Inalienables do not.

(8) Le médecin leur a radiographié l'*estomac* à toutes
et il a constaté qu'*ils* avaient des images normales.
"The doctor x-rayed their *stomach(s)* [of all the females]
and he saw that *they* looked normal".

(9) Le médecin leur a examiné la gorge [aux enfants].
The doctor to them examined the throat [to the children].

(10)Le médecin a examiné leurs gorges.
"The doctor examined their throats".

In (10) the inalienable DP is plural and has only a *token* interpretation, whereas in (9) the inalienable DP has a *type* interpretation as the computer in (11).

(11)On a donné le même *ordinateur* à Sophie, à Justine et à Cléa,
et *ils* sont tous tombés en panne.
"Someone gave the same *computer* to Sophie, Justine and Clea
and *they* all broke down".

V&Z (1992:649) propose that possessive determiner inalienables (int[ernal] poss[essor] constructions whose possessor is expressed internally) are DPs which denote tokens, whereas "the inalienable phrase in the ext[ernal] poss[essor] construction [whose possessor is expressed external to the NP] is a type-denoting phrase headed by an expletive determiner". They describe the distinction between DP and NP by the Correspondence Law (ibid.:612) (12).

(12)*Correspondence Law*
When a DP or an NP denotes, the DP denotes a token and the NP denotes a type.

Inalienables are semantically dependent on a possessor who, in the case of ext-poss constructions, must be determined by predication that binds the inalienable NP to its subject.[2]

---

[2] "Either the subject is realized within the maximal projection of the argument-taking category as the Specifier of that category, in which case Predication does not apply; or the subject is realized outside the maximal projection of the argument-taking category and Predication does apply, binding that maximal projection to its subject" (V&Z:608).

V&Z use a small clause representation to describe the predicational relationship that must obtain between the body part and the possessor (13).

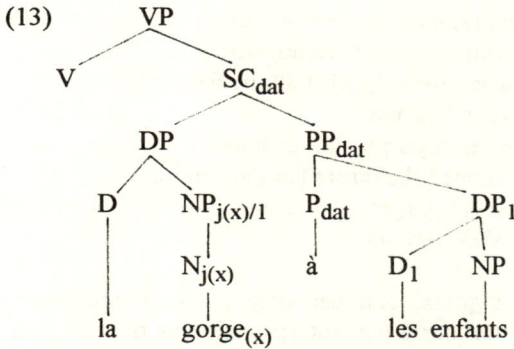

(13)

```
              VP
           /      \
          V        SC_dat
                  /      \
               DP         PP_dat
             /    \       /     \
            D   NP_j(x)/1  P_dat   DP_1
            |     |        |      /   \
            |    N_j(x)     à    D_1    NP
            |     |              |       |
           la  gorge_(x)       les    enfants
```

The inalienable *gorge* with its subscripted letter indicating its type denotation, requires predication; the arabic number indicates a token (actually it is the determiner that is denotational) from which the inalienable obtains the denotational index. The binding relationship between the inalienable and the possessor obeys strict locality constraints as an instance of mutual m-command.

(14) *M-command* (Chomsky 1986b:8)
    α m-commands β iff α does not dominate β and every maximal projection that dominates α dominates β.

The possessor binder must m-command the body part inalienable. It is necessary that the command be mutual because the two internal arguments are equal in prominence for purposes of anaphoric binding; superficially both orderings, antecedent before anaphor and anaphor before antecedent, obtain.[3] The predicational relationship must be established at LF.

---

[3] The first ordering is shown in (i) and the second in (ii).
   (i) a   Marc me / lui lave les mains. "Mark washes my / her hands".
      b   Marc me les lave. "Mark washes them for me".
   (ii) a   Marc lave les mains à l'enfant. "Mark washes the child's hands".
      b   Marc les lui lave. "Mark washes them for her".
This variation is a problem for a literal interpretation of binding theory either for a traditional formulation or the minimalist definition (Chapter 1). The variation is reminiscent of the equal prominence of direct and indirect objects for backward binding with psych verbs (cf. Chapter 4).

Herschensohn (1992a) presents additional syntactic evidence indicating that inalienables must be locally bound and that they are in complementary distribution with possessives subject to Binding Condition B.[4] Inalienables must be locally bound by their antecedents (14)–(17), whereas possessives must be locally free. Sentences (15)–(16) are acceptable with a possessive, but are ungrammatical with an inalienable determiner because it is not locally bound by its antecedent.

(15) a $Sa_{i,j}$ / *La_i main a été levée par $Pierre_i$.
      "His hand was raised by Peter".
   b   Sur la lune $son_{i,j}$ / *le_i pied était facile à PRO_i lever.
      "On the moon his foot was easy to raise".
(16) La photo de $Jean_i$ a réjoui $ses_{i,j}$ / *les_i yeux.
     "John's photo rejoiced his eyes".

When the inalienable is locally bound by its possessor, the sentence is acceptable as (17) shows.

(17) Sur la lune il était facile de PRO_i lever le_i pied.
     On the moon it was easy to raise one's foot".

Inalienables also show Tensed Sentence Condition (18)–(19) and Specified Subject Condition (20)–(21) effects that possessives don't.

(18) $Elle_i$ croit PRO_i avoir [la jambe enflée]$_i$.
     "She believes her leg to be swollen".
(19) $Elle_i$ dit que $sa_{i,j}$ / *la_i jambe est enflée.
     "She says that her leg is swollen".
(20) $Pierre_i$ est capable de PRO_i lever [la main]$_i$.
     "Peter is capable of raising his hand".
(21) $Pierre_i$ me_j croit capable de PRO_j lever sa_i / *la_i main.
     "Peter thinks me capable of raising his hand".

As in (19) the possessive determiner is acceptable in (21) because it is free in the embedded clause.

The evidence presented indicates clearly that inalienables are locally bound whereas possessive determiners behave as pronominals with regard to binding

---

[4] Guéron (1986:48) observes evidence for the anaphoric nature of inalienables, although she doesn't contrast them with possessives.

conditions. V&Z's proposal of mutual m-command between the inalienable and a dative accounts for standard cases (2)–(3); the exceptional (4), which superficially appears to contradict this proposal, is the focus of the next section.

6.2 *Dative and undative inalienable verbs*

The evidence presented thus far indicates that ext-poss definite inalienables must be bound in a local domain. This section examines the syntactic configuration of the inalienable / possessor relationship. The investigation is restricted to cases where the inalienable noun phrase is an argument of the verb.[5] It is argued that in the paradigm case, inalienable direct objects initially in Spec VP_2 must be bound to the argument originating in the Spec of VP_3. This discussion runs counter to Guéron's (1986:45) claim that there is an "absence of any syntactic position systematically associated with the 'possessor' NP". Two kinds of evidence show that the Spec VP_3 must be the subject for the inalienable. First, as V&Z show, inalienable subjects of accusative and unaccusative verbs clearly require indirect object antecedents. A second category of evidence is found in the verbs that V&Z do not dwell on, the *lever* verbs exemplified in (4). Section 6.2.2 will argue that these verbs are trivalent—they may be unaccusative or undative—and also require an inalienable subject in the Spec VP_3.

6.2.1 *Dative inalienable constructions*

Common accusative and unaccusative verbs which allow indirect objects indicate that the definite inalienable is bound to the possessor originating in the Spec VP_3. French indirect objects are realized at S-structure as full DPs preceded by *à* or as the clitics *lui, leur*, etc. (Kayne 1975), Burzio 1986). Barnes (1980, 1985) and Rooryck (1988) discuss the inalienable dative as a nonlexical dative which contrasts with lexical datives subcategorized by a large class of verbs allowing full DPs as well as pronominal datives. The verbs which allow inalienables are not strictly subcategorized for indirect objects, but are capable of optionally taking "affected" indirect objects (Cheng &

---

[5] Cases such as (i) which Guéron terms IA [inalienable]-2 are not considered in this chapter.

    (i) Elle l'a embrassé sur la bouche. "She kissed him on the mouth".

In cases of IA-2 the phrase containing the inalienable is optional and may be deleted without affecting the argument structure of the sentence. V&Z discuss prepositional inalienables in terms of metonymy. "Verbs that can appear in the PP construction are *verbs that license metonymy*. More precisely, such verbs allow the part (the PP complement) to be identified with the whole (the direct object)" (V&Z:639).

Ritter 1987) in constructions with body parts. The lexical / non-lexical distinction is not relevant to the present discussion.

The most frequent possessor for inalienables is the indirect object (2), (3). Common examples of this type are body care verbs (usually reflexive) such as *(se) brosser, (se) peigner, (se) laver*, etc. "to brush, comb, wash" and injury verbs such as *casser, tordre*, etc. "to break, twist". Sentences with these verbs are ungrammatical without an indirect object possessor, unless a possessive determiner is used. In the absence of an indirect object, the sentential subject cannot be taken as the possessor of the inalienable.[6] Sentences with inalienables in non-argument PPs often have the indirect object as the binder (22).

(22) a   Le vent lui soufflait au visage.
        "The wind blew in his face".
    b   Elle lui plongea le poignard dans le coeur.
        "She plunged the dagger into his heart".

Unaccusative verbs also have indirect object antecedents for the inalienable. These verbs allow movement of the direct object to subject position, as in (23).

(23) a   IL lui manque le pouce gauche.
        "There is missing his left thumb [to him]".
    b   Son / Le pouce gauche lui manque.
        "His left thumb is missing [to him]".

The inalienable antecedent in (23) is the indirect object. As noted earlier, the use of the possessive is usually required for an inalienable in subject position.[7]

Verbs which do not permit "affected themes" allow only possessive, not inalienable determiners.[8] Cheng & Ritter (1987:67) describe the notion of

---

[6]   For example, in (i) only the possessive is grammatical.
     (i)   Jean a lavé ses / *les mains. "John washed his hands".
[7]   The apparent relaxation of the m-command requirement with *manquer* is quite lexically specific, since other unaccusatives don't allow the violation (ii, iii).
     (i)   Le bras lui manque. "His arm is missing".
     (ii) a   *La tête lui tombe sur l'épaule.
         b   Sa tête tombe sur son l'épaule. "His head falls on his shoulder".
[8]   For example *apercevoir* "to perceive" is more acceptable with a possessive than an inalienable determiner.
     (i)   ?Pierre lui a aperçu la main dans la glace.

"affected theme" as the property of a verb which "effects some change in its direct object, breaking it, peeling it, etc". They discuss inalienable possession in French and Chinese, stating that "this construction is ungrammatical with verbs which do not select an affected theme such as *admire, see, smell* or *want*". Although the subject is available as a possessor for verbs such as *voir, entendre, reconnaître* "to see, hear, recognize," it cannot be taken as such. As in other cases when clausal binding fails, the possessive determiner ext-poss construction must be used to indicate the possessor of the body part. The resistance of verbs such as *admirer* to allow inalienable anaphors (less for French than Cheng & Ritter claim) points up a lexical property of verbs that do allow inalienables: verbs which allow body parts to be affected require a second internal argument of the verb to absorb the effect.

6.2.2 *Two dilemmas*

An apparent counterexample to the claim that inalienables are unable to be bound to the sentential subject is the class of verbs such as *lever* in (4); quite to the contrary, these verbs require binding to the subject by the inalienable. V&Z (1992:622) do not investigate this construction in much detail and adopt Guéron's reanalysis treatment: "because of reanalysis, the VP is interpreted as a projection of the complex predicate *lever le bras*".[9] A more complete examination of this verb type reveals that it conforms to V&Z's predicational proposal of m-command of the body part by the possessor. It will be shown that it is precisely the suspension of dative Case which forces the argument in the Spec of VP_3, the structural position usually linked to dative Case, to move to Spec Agr_S with nominative Case in these constructions.

There are a number of verbs like *lever* that have a sentential subject binder for the ext-poss inalienable. Hatcher (1944:460–461) lists the following verbs which allow possessor subjects: *agiter, allonger, avancer, baisser, balancer, bomber, bouger, branler, claquer, contracter, crisper, croiser, creuser, desserrer, détourner, (re)dresser, écarter, élever, enfler, étendre, fermer, hausser, hocher, incliner, (re)jeter, joindre, (re)lever, montrer, ouvrir, pencher, plier, raidir, remuer, renverser, secouer, serrer, tourner, trainer* "to agitate, stretch, advance, lower, balance, swell, budge, shake, flap, contract,

---

(ii) Pierre a aperçu sa main dans la glace.
  "Peter perceived her hand in the mirror".
Informants did not reject (iii) out of hand (cf. Appendix), despite Cheng & Ritter's observation.
(iii) Paul s'est vu la main dans la glace. "Paul saw his hand in the mirror".
[9] V&Z note (p.621) that "this construction is lexically restricted. In French it is found only with verbs that denote body movements".

stiffen, cross, hollow out, loosen, turn away, straighten up, spread out, lift, enflame, stretch, close, shrug, nod, incline, throw back, join, raise, show, open, lean, bend, stiffen, wiggle, overturn, jolt, clasp, turn, drag". The verbs *donner, offrir, passer, tendre* "to give, offer, pass, tender" allow possessor subjects and also take lexical dative objects, but only permit inalienable binding with *hand* and metonymically related parts.

(24) a Marc$_i$ lui$_j$ a donné / offert / tendu la main$_{i/*j}$.
　　　 "Mark gave / offered / extended him his hand".
　　 b Marc$_i$ lui$_j$ a donné un coup dans le dos$*_{i/j}$.
　　　 "Mark hit him a blow to the back".

Expressions such as *donner la main, le petit doigt* "to gives one's hand, little finger" are fixed (Grevisse 1993:910 refers to them as *formules traditionnelles*) and are not productive as subject antecedent inalienable verbs. (24b) shows that they usually have an indirect object antecedent for the inalienable.

Three kinds of evidence show that *lever* type verbs are best analyzed as having a triple subcategorization, one of which has a nonthematic external argument structure with an inalienable possessor that is the verb's second internal argument. First, *lever* verbs have an true transitive subcategorization frame with an underlying thematic agent in Spec VP$_1$, distinct from sentence type (4). Second, they also have an unaccusative subcategorization frame with a nonthematic external argument, as unaccusative tests indicate. Finally, the inalienable binding configuration of these verbs and solutions to two other anomalies fall out from an analysis which posits base generation of the possessor argument in Spec VP$_3$ with possible movement of either the direct or indirect object to Spec Agr$_s$.

The verbs that can select inalienable arguments and have a superficial subject antecedent for the inalienable are exemplified by (4).

(4) Pierre a levé la main.
　　"Peter raised his hand".

These verbs appear to contradict the proposal that the antecedent of the inalienable must be the indirect object of the clause. At first glance, one wonders why they should allow subject antecedents when other verbs do not (6), (22). On closer inspection, one notes that these verbs—including *lever, passer, ouvrir* "to raise, pass, open"—display different thematic roles in inalienable constructions like (4) than with other direct objects.

Alongside sentences like (4), there are sentences like (1), (3a), (25), and (26) which manifest a paradigmatic agent / theme relation between the superficial subject and direct object.

(1) Jean a lavé son / le verre.
   "John washed his / the glass".
(3a) Pierre$_i$ lui$_j$ a lavé [les mains]$*_{i/j}$.
   "Peter washed her hands".
(25) Pierre a levé son / le verre.
   "Peter raised his / the glass".
(26) Elle$_i$ lui$_j$ a levé [la tête]$*_{i/j}$.
   "She raised his head".

In all these sentences an agent performs an action affecting a theme. For both *laver* and *lever* in (3a) and (26) the agent performs an action on the body part and indirectly on the possessor. Further support for the transitive or agentive nature of these sentences is the fact that (1) and (25) may be passivized with the agent in the *par* "by" phrase (27).

(27) Le verre a été lavé / levé par Pierre.
   "The glass was washed / raised by Peter".

Lever in these constructions, like *laver*, clearly has an accusative or true transitive subcategorization. In (4), by contrast, *Peter's* raising his own hand is not an action applied to an external object, such as washing a glass (1), seeing a hand (6), raising a glass (25) or raising someone else's head (26).[10] *Peter* is a thematic agent in (25) and (26) as in (1), but *Peter* is not an agent in (4). This phenomenon can be referred to as the thematic dilemma.

There is a second difference between *lever* and *laver* verb types. If the possessor is the superficial subject, *laver*, as might be expected, has a pronominal reflexive form parallel to the nonpronominal indirect object *lui* (3), whereas *lever* is ungrammatical with a pronominal reflexive (28).

(28) *Pierre s'est levé la main.
   "Peter raised his hand".

---

[10] Hatcher observes (1944:462): "all these phrases are essentially 'intransitive': though the part is the object of the verb, it is not the object of activity. For the subject of *il lève la tête* does not 'do something' to his head [...] rather, he does something with his head: he makes a movement that is determined by the head".

This phenomenon can be referred to as the pronominal dilemma. It appears that *lever* verbs have an accusative subcategorization frame, but manifest two problems with respect to sentences like (4)—which look like transitive sentences, but are not—the thematic dilemma and the pronominal dilemma.

6.2.3 *Undative inalienable verbs*

The solution to the two dilemmas is the proposal that *lever* verbs have, in addition to the accusative subcategorization, a subcategorization by which the Spec VP$_1$ is nonthematic and either accusative or dative Case can be suspended. Diagnostics indicate that this proposal is true for an unaccusative subcategorization frame whereby the direct object can move into superficial subject position with an intransitive interpretation.[11] First, these verbs, as other unaccusatives (lexical and pronominal), allow movement of the direct object to the subject position (29).[12]

(29) a Deux têtes se sont levées.
       "Two heads were raised".
     b Ses sourcils se sont froncés.
       "His eyebrows knitted".
     c Ses membres (se) raidissent.
       "His members stiffen".
     d Cette dent remue.
       "This tooth is loose".

The analysis proposed here is that in the sentences in (29) the external argument is nonthematic and the direct object (in Spec VP$_2$) raises to subject position. Second, although the reciprocal diagnostic is essentially inapplicable with inanimate body parts as subjects, the *lever* verbs are totally impossible (30a), while the *laver* reciprocals are at least comprehensible under a metaphorical reading with the hands representing those who wash each other.

---

[11] The *on* and reciprocal diagnostics are inapplicable since the direct object affected theme body part is always inanimate.

[12] Accusative *lever, raidir* "raise, stiffen" alternate with ergative *se lever, (se) raidir* as do Burzio's (1986:38) examples of *romper / rompersi* "to break". He points out that the morphological reflex *si* is unpredictable in ergative verbs: "we find no principled way to predict when in a transitive–ergative alternation *si* will appear. We may regard this as governed by lexical idiosyncrasies".

(30) a   *Les têtes se sont levées l'une l'autre.
          "The heads raise one another".
     b   ?Les mains se sont lavées l'une l'autre.
          "The hands washed one another".

Third, *lever* verbs meet the causative diagnostics for nonthematic external argumenthood. Dative cliticization in causatives with embedded thematic external arguments causes a binding violation (31).

(31) a   Jean téléphone à ses parents.
          "John phones [to] his parents".
     b   *On leur a fait téléphoner Jean.
          "We made John phone them".

The *lever* inalienables do not manifest these binding violations with dative clitics (32).

(32) a   Le froid lui a fait croiser les bras.
          "The cold made him cross his arms".
     b   Cette drogue lui a fait froncer les sourcils sans le vouloir.
          "This drug made him knit his eyebrows without wanting to".
     c   Pour amuser les enfants, on lui a fait remuer les oreilles".
          "To amuse the children, we had him wiggle his ears".
     d   Cette nouvelle lui a fait lever le bras de désespoir.
          "This news made him lift his arm in dispair".

The grammaticality of (32) is predicted by a nonthematic external argument with *lever* verbs.

When embedded in causative constructions, true external arguments can be null (33a), but derived subjects cannot be. The ungrammaticality of (33b–d) indicates that the intransitive subjects of (29) are derived.

(33) a   Une nouvelle joyeuse fait téléphoner tout de suite.
          "Joyful news makes [someone] phone right away".
     b   Le froid fait croiser *(les bras).
          "The cold makes [someone / something] cross (their arms).
     c   Une telle nouvelle fait froncer *(les sourcils).
          "Such news makes [someone / something] knit (their brows)".
     d   *Cela a fait remuer.
          "That made [someone / something] wiggle".

(33b–d) would be acceptable if the superficial subject of sentences such as (29) were included (as in parentheses), but they are not grammatical without it. These verbs do not have thematic external arguments although they, like *téléphoner* are superficially intransitive in (29). When the body part is present as in (33b,c) without parentheses, the sentence is acceptable because selected direct objects are not expendable whereas external arguments are. *Lever* then has two subcategorization frames, the accusative and the unaccusative. In the first subcategorization (25–27) the verb assigns a theta role to its external argument; in the second (29, 30, 32, 33) it does not.

Usually sentences which have no indirect object do not permit the sentential subject to be the inalienable antecedent. With *lever* verbs, however, the subject may be the possessor (4). The fact that *lever* verbs may have a nonthematic external argument offers precisely the reason why they are different. With *lever* verbs either the first *or* second internal argument may be the superficial subject. This analysis of triple valence provides an account of inalienable binding, the thematic dilemma and the pronominal dilemma.

The same diagnostics used above can be applied to sentence type (4), (34) to show that *Pierre* is also a derived subject.

(34) a   Pierre a froncé les sourcils.
        "Peter knit his brows".
   b   Pierre a remué les oreilles.
        "Peter wiggled his ears".
   c   Pierre a ouvert la bouche.
        "Peter opened his mouth".
   d   Pierre a levé la tête.
        "Peter raised his head".

The derivation giving (29) is unaccusative whereas the one giving (34) is undative. Presentational *IL* and *en* extraction are inapplicable with undatives (cf. Chapter 5). Arbitrary *on* (35), reciprocal and the causative diagnostics do support the derived status of the subjects of (34).

(35) a   On a levé la main.
        "We / *Someone raised his hand".
   b   On a froncé les sourcils.
        "We / *Someone knitted his eyebrows".
   c   On a remué les oreilles.
        "We / *Someone wiggled his ears".

    d   On a ouvert la bouche.
       "We / *Someone opened his mouth".

Although judgments on *on* are subtle, informants did not readily accept the arbitrary reading with the inalienable verbs (cf. Appendix). The reciprocal sentences are not good with the meaning of (34), they are only acceptable with the transitive meaning. The verbs in (36) can only have the accusative interpretation, for example of the children raising each other's hand, not of each raising his own hand.

(36) a Les élèves se sont levé les mains l'un à l'autre.
        "The pupils raised each other's hands".
        "*Each pupil raised his hand to the other".
    b Ils se sont froncé les sourcils l'un à l'autre.
        "They wrinkled each other's brows".
        "*Each wrinkled his brow to the other".
    c Ils se sont remué les oreilles l'un à l'autre.
        "They wiggled each other's ears".
        "*Each wiggled his ear to the other".
    d Ils se sont ouvert la bouche l'un à l'autre.
        "They opened each other's mouth".
        "*Each opened his mouth to the other".

The inapplicability of the causative binding diagnostics in dative cliticization with causatives (32) confirms that the possessor is not a thematic external argument, but an internal argument (see the discussion above).

(32) a Le froid lui a fait croiser les bras.
        "The cold made him cross his arms".
    b Cette drogue lui a fait froncer les sourcils sans le vouloir.
        "This drug made him knit his eyebrows without wanting to".
    c Pour amuser les enfants, on lui a fait remuer les oreilles.
        "To amuse the children, we had him wiggle his ears".
    d Cette nouvelle lui a fait lever le bras de désespoir.
        "This news made him lift his arm in dispair".

The apparently anomalous binding of the inalienable with the subject rather than the indirect object is clarified by this proposal. The inalienable in sentences like (4) actually does have a second argument possessor, but in this case it is unusually moved to subject position. The thematic differences between true transitives and *lever* type verbs in (4) are attributed to the unaccusative / accusative difference. The accusative (true transitive) sentences (1), (25) and (26) with agent subjects contrast with (4), because in (4) the subject is really the verb's second internal argument. The second argument is usually the indirect object as in (26), but in the limited class of trivalent verbs, it may raise to subject position (4).

Finally, the pronominal dilemma is resolved: trivalent *lever* type verbs allow realization of the second argument in subject position, rather than replication of the accusative subcategorization with a reflexive pronominal form as *laver* does. The distinct behavior of *lever* verbs and the inalienable binding configuration are both explicable as a consequence of the fact that these verbs are trivalent. *Lever* type verbs are trivalent since they permit as derived subjects both the inalienable (29) and the possessor (4).

6.3 *Binary internal argument structure*

The existence of a class of undative verbs which can be analyzed in the same manner as psych undatives can be seen to offer further support for the binary approach to Case and argument projection. Section 6.3.1 outlines the derivation of the two classes of inalienable verbs, while Section 6.3.2 discusses the significance of inalienables to the binary hypothesis.

6.3.1 *Derivation of ext-poss inalienable constructions*

Given the analysis of inalienable verbs proposed in section 6.2, standard inalienables behave syntactically like other transitive verbs, while trivalents have an unaccusative or undative derivation. The standard *laver* (37) has an external argument in Spec VP_1 which raises to the Spec of Agr_s. The body part in Spec VP_2 is bound by predication to its possessor subject originating in Spec VP_3. The transitive verb assigns both accusative and dative Case to DP_2 and DP_3 respectively.

(37) *Standard inalienable.*
   Jean s'est lavé les mains. Marie lui a levé les mains.
   "John washed his hands. Mary lifted his hands".

(37)

$$
\begin{array}{c}
\text{Agr}_{O2}'' \\
\overbrace{} \\
\text{Spec} \qquad \text{Agr}_{O2}'
\end{array}
$$

Agr$_{O2}''$

Spec   Agr$_{O2}'$

     Agr$_{O2}$ Agr$_{O3}''$

     V   Agr

       Spec   Agr$_{O3}'$
       lui$_i$ / *se*$_i$

         Agr$_{O3}$ VP$_1$

         V   Agr

             Spec   V$_1'$
             Marie / Jean

                V   VP$_2$

                   Spec   V$_2'$
                   les mains

                      V   VP$_3$

                         Spec   V$_3'$
                         pro$_i$

                              V

                         levé / lavé

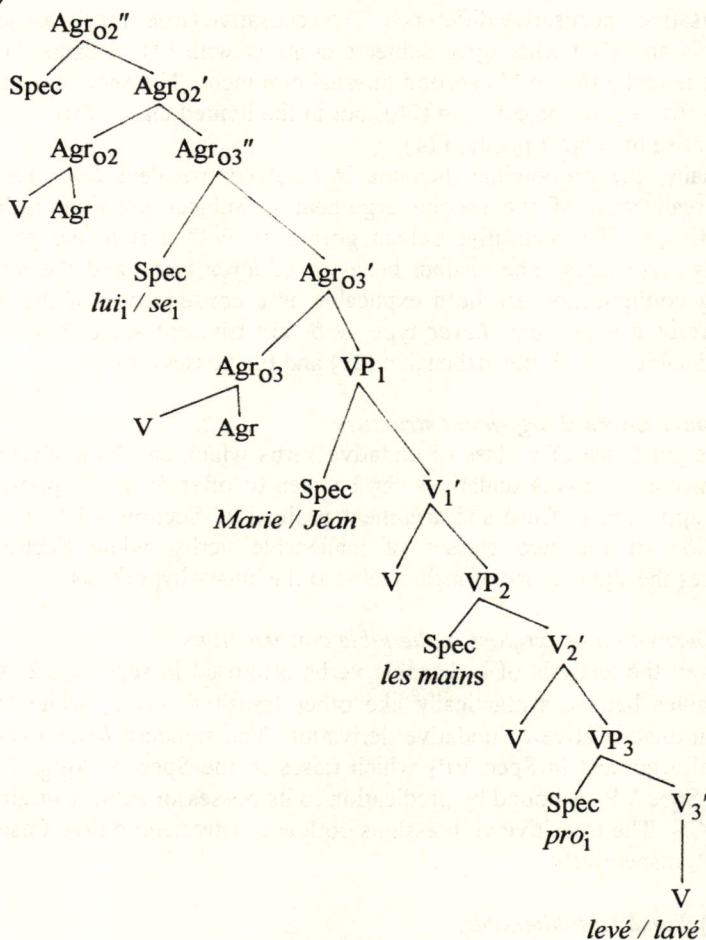

The trivalent *lever* has in addition to the transitive realization (37) a nonthematic Spec VP$_1$ and may have either an unaccusative derivation (38) or an undative derivation (39). In (38) accusative Case is suspended and DP$_2$ is forced to raise to subject position (Spec Agr$_s$) with nominative Case. The unaccusative variant is often pronominal.

(38)*Unaccusative inalienable*
   Plusieurs mains se sont levées. Sa dent remuait.
   "Several hands were raised. His tooth wiggled".

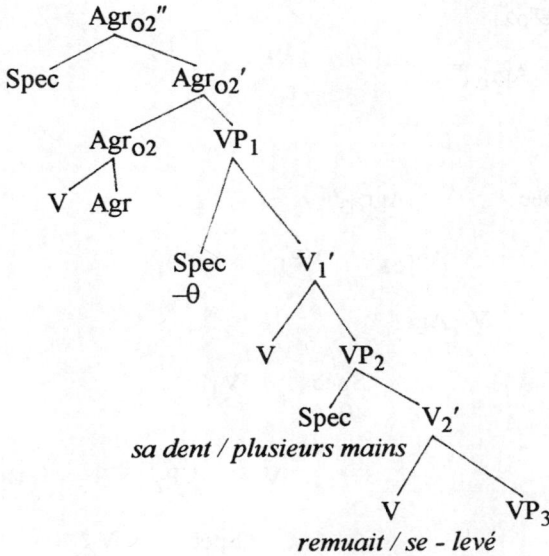

```
                Agr_O2"
              /        \
          Spec          Agr_O2'
                       /        \
                  Agr_O2          VP_1
                 /     \         /    \
               V      Agr     Spec     V_1'
                               -θ     /    \
                                     V      VP_2
                                           /    \
                                        Spec     V_2'
                                sa dent / plusieurs mains
                                                /    \
                                               V      VP_3
                                        remuait / se - levé
```

In the undative derivation (39) the Spec VP_1 is nonthematic and the inalienable DP in Spec VP_2 raises covertly with accusative Case to Agr_{O2}. The possessor DP in Spec VP_3 cannot receive dative Case because dative is suspended; the DP must raise through Spec Agr_{O2} to Spec Agr_S with nominative Case. The inalienable undative (39) contrasts with both the standard inalienable (37) and the unaccusative (38).

(39) *Undative inalienable*
   Pierre a levé la main.
   "Peter raised his hand".

(39)

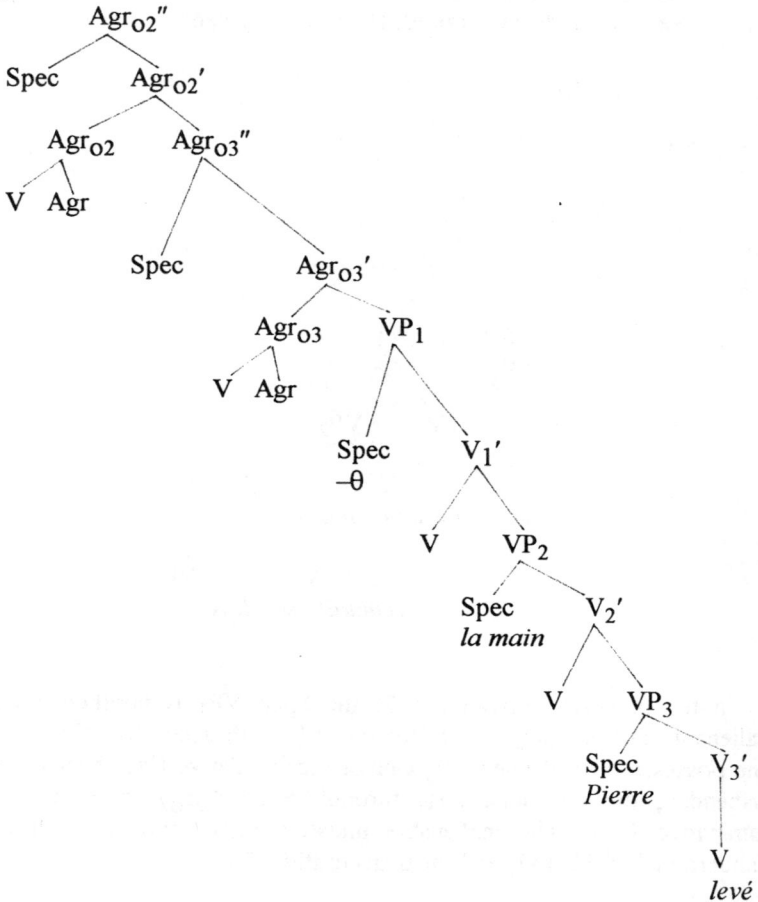

6.3.2 Divergence of syntactic and thematic structure

Undative inalienables are multivalent verbs in that they have variable Case assigning properties like *fondre* "to melt": *lever* can be transitive (26) assigning accusative Case to its Spec of VP_2 and dative to its Spec of VP_3, but if the action designated by the verb indicates a kind of intransitive movement on the part of the body part, the verb has a nonthematic external argument position in Spec VP_1 and one Case, accusative or dative, suspended in accordance with Burzio's extended generalization. These inalienable verbs are lexically quite complex since they have three subcategorization frames, the transitive, the unaccusative and the undative. Psych undatives are like unaccusatives in that they have one defective Case; inalienable undatives are multivalent like *Abs se* in that they have one suspended Case. In all instances, the suspended or defective Case correlates with a nonthematic external argument as Burzio's generalization predicts. If other internal Cases were available, movement to subject position would not be required. Therefore the behavior of these several classes of verbs supports the extended generalization and two structural Cases in French.

As for argument structure, it has been shown repeatedly that while internal argument structure and Case are each limited to no greater than two, they are not always linked. There may be two internal arguments but only one internal Case, as in all the nonthematic external argument constructions. Is it possible to have more than two internal arguments in inalienable constructions? Given the analysis proposed for undative inalienable verbs, the ungrammaticality of (26) is predicted by the limitation on internal arguments.

(26) *Pierre s'est levé la main.
     Peter self is raised the hand

Assuming a nonthematic external argument in Spec VP_1, *la main* in Spec of VP_2 and *Pierre* in Spec of VP_3, the *se*, which it has been shown must constitute an argument in French, would be a third internal argument, either as part of the verbal morphology or in an additional maximal projection. The ungrammaticality of an additional argument in this nonthematic external argument construction lends further support for the binary limit.

The duality hypothesis demonstrates the syntactic limits imposed on argument projection. The congruence approach to theta role / argument correspondence is supported by evidence that the possessor experiencer whose theme body part is affected is in the Spec VP_3, both with *lever* and *laver* type verbs. The standard configuration of inalienable constructions has the body part in Spec VP_2 and the possessor in Spec of VP_3. However, the restrictions on the distribution of these two related arguments are predicted by certain syntactic, but not thematic constraints. The definite body part generally is not found in subject position because it cannot be properly bound, not because it is thematically excluded. Indeed, a sentence such as (40) is grammatical when reference is arbitrary (V&Z 1992:598).[13]

(40) Pendant le saut les mains ne doivent pas toucher les cuisses.
"During the dive the hands must not touch the thighs".

More importantly, the appearance of a dative or nominative experiencer is shown to be a function of Case suspension with subsequent movement of an internal argument. There is also occasional variability in syntactic positioning of inalienable and possessor (41).

(41) a   Elle s'[dat] est coupé le doigt.
         "She cut her finger".
     b   Elle s'[acc] est blessée au doigt.
         "She hurt her finger".

The sentences in (41) are reminiscent of the *spray / load* alternations. A syntactic treatment such as that proposed by V&Z accounts for both the standard argumental varieties of inalienables and the exceptional cases. While there is clearly a regularity in the projection of inalienable and possessor roles onto arguments, a strictly thematic approach will only predict the standard configuration and will have to resort to secondary thematic roles or ad hoc solutions to deal with the exceptional cases.[14] A syntactic treatment, the predicational approach proposed by V&Z, is to be preferred on empirical and theoretical grounds.

6.4 *Conclusion*

French then has two options for realizing inalienable possession—a referential subject within the DP in the form of the possessive determiner, or a nonreferential inalienable definite determiner which takes its reference from a

---

[13] Cinque (1988:547) discusses the "arb" or generic interpretation with respect to sentences containing *si*. "It seems plausible to assume that *arb* (or impersonal) indeterminate subjects acquire the two different interpretations of quasi-universal and quasi-existential quantification as a function of the different time reference [...] In other words, they can be seen as two contextual variants of a single *arb* entity".

[14] Jaeggli (1982:33–40), in noting that the dative clitic acts as the inalienable possessor, proposes: "Verbs that do allow the inalienable construction will then be listed in the lexicon as assigning a special theta role, theta$_p$, to dative clitics attached to them" (1982:36). Guéron gives convincing arguments that the distinct theta role proposed by Jaeggli is unjustified (1986:45,80).

coindexed possessor outside the DP. The class of body part nouns requires a possessor which may be realized either DP internally in the case of possessives or DP externally in the case of the ext-poss construction, usually bound by predication to the second argument of the verb. The analysis proposed here shows that the requirement of second argument possessors for inalienables delineates a class of trivalent verbs, capable of being accusative, unaccusative or undative. Verbs such as undative *lever* have a second internal argument possessor that raises to subject position due to a lack of dative Case, a lack that explains the ungrammaticality of pronominal *se* with these verbs and confirms the dual limit on argument structure. Finally, this analysis offers a motivated proposal for the differences in interpretation and binding of possessive and definite inalienable determiners.

CHAPTER 7

CASE SUSPENSION AND COMPLEMENT STRUCTURE

7.0 *Introduction*

A major enterprise that generative theory proposes is the determination of how language acquisition is accomplished, how a young child achieves phonological and syntactic mastery of a language to which she has imperfect input, the less than complete corpus to which she is exposed (cf. Goodluck 1991). The current generative model holds that the linguistic facts of a particular language are learnable because it has a core, universal grammar, comprising principles which are invariant across languages, and parameters whose differing values permit an explanation of variation from language to language. Research in the principles and parameters paradigm has elucidated a model accommodating both the expected or unmarked core case as well as the unexpected or marked peripheral one. "The resulting interaction between value–fixed parameters and UPGs [universal principles of grammar] results in a *core grammar*—one of the particular grammars made possible by the innate schema of parameters and the innate universal principles" (Jaeggli & Safir 1989:3).

The central question investigated in this book is what role Case plays in determining the distribution and movement of syntactic arguments. A long tradition of work—ranging from Fillmore's Case theory to Baker's Uniformity of Theta Assignment—has established the significance of thematic relations as a primary determinant in argument projection, and finer grained semantic studies (e.g. Grimshaw 1992, Hale & Keyser [H&K] 1993, Pesetsky 1995) have elucidated the lexical subtleties that can contribute to apparent reversals in argument relations. No previous study has looked specifically at the role of Case as a factor in argument representation. Section 7.1 discusses the central hypothesis of the book and Section 7.2 summarizes the arguments presented in each chapter.

7.1 *Binary Case and internal argument structure*

The present study argues that in addition to thematic considerations, argument projection is influenced by the Case system of a language. More particularly, the language of investigation, French, is shown to have a maximum of two internal argument positions that correlate with the two potential structural Cases its verbs can assign. The two Case potential is not always realized in a direct correspondence to argument structure because there are Caseless arguments (e.g. CP complements not requiring Case or the objects of unaccusative and undative verbs that must seek Case elsewhere) and Case marked nonarguments (e.g. affected datives or exceptionally Case marked complements). The limit on the number of argument positions is supported by data presented throughout the book. The Case assigning potential of a language is then argued to determine its potential argument structure. The proof of this hypothesis is sought in constructions where one Case is suspended, and yet where there are two argument positions available.

The interaction of structural Case and internal argument projection raises three questions first posed in Chapter 1.

(1) a   Is there a link between potential Case and argument position?
    b   Can either Case or argument be missing?
    c   Is the projection potential limited in any way?

The answer to the first question appears obvious in ditransitive sentences that show no Case suspension and no movement, but it is the second question that points up the key issue for investigating the problem. If the two are dissociable, then they can be studied independently and are not simply a function of one another. The third question seeks a response to Williams's (1994:32) comment that "there can be an indeterminate number of internal arguments". The theoretical underpinnings of the three issues under investigation are the Larsonian approach to argument projection and Burzio's generalization. Two aspects of the Larsonian approach are significant, first the multitiered VP shell adapted from his treatment of double object constructions to accommodate Case marking and agreement phenomena within the minimalist framework; and second, his single complement hypothesis that justifies that structure as well as the binary limit on argument structure and Case. The single complement hypothesis accounts for the syntactic configurations described as well as their predicational relationships: the internal VP is predicated of the sentence's subject, while the indirect object is predicated of the direct object (the "subject" of the internal VP). Burzio's generalization describes the link between missing Case and missing argument, the engine of syntactic movement of internal arguments. He claims that a lack of accusative Case is correlated with a lack of thematic external argument; nominative Case is thus freed up for the Caseless argument. His generalization is extended in the presence of two internal structural Cases, dative and accusative. The minimalist program provides a motivated framework for linking Case and arguments, offering a unified treatment of Case as Spec–head agreement and accommodating variation in syntactic configuration as a function of overt vs. covert movement. Argument projection, determined lexically by strict syntactic principles (H&K 1993b), translates conceptual structures into syntactic form while defining the syntactic derivation through the morphosemantic exigencies of the lexical item.

Previous work on argument structure (e.g. Grimshaw 1992, Baker 1988, Williams 1994, Pesetsky 1995) does not take into account the crucial role played by Case, but fleshes out the importance of thematic / semantic relations to the establishment of syntactic representation. Their work has not asked whether there is a link between Case and argument structure, nor whether there is an upper limit to the number of arguments / Cases permitted. Considerations of the role of Case in the syntactic realization of arguments complement the analyses of argument structure that trace the translation of lexical conceptual structure to syntactic configuration. This book has described the role in terms of the overt syntax, looking at argument movement as a function of available Case; nonthematic external arguments thus permit mobility in the syntactic derivation. If a language defines by its Case options a certain hierarchy of possible arguments, then the mapping may take into account the "meaning" of Case in projecting arguments to syntactic structure. Dixon (1994:112–114) alludes to this kind of correspondence in speaking of the universality of the notion "subject" and the fact that "the same semantic roles are mapped onto the basic syntactic relation A [subject of a transitive verb] in just about every language".

7.2 *Overview*

The apparently peripheral constructions examined in this book involving unaccusative and undative verbs lacking a thematic external argument require that Agr_O check two structural Cases and that Burzio's generalization linking nonthematicity and Case suspension be extended to accommodate the two internal Cases. Following Burzio, defective internal Case requires that nominative Case be available (not assigned to the external argument) so that the Caseless argument can move with nominative Case. The prototypical construction, the unaccusative verb, provides diagnostics for other nonthematic subject constructions studied. The extended generalization is supported by the constructions examined in subsequent chapters, for all of them show a lack of thematic external argument and correlated lack of internal Case.

The first three chapters of the book lay the theoretical foundation and present the empirical problems. Chapter 1 outlines the tenets of the minimalist program and Chapter 2 spells out the details of a minimalist treatment of Case in French. It is argued that French has two internal structural Cases, objective and dative; objective Case is usually realized as accusative, but a DP deprived of accusative Case may be saved by partitive Case, a variant of objective Case that is 'built in' to the indefinite DP by its preposition *de*. The Larsonian triple tier VP is linked to three agreement nodes where Case may be checked in the minimalist framework: Agr_s for nominative, Agr_{o2} for objective, and Agr_{o3} for dative. Larson's single complement hypothesis theoretically limits the number of internal arguments and Cases to two; this binary limit is one of the areas of investigation in the remaining chapters.

The third chapter reviews indications of the nonthematicity of the external argument in its reexamination of unaccusative verbs, and extends Burzio's generalization in the light of dual internal Case. This extension claims that a nonthematic external argument is linked to a lack of either accusative or dative Case. Unaccusative verbs are shown to respect the dual limit in that they can take two internal arguments (despite the lack of accusative Case) but can take no more than two as cognate object sentences (2) show.

(2) a *Marc a / est resté un séjour agréable à Rome.
        "Mark stayed a pleasant stay in Rome".
    b   *Marc lui a / est tombé une chute terrible.
        "Mark fell a terrible fall to him".

The sentences in (2) are ungrammatical not only due to a lack of Case (partitive cannot save the derivation here), but also to the fact that there are three internal arguments for two internal positions.

The next three chapters examine verbs whose dative Case is suspended, psych experiencer, absorber pronominals and inalienables. In all three classes there are related unaccusative verbs. Psych experiencer verbs such as *amuser* are argued to be undative (incapable of assigning Case to lexical or affected datives and Case incompatible with dative assigning *faire*) and thus to corroborate the extension of Burzio's generalization with a nonthematic external argument. Their second internal argument is forced to raise to subject position with nominative Case. They also conform to the duality limit in allowing only up to two internal arguments, although they may select three thematically distinct internal arguments (3,4).

(3) a   Ce bar dégoûte Marie.
        "This bar disgusts Mary".
    b   Marie se dégoûte de la bière.
        "Mary is disgusted by beer".
    c   *Ce bar dégoûte Marie de la bière.
        "This bar disgusts Mary of beer".
(4) a   Les maths intéressent Pauline.
        "Math interests Pauline".
    b   Pauline s'intéresse à ce problème.
        "Pauline is interested in this problem".

c   *Les maths intéressent Pauline à ce problème.
"Math interests Pauline in this problem".

The overload sentences (3,4c) show that even if Case (here prepositionally assigned inherent) is available for thematically selected arguments, only two internal arguments are allowed.

Chapter 5 treats absorber *se*, (intrinsic, neutral, middle and psych), another construction with a nonthematic external argument. This *se* lexically absorbs one thematic argument (usually the external argument) and accusative Case, thus creating another class of unaccusative verbs. Uniquely, psych *se*, attached to an already undative verb, absorbs an *internal* thematic argument, the causer of the psychological experience such as *ce bar, les maths* in (3,4). *Abs se* supports Burzio's generalization and the binary limit. With three internal thematic arguments available, only two can possibly be realized (5).

(5) a   *Marie se dégoûte un bar de la bière.
"Mary is disgusted a bar of beer".
b   ?IL se dit des choses facilement des stars au public.
"There are things said easily of stars to the public".

The sentences in (5) can conceivably be Case marked (assuming partitive redemption), but are ungrammatical because they have too many internal arguments. Furthermore, sentences such as (5a) verify the specificity of VP to agreement node link and the path of arguments raised.

Chapter 6 examines inalienable constructions, arguing that verbs such as *lever* are triple valent in having three subcategorizations: they may be transitive, unaccusative or undative. In the last valence they have a nonthematic external argument and a second internal argument that lacks dative Case. They show the distinctive subject possessor characteristics (6a) that render dative possessor (the usual structure for inalienables (6c)) ungrammatical (6b).

(6) a   Pierre a levé la main.
"Peter raised his hand".
b   *Pierre s' [dat] est levé la main.
"Peter raised his hand".
c   Pierre s' [dat] est lavé les mains.
"Peter washed his hands".

(6b) is ungrammatical because *lever* is here undative and cannot assign dative Case to *se*; it has a nonthematic external argument, so has two internal positions for three internal arguments. Once again, the limit on arguments is borne out. Psychological experiencer verbs fall into three categories, transitive, unaccusative, and undative. The undative psych verbs corroborate Burzio's extended generalization in having a nonthematic subject and defective dative Case (forcing movement of the nonaccusative argument to subject position). A second class of undatives, inalienable verbs such as *lever*, have a possessor that is raised to subject from internal argument position. An analysis of intrinsic–middle–neutral–psych *se* distinguishes these lexically determined absorber constructions from syntactic reflexive–reciprocal *se*.

The book shows then an affirmative answer to all three questions raised in (1). In response to (1c), the data presented to support the limit on argument structure demonstrate that despite selectional features of the verb (e.g. psych verbs selecting three internal thematic arguments) or possible Case redemption (e.g. partitive or non Case marked CP), the number of internal arguments can be as many as two, but no more in French. The argument limit is independent of the actual Cases that are available . These facts answer (1b) since they point to the possible dissociation of Case and argument in Case defective constructions (unaccusative and undative). Finally, the facts confirm the necessary abstract link between the argument position and its Case checking agreement node. The specificity of this link is verified by proof such as the passage of the direct object from VP_2 through $Agro_2$ on its way to Agr_s with nominative Case. The specificity supports the linking and its syntactic representation by the Larsonian shell with its paired agreement nodes.

7.3 *Conclusion*

This book has investigated Case theory as a central component of core grammar, and has uncovered previously unnoticed regularities. The generalities concerning Case theory are consonant with other components of the grammar and contribute to the simplicity and universality of the generative model. The central claim is that Case theory requires as the core realization a limitation to no greater than two internal structural Cases. The minimalist program provides the framework for this generalization in its proposal that object and subject agreement are parallel. The book has developed this notion in proposing a specificity of the tiered VPs corresponding to the core arguments and to the agreement nodes, required in French to accommodate the two internal structural Cases, objective and dative. It is argued that the dual Case limit is echoed in a parallel limit on internal argument projection. The limitation to Case and argument structure is borne out empirically in straightforward transitive sentences, but more importantly in a set of superficially unrelated constructions common to the Romance languages.

White (1989:118) discusses the implications of syntactic markedness, pointing out that core grammar provides an evaluation metric as the unmarked case. "Core grammar is often thought of as unmarked because it is acquired with minimal evidence or triggering data". Language specific deviations are more highly marked in universal terms, therefore more peripheral, and yet marked syntax is "only acceptable when lexical and structural complexities are minimal" (Koster 1978:59). The French constructions examined here underscore the unmarked character of core grammar and the tight limitations of variation allowed in the periphery. Nonthematic subject constructions are peripheral both in their syntax and their lexical restriction; nevertheless, they keep structural complexities to a minimum in that the superficial structure resembles that of a standard transitive or intransitive sentence. An examination of these constructions in French has at once revealed what constitutes periphery in the grammar and pointed up the very limited degree of markedness allowed in syntactic deviance from core grammar. The tight limitations of core grammar are indicative of a kind of economy: the grammar usually exemplifies the case that is more easily learnable given a genetic predisposition. But the grammar also allows peripheral phenomena precisely because they as well are restricted and hence learnable.

APPENDIX

GRAMMATICALITY SURVEY

The following survey was given to 17 speakers of French (10 continental and 7 Québécois). Results of the survey are discussed below.

Survey introduction: I would greatly appreciate your rendering grammaticality judgments on the following sentences. If the sentence sounds fine to you, you needn't mark it. If it is totally unacceptable, place an asterisk (*) before it. If it is questionable, place a question mark (?) before it. The sentences below are not necessarily acceptable in all registers (levels of formality): the "affected datives" (*Le gosse lui a attrapé un rhume.*) are very popular / spoken, while the presentational sentences (*IL est arrivé plusieurs Anglais.*) are more stilted. I am not interested in unacceptability due to register, so please judge the sentences with respect to other sentences of the same category, not level of formality. Please indicate the dialect of French that you speak (e.g. Belgian, Québécois). Thank you very much for your help in this matter.

A. *Presentational* (capitalized *IL* = 'it, there' as in *IL y a...* or *IL existe...*)
1.   Plusieurs Anglais sont arrivés. 0^1 $(0, 0)^2$
2.   IL est arrivé plusieurs Anglais. *0* (0, 0)
3.   Les Anglais sont arrivés. *0* (0, 0)
4.   *[3] IL est arrivé les Anglais. *2.0* (2.0, 2.0)
5.   Beaucoup de jupes ont été vendues. *0* (0, 0)
6.   IL a été vendu beaucoup de jupes. *.18* (.29, .10)
7.   Ces jupes se sont bien vendues. *0* (0, 0)
8.   IL s' est vendu beaucoup de jupes. *0* (0, 0)

---

[1]   Grammaticality as judged by informants was rated in the following manner: * = 2, ? = 1, ok = 0. The averages for each sentence are listed after the sentence: *number in italics* = total average for the 17 respondents.

[2]   The numbers in parentheses are the averages of each of the two groups of informants (average of 7 Québécois, average of 10 continental speakers).

[3]   The averages of the totals (the number in italics) were interpreted to give a rating at the beginning of the sentences: * [before the sentence] = *a total average of 1.25–2*; ? [before the sentence] = *a total average of .50–1.24*. The exact average can be verified by looking at the end of the sentence. Averages below *.50* were considered inconsequential for ungrammaticality.

9. *IL a dormi trois garçons. *1.94* (1.86, 2.0)
10. IL manque plusieurs livres. *0* (0, 0)
11. *IL a été adoré plusieurs idoles. *1.24* (1.17, 1.5)
12. IL a été mangé beaucoup de pommes. *.41* (.29, .5)
13. ?IL a été beaucoup parlé de Paul. *1.06* (.57, 1.4)
14. *IL a été amusé beaucoup d'enfants. *1.76* (1.86, 1.7)
15. *IL s'est amusé beaucoup d'enfants. *1.29* (.86, 1.6)
16. ?IL s'est levé deux têtes. *.71* (.71, .7)
17. IL s'est froncé plusieurs sourcils. *.47* (0, .8)

B. *ON* Some speakers report a variability of interpretation of *on:* while the 'we' interpretation is always available, speakers sometimes find the indefinite ('one, someone') interpretation unacceptable. If you cannot get the 'someone' (SO) interpretation, please indicate this by crossing out SO at the beginning of the sentence.
1. 'we / SO' On a téléphoné à Pierre. *0* (0, 0)[4]
2. 'we / SO' On critique beaucoup le nouveau gouvernement. *.35* (.29, .4)
3. 'we / *SO' On est allé au cinéma. *1.35* (1.57, 1.2)
4. 'we / ?SO' On a survécu au tyran. *.94* (1.14, .8)
5. 'we / SO' Dans ce pays lointain on adore les idoles. *.12* (0, .2)
6. 'we / *SO' Depuis qu'il est seul, il trouve qu'on lui manque beaucoup. *1.53* (1.71, 1.4)
7. 'we / ?SO' On a beaucoup amusé les enfants hier soir. *.82* (.86, .8)
8. 'we / *SO' On lui est apparu déguisé en soldat. *.76* (1.57, .2)
9. 'we / SO' On s'évanouit en apprenant une nouvelle pareille. *.35* (0, .6)
10. 'we / SO' On s'amuse bien au Parc Astérix. *.24* (.29, .2)
11. 'we / SO' A la réunion on a souvent levé la main. *.47* (.29, .6)
12. 'we / ?SO' On a froncé les sourcils après avoir entendu les résultats. *.64* (1.0, .4)
13. 'we / ?SO' On a remué les oreilles pour amuser les enfants. *.94* (1.43, .6)

C. *Affected datives*: please judge the following sentences as examples of a very popular spoken, not written form. Do not judge whether they are proper and correct prescriptively, but rather if they could be uttered in informal speech.
1. Je lui ai trouvé un emploi. *0* (0, 0)
2. Le chiot lui a pissé dans ses laitues. *.18* (.43, 0)
3. Le gosse lui a attrapé un rhume. *.24* (.14, .3)
4. Paul lui a fait une bronchite. *.18* (0, .2)
5. *Paul lui a eu une bronchite. *1.53* (2.0, 1.2)
6. Le voleur leur a tiré dessus. *0* (0, 0)
7. ?Tonton Jean lui a amusé ses enfants. *1.0* (.86, 1.1)
8. La voiture rouge lui a écrasé son chat. *0* (0, 0)
9. *Son mari lui a ennuyé les invités embêtants. *1.47* (1.71, 1.3)

---

[4] The numbers in this section refer to the averages of informants who could *not* get the arbitrary reading.

10. *On lui a humilié l'ingrat paresseux. *1.71* (2.0, 1.5)
11. Son frère va lui cirer le plancher avant midi. *0* (0, 0)
12. *Le nouveau patron lui a intéressé les employés. *1.76* (2.0, 1.6)
13. ?Mon grand–père, on lui aimait bien son béret noir et son air un peu paysan. *.59* (.86, .4)
14. *Le plat peu appétissant leur a dégoûté les clients. *1.88* (1.86, 1.9)
15. Elle lui regarde la tête. *.06* (.14, 0)
16. *Les gosses lui craignaient son visage farouche. *1.35* (1.43, 1.3)
17. *Les plats si bien présentés leur ont impressionné les clients. *1.76* (1.86, 1.7)
18. ?Bien qu'on les trouve compétents, on leur déteste cette attitude pompeuse. *.82* (1.29, .5)
19. *Malgré ses propres allergies, Marc lui a supporté son petit chaton. *1.41* (1.71, 2.0)
20. *Le plan de la ville lui a préoccupé l'architecte qui s'intéresse au projet. *1.88* (1.71, 2.0)
21. La coiffeuse lui a coupé les cheveux. *0* (0, 0)
22. ?La bourgeoise bien habillée lui a déploré ce manteau usé. *1.12* (1.29, 1.0)

D. *Other*

1. ?Cette nouvelle choquante fait s'évanouir. *.88* (.71, 1)
2. Le prêtre faisait adorer les idoles. *.18* (.14, .2)
3. Il a fait réparer ses chaussures. *0* (0, 0)
4. Ces somnifères font dormir sans difficulté. *0* (0, 0)
5. ?Cet autobus fait arriver à l'heure. *.65* (.71, .6)
6. *Cette chanson faisait manquer à Marie. *1.71* (1.86, 1.6)
7. *Cette blague faisait amuser les enfants. *1.29* (1.43, 1.2)
8. *Cette blague fait s'amuser. *1.29* (1, 1.5)
9. *Le vent a fait se briser. *1.88* (1.71, 2.0)
10. Il me donnera des stylos pour Paul au bureau. *0* (0, 0)
11. *Il me lui en donnera au bureau. *1.53* (1.43, 1.6)
12. *Il me lui y en donnera. *1.71* (1.71, 1.7)
13. Je t'ai demandé ce service à la maison. *0* (0, 0)
14. ?Je te l'y ai demandé. *.53* (.71, .4)
15. *Je te le lui y ai demandé. *1.47* (1.71, 1.3)
16. Pierre a vu sa main dans la glace. *0* (0, 0)
17. Pierre a vu la main dans la glace. *.24* (.57, 0)
18. Pierre s'est vu la main dans la glace. *.41* (.43, .4)
19. Deux têtes se sont levées. *.18* (.29, 0)
20. Ses sourcils se sont froncés. *.18* (.29, 0)
21. Ses membres (se) raidissent. *.18* (.29, 0)
22. Cette dent remue. *.06* (.14, 0)

Commentary on survey procedures and results

The *Presentational sentences* (A), a class that is amply documented in traditional grammars, demonstrate that speakers are more clear in accepting unaccusatives (#2, 10), in respecting the definiteness restriction (#4), and in rejecting unergatives (#9) than they are in judging middle voice and passive impersonals. There is a greater acceptance of middle impersonals than passives, and some informants even rejected the typical passive impersonal phrases cited by traditional grammars (#12, 13).

The *on* (B) sentences were not screened for the generic reading, so even the same lexical item *amuser* evokes a range of responses (#7, 10). Although the diagnostic appears somewhat elusive, there is a clear preference for the arbitrary reading with transitives (#2, 5), a range of rejection with unaccusatives (#3, 4, 6, 8), and a level of discomfort with undatives (#7, 11, 12, 13). The arbitrary interpretation is used as a diagnostic for nonthematicity by Legendre for French and Belletti & Rizzi for Italian.

The *affected dative* section (C) contrasts undative object experiencer psych verbs with transitive subject experiencer psych verbs. The clear grammaticality of affected datives with regular transitives (#1–4, 6, 8, 11) is a benchmark of comparison. The subject experiencer would be predicted to be questionable since it represents a stative verb that resists a priori (cf. #5 a nonpsych stative) the affected dative construction. Object experiencer verbs resemble the typical transitive in having a causer subject and could be predicted to be acceptable with affected datives for that reason. The survey indicates the contrary: the results clearly group the undative object experiencer verbs (#7, 9, 10, 12, 14, 17, 20) as far less grammatical than the subject experiencer transitive verbs (#13, 16, 18, 19, 22). The average for the object experiencer verbs is 1.63 (or 1.74 without the outlyer) as opposed to 1.06 for the subject experiencer verbs.

The last group (D) includes causative constructions and clitic sequences. The causatives bear out the claim that thematic external arguments (#2, 3, 4) can be omitted when embedded under *faire*, whereas derived subjects (original internal arguments) cannot be (#5–9). The clitic sequences indicate that three clitics (#11, 14) are questionable and four clitics (#12, 15) clearly rejected.

REFERENCES

Ackema, Peter. 1995. "Middles and Nonmovement". *Linguistic Inquiry* 26.173–197.

Adams, Marianne. 1987. "From Old French to the Theory of Pro–Drop". *Natural Language and Linguistic Theory* 5.1–32.

Anderson, Mona. 1983. "Prenominal Genitive NPs". *Linguistic Review* 3.1–24.

Aoun, Joseph. 1985. *A Grammar of Anaphora*. Cambridge, Mass.: MIT Press.

————— & Dominique Sportiche. 1982. "On the Formal Theory of Government". *Linguistic Review* 2.211–236.

Arteaga, Deborah. 1990. *The Disjoint Reference Requirement in Subjunctive Clauses: Diachronic evidence from Romance*. Unpub. Ph.D. Dissertation, Univ. of Washington, Seattle.

—————. 1994. "Impersonal Constructions in Old French". Mazzola 1994. 141–158.

—————. 1995a. *Obviation in Romance: Diachronic and synchronic perspectives*. Lanham, Md.–New York–London: University Press of America.

—————. 1995b. "Sobre la construcción de complemento objeto doble en el francés antiguo. Unpub. ms., Univ. of Nevada, Las Vegas.

Atkinson, James C. 1973. *The Two Forms of Subject Inversion in Modern French*. The Hague: Mouton.

Authier, J.-Marc. 1989. "Arbitrary Null Objects and Unselective Binding". Jaeggli & Safir 1989.45–67.

—————. 1991. "V–Governed Expletives, Case Theory and the Projection Principle". *Linguistic Inquiry* 22.721–740.

—————. 1992a. "A Parametric Account of Verb Governed Arbitrary Null Arguments". *Natural Language and Linguistic Theory* 10.345–374.

—————. 1992b. "Is French a Null Subject Language in the DP?". *Probus* 4.1–16.

————— & Lisa Reed. 1991. "Ergative Predicates and Dative Cliticization in French Causatives". *Linguistic Inquiry* 22.197–205.

————— & —————.1992. "On the Syntactic Status of French Affected Datives". *Linguistic Review* 9.295–311.

————— & —————. 1993. "Remarks on Binding Theory". Unpub. ms., Univ. Ottawa.

Bach, Emmon. 1980. "In Defense of Passive". *Linguistics and Philosophy* 3.297–341.

————— & Robert T. Harms, eds. 1968. *Universals in Linguistic Theory*. New York: Holt, Rinehart & Winston.

Bailard, Joelle. 1981. "A Functional Approach to Subject Inversion". *Studies in Language* 5.1–30.

Baker, Mark C. 1988. *Incorporation: A theory of grammatical function changing.* Chicago: Univ. of Chicago.

———, Kyle Johnson & Ian Roberts. 1989. "Passive Arguments Raised". *Linguistic Inquiry* 20.219–252.

Baltin, Mark & Anthony S. Kroch, eds. 1989. *Alternative Conceptions of Phrase Structure.* Chicago: Univ. of Chicago Press.

Barnes, Betsy. 1980. "The Notion of 'Dative' in Linguistic Theory and the Grammar of French". *Lingvisticae Investigationes* 4.245–292.

———. 1985. "A Functional Explanation of French Nonlexical Datives". *Studies in Language* 9.159–195.

Belletti, Adriana. 1982a. "On the Anaphoric Status of the Reciprocal Construction in Italian". *Linguistic Review* 2.101–137.

———. 1982b. "Morphological Passive and Pro–Drop: The impersonal construction in Italian". *Journal of Linguistic Research* 2.1–34.

———. 1988. "The Case of Unaccusatives". *Linguistic Inquiry* 19.1–34.

———. 1990. *Generalized Verb Movement: Aspects of verb syntax.* Turin: Rosenberg & Sellier.

Belletti, Adriana & Luigi Rizzi. 1981. "The Syntax of *ne*: Some theoretical implications". *The Linguistic Review* 1.117–154.

———. 1988. "Psych Verbs and Theta Theory". *Natural Language and Linguistic Theory* 6.291–352.

Benveniste, Emile. 1966. *Problèmes de linguistique générale.* Paris: Gallimard.

Birdsong, David & Jean-Pierre Montreuil, eds. 1988. *Advances in Romance Linguistics.* Dordrecht: Foris.

Blanche-Benveniste, Claire, José Delofeu, Jean Stéfanini & K. Van den Eynde. 1984. *Pronom et syntaxe.* Paris: Selaf.

Bley-Vroman, Robert, Sascha W. Felix & Georgette Ioup. 1988. "The Accessibility of Universal Grammar in Adult Language Learning". *Second Language Research* 4.1–32.

Bloomfield, Leonard. 1933. *Language.* New York: Henry Holt & Co.

Boas, Franz. 1938. "Language". *General Anthropology* ed. by Franz Boas, 124–145. Boston: D. C. Heath.

Bordelois, Ivonne, Heles Contreras & Karen Zagona, eds. 1985. *Generative Studies in Spanish Syntax.* Dordrecht: Foris.

Borer, Hagit. 1984. *Parametric Syntax.* Dordrecht: Foris.

———, ed. 1986a. *The Syntax of Pronominal Clitics.* (= *Syntax and Semantics,* 19.) Orlando, Fla.: Academic Press.

———. 1986b. "I–Subjects". *Linguistic Inquiry* 17.375–416.

———. 1989. "Anaphoric Agr". Jaeggli & Safir 1989.69–110.

———. 1993. "The Projection of Arguments". (= *Univ. of Massachusetts Occasional Papers in Linguistics,* 17.) Amherst: Univ. of Massachusetts.

———. 1994. "The Ups and Downs of Hebrew Verb Movement". *Natural Language and Linguistic Theory* 13.527–606.

————— & Yosef Grodzinsky. 1986. "Syntactic Cliticization and Lexical Cliticization: The case of Hebrew dative clitics". Borer 1986.175–217.

Bouchard, Denis. 1984. *On the Content of Empty Categories*. Dordrecht: Foris.

—————. 1988a. "*En* Chain". Birdsong & Montreuil 1988.33–49.

—————. 1988b. "French *voici / voilà* and the Analysis of Pro–Drop". *Language* 64.89–100.

—————. 1992. "Psych Constructions and Linking to Conceptual Structures". Hirschbühler & Koerner 1992.25–44.

Bowers, John. 1981. *The Theory of Grammatical Relations*. Ithaca, N.Y.: Cornell Univ. Press.

—————. 1993. "The Syntax of Predication". *Linguistic Inquiry* 24.591–656.

Brame, Michael. 1978. *Base Generated Syntax*. Seattle: Noit Amrofer.

Branchadell, Albert. 1990. "A Proposal for the B Dative". Unpub. ms., M.I.T., Cambridge, Mass.

—————. 1991. "Against Argument Argumentation". Unpub. ms., Univ. of Barcelona.

—————. 1992. *A Study of Lexical and Nonlexical Datives*. Unpub. Ph.D. Dissertation, Universitat Autònoma de Barcelona.

Brekke, Magnar. 1988. "The Experiencer Constraint". *Linguistic Inquiry* 19. 169–180.

Brody, Michael. 1993. "Thematic Theory and Arguments". *Linguistic Inquiry* 24.1–24.

Browning, M. A. 1991. "Bounding Conditions on Representation". *Linguistic Inquiry* 22.541–562.

Burston, Jack. 1979. "The Pronominal Verb Construction in French". *Lingua* 48.147–176.

Burton, Strang & Jane Grimshaw. 1992. "Coordination and VP Internal Subjects". *Linguistic Inquiry* 23.305–313.

Burzio, Luigi. 1983a. "D–structure Conditions on Clitics". *Journal of Linguistic Research* 2/2.23–54.

—————. 1983b. "Conditions on Representation and Romance Syntax". *Linguistic Inquiry* 14.193–221.

—————. 1986. *Italian Syntax: A government–binding approach*. Dordrecht: Reidel.

—————. 1991. "The Morphological Basis of Anaphora". *Journal of Linguistics* 27.81–105.

—————. 1992. "On the Morphology of Reflexives and Impersonals". Laeufer & Morgan 1992.399–414.

Campos, Hector. 1989. "Impersonal Passive *se* in Spanish". *Lingvisticae Investigationes* 13.1–21.

————— & Paula Kempchinsky. 1991. "Case Absorption, Theta Structure and Pronominal Verbs". Wanner & Kibbee 1991.171–185.

Carrier, Jill & Janet Randall. 1992. "The Argument Structure and Syntactic Structure of Resultatives". *Linguistic Inquiry* 23.173–234.

Cheng, Lisa lai–Shen & Elizabeth Ritter. 1988. "A Small Clause Analysis of Inalienable Possession in Mandarin & French". *Papers from the 18th Meeting of the Northeast Linguistics Society* ed. by James Blevins & Juli Carter, 65–88. Amherst, Mass.: Graduate Student Linguistic Association.

Chevalier, Jean–Claude, Claire Blanche–Benveniste, Michel Arrivé & Jean Peytard. 1988. *Grammaire Larousse du français contemporain.* Paris: Larousse.

Chomsky, Noam. 1957. *Syntactic Structures.* The Hague: Mouton.

———. 1965. *Aspects of the Theory of Syntax.* Cambridge, Mass.: MIT Press.

———. 1981. *Lectures on Government and Binding.* Dordrecht: Foris.

———. 1986a. *Knowledge of Language.* New York: Praeger.

———. 1986b. *Barriers.* Cambridge, Mass.: MIT Press.

———. 1991. "Some Notes on Economy of Derivation and Representation" Freidin 1991.417–454.

———. 1993. "A Minimalist Program for Linguistic Theory". Hale & Keyser 1993.1–52.

———. 1994. "Bare Phrase Structure". (=*MIT Occasional Papers in Linguistics,* 5.) Cambridge, Mass.: Dept. of Linguistics & Philosophy, M.I.T.

———. 1995. "Categories and Transformations". *The Minimalist Program*(Chapter 4). Cambridge, Mass.: MIT Press.

Cinque, Guglielmo. 1988. "On *si* Constructions and the Theory of *arb*". *Linguistic Inquiry* 19.521–581.

———. 1990a. *Types of A' Dependencies.* Cambridge: MIT Press.

———. 1990b. "Agreement and Head to Head Movement in the Romance Noun Phrase". Paper presented at the Twentieth Linguistic Symposium on Romance Languages, Ottawa.

Clahsen, Harald & Pieter Muysken. 1986. "The Availability of Universal Grammar to Adult and Child Learners: A study of the acquisition of German word order". *Second Language Research* 2.93–119.

Clark, Robin & Ian Roberts. 1993. "A Computational Model of Language Learnability and Language Change". *Linguistic Inquiry* 24.299–346.

Contreras, Heles. 1984. "A Note on Parasitic Gaps". *Linguistic Inquiry* 15. 698–701.

———. 1987. "Small Clauses in Spanish and English". *Natural Language and Linguistic Theory* 5.225–243.

———. 1989a. "Closed Domains". *Probus* 1.163–180.

———. 1989b. "On Spanish Empty N' and N*". Kirschner & Decesaris 1989.83–95.

———. 1990. "Two Kinds of Minimality". *Linguistic Inquiry* 21.467–470.

———. 1991. "On the Position of Subjects". Rothstein 1991.63–79.

———. 1993. "On Null Operator Structures". *Natural Language and Linguistic Theory* 11.1–30.

————. 1994. "Economy and Projection". Paper presented at the Twenty–fourth Linguistic Symposium on Romance Languages, University of Southern California, Los Angeles.

Couquaux, Daniel. 1979. "Sur la syntaxe des phrases prédicatives en français". *Lingvisticae Investigationes* 3.245–284.

————. 1981. "French Predication and Linguistic Theory". May & Koster 1981.33–64.

Culicover, Peter & Wendy Wilkins. 1986. "Control, *pro* and the Projection Principle". *Language* 62.120–153.

Cummins, Sarah & Yves Roberge. 1994. "A Morphosyntactic Analysis of Romance Clitic Constructions". Mazzola 1994.239–258.

Damourette, Jacques & Edouard Pichon. 1930–43. *Des mots à la pensée: Essai de grammaire de la langue française*, Vol. IV. Paris: Collection des Linguistes Contemporains.

Davis, Lori. 1986. "Remarks on the Theta Criterion and Case". *Linguistic Inquiry* 17.564–568.

Demonte, Violeta. 1992a. "Linking and Case: The case of prepositional verbs". Laeufer & Morgan 1992.415–456.

————. 1992b. "El clitico dativo y la construcción de doble objeto". Unpub. ms., Univ. Autónoma de Madrid.

Díaz-Insensé, Natàlia. 1994. "Catalan Possessives: Extraction from DP and strong crossover". Mazzola 1994.285–302.

DiSciullo, Anna-Maria. 1991. "Modularity and the Mapping from the Lexicon to the Syntax". *Probus* 2.257–290.

———— & Elizabeth Klipple. 1994. "Modifying Affixes". Unpub. ms., Univ. du Québec, Montréal.

———— & Edwin Williams. 1987. *On the Definition of Word*. Cambridge, Mass.: MIT Press.

Dixon, R[obert] M.W. 1994. *Ergativity*. Cambridge: Cambridge Univ. Press.

Dobrovie-Sorin, Carmen. 1990. "Clitic Doubling, Wh–Movement and Quantification in Romanian". *Linguistic Inquiry* 21.351–397.

————. 1995. "Impersonal *si* Constructions in Romance and the Passivization of Intransitives". Unpub. ms., Univ. Paris VII.

Dowty, David R. 1979. *Word Meaning and Montague Grammar*. Dordrecht: Reidel.

————. 1991. "Thematic Proto–Roles and Argument Selection". *Language* 67.547–619.

Dresher, B. Elan & Norbert Hornstein. 1979. "Trace Theory and NP Movement Rules". *Linguistic Inquiry* 10.65–82.

Drijkoningen, Frank. 1990. "Functional Heads and the Unification of French Word Order". *Probus* 2.291–320.

Dubois, John W. 1987. "The Discourse Basis of Ergativity". *Language* 63.805–855.

DuPlessis, Jean, Doreen Solin, Lisa Travis & Lydia White. 1987. "UG or Not UG, That is the Question: A reply to Clahsen & Muysken". *Second Language Research* 3.56–75.

Emonds, Joseph. 1975. "A Transformational Analysis of French Clitics without Positive Output Constraints". *Linguistic Analysis* 1.3–24.

––––––. 1976. *A Transformational Approach to English Syntax*. New York: Academic Press.

––––––. 1978. "The Verbal Complex V'–V in French". *Linguistic Inquiry* 9.151–175.

––––––. 1980. "Word Order in Generative Grammar". *Journal of Linguistic Research* 1.33–54.

––––––. 1985. *A Unified Theory of Syntactic Categories*. Dordrecht: Foris.

––––––. 1989. "The Passive and Past Participle". Unpub. ms., Univ. of Washington, Seattle.

––––––. 1991. "The Autonomy of the (Syntactic) Lexicon and Syntax: Insertion conditions for derivational and inflectional morphemes". Georgopoulos & Ishihara 1991.119–148.

––––––. 1995. "Secondary Predication, Stationary Particles and Silent Prepositions". *Essays in Linguistics and Philology Presented to Professor Kinsuke Hasegawa on the Occasion of his Sixtieth Birthday February 8, 1995*. ed. by Editorial Committee of a Festschrift for Professor Kinsuke Hasegawa, 1–20. Tokyo: Tokyo University of Foreign Studies.

Enç, Mürvet. 1991 "The Semantics of Specificity". *Linguistic Inquiry* 22.1–25.

Epstein, Samuel. 1995. "Un–Principled Syntax and the Derivation of Syntactic Relations". Unpub. ms., Harvard Univ., Cambridge, Mass.

Everett, Daniel. 1989. "Anaphoric Indices and Inalienable Possession in Brazilian Portuguese". *Linguistic Inquiry* 20.491–497.

Fagan, Sarah. 1988. "The English Middle". *Linguistic Inquiry* 19.181–204.

Fee, E. Jane & Katherine Hunt, eds. 1989. *Proceedings of the Eighth West Coast Conference on Formal Linguistics*. Stanford, Cal.: Stanford Linguistics Association. (Center for the Study of Language and Information).

Fillmore, Charles. 1968. "The Case for Case". Bach & Harms 1968.1–90.

Flynn, Suzanne & Wayne O'Neil. 1988. *Linguistic Theory in Second Language Acquisition*. Dordrecht: Kluwer.

Franks, Steven. 1993. "On Parallelism in Across the Board Dependencies". *Linguistic Inquiry* 24.509–529.

––––––. 1995. *Parameters of Slavic Morphosyntax*. New York: Oxford Univ. Press.

––––––. Forthcoming. "Empty Subjects and Voice Altering Morphemes in Slavic". *International Journal of Slavic Linguistics and Poetics*.

–––––– & Gerald Greenberg. 1991. "A Parametric Approach to Dative Subjects and Second Datives in Slavic". *Slavic and East European Journal* 35.71–97.

Freidin, Robert. 1975. "The Analysis of Passives". *Language* 51.384–405.

––––––, ed. 1991. *Principles and Parameters in Comparative Grammar*. Cambridge, Mass.: MIT Press.

––––––. 1992. *Foundations of Generative Syntax*. Cambridge, Mass.: MIT Press.

————, ed. 1995. *Current Issues in Comparative Grammar*. Dordrecht: Kluwer.

———— & Rex Sprouse. 1991. Freidin 1991.392–416.

Fukui, Naoki. 1993. "Parameters and Optionality". *Linguistic Inquiry* 24.399–420.

———— & Margaret Speas. 1986. "Specifiers and Projection". *MIT Working Papers* 8. 128–172.

Furukawa, Naoyo. 1987. "Sylvie a les yeux bleus: Construction à double thème". *Lingvisticae Investigationes* 11.283–302.

Garvin, Paul, ed. 1964. *A Prague School Reader on Esthetics, Literary Structure and Style*. Washington D.C.: Georgetown Univ. Press.

Georgopoulos, Carol & Roberta Ishihara, eds. 1991. *Essays in Honor of S-Y Kuroda*. Dordrecht: Kluwer.

Gibson, Edward & Kenneth Wexler. 1994. "Triggers". *Linguistic Inquiry* 25.407–454.

Giorgi, Alessandra & Giuseppe Longobardi. 1989. "Null Pronominals within NPs and the Syntax of DPs". *Probus* 1.181–209.

————. 1991. *The Syntax of NPs*. Cambridge: Cambridge Univ. Press.

Giusti, Giuliana. 1991a. "La sintassi dei nominali quantificati in Romeno". *Rivista di Grammatica Generativa* 16.29–57.

————. 1991b. "The Categorial Status of Quantified Nominals". *Linguistische Berichte* 136.438–454.

Godard, Danièle. 1992. "Extraction out of NP in French". *Natural Language and Linguistic Theory* 10.233–277.

Goodall, Grant. 1993. "On Case and the Passive Morpheme". *Natural Language and Linguistic Theory* 11.31–44.

Goodluck, Helen. 1991. *Language Acquisition: A linguistic introduction*. Oxford: Blackwell.

Grammont, Maurice. 1960 [1933]. *Traité de phonétique*. Paris: Delagrave.

Grevisse, Maurice. 1993. *Le bon usage: Grammaire française*. 13th ed.. Paris: Duculot.

Grimshaw, Jane. 1980. "On the Lexical Representation of Romance Reflexive Clitics". (=*Occasional Papers*, 5.) Cambridge, Mass.: Center for Cognitive Science, MIT.

————. 1988. "Adjuncts and Argument Structure". (=*Lexical Project Working Papers*, 21.) Cambridge, Mass.: Center for Cognitive Science, MIT.

————. 1992. *Argument Structure*. Cambridge, Mass.: MIT Press.

Gross, Maurice. 1986. *Grammaire transformationnelle du français 1: Syntaxe du verbe*. Paris: Cantilène.

Gruber, Jeffrey. 1965. *Studies in Lexical Relations*. Unpub. Ph.D. Dissertation, M.I.T., Cambridge, Mass.

Guéron, Jacqueline. 1980. "On the Syntax and Semantics of PP Extraposition". *Linguistic Inquiry* 11.637–678.

————. 1983. "L'emploi possessif de l'article défini en français". *Langue Française* 58.23–35.

————. 1986. "Inalienable Possession, Pro–Inclusion and Lexical Chains". Guéron, Obenauer & Pollock 1986.43–86.

————. 1991. "La possession inaliénable et l'aspect locatif". Unpub. ms., Univ. de Paris X.

————, Hans Obenauer, & Jean-Yves Pollock, eds. 1986. *Grammatical Representation*. Dordrecht: Foris.

Haegeman, Liliane. 1994. *Introduction to Government and Binding Theory*. 2nd ed. Oxford: Basil Blackwell.

Hale, Kenneth & Samuel Jay Keyser. 1986. "Some Transitivity Alternations in English". (=*Lexicon Project Working Papers*, 7.) Cambridge, Mass.: Center for Cognitive Science, MIT.

———— & ————. 1987. "A View from the Middle". (=*Lexicon Project Working Papers*, 10.) Cambridge, Mass.: Center for Cognitive Science, MIT.

———— & ————. 1988. "Explaining and Constraining the English Middle". *Studies in Generative Approaches to Aspect* (=*Lexicon Project Working Papers*, 24) ed. by Carol Tenny. Cambridge, Mass.: Center for Cognitive Science, MIT.

———— & ————, eds. 1993a. *The View from Building 20*. Cambridge, Mass.: MIT Press.

———— & ————. 1993b. "On Argument Structure and the Lexical Expression of Syntactic Relations". Hale & Keyser 1993.53–110.

Halle, Morris & Alec Marantz. 1993. "Distributed Morphology and the Pieces of Inflection". Hale & Keyser 1993.111–176.

Halpern, Aaron, ed. 1990. *The Proceedings of the Ninth West Coast Conference on Formal Linguistics*. Stanford, Cal.: Stanford Linguistics Association. (Center for the Study of Language and Information).

Hatcher, Anna Granville. 1944. "Il tend les mains vs Il tend ses mains". *Studies in Philology* 41.457–481.

Herschensohn, Julia. 1980. "On Clitic Placement in French". *Linguistic Analysis* 6.187–219.

————. 1981. "French Causatives: Restructuring, Opacity, Filters and Construal". *Linguistic Analysis* 8.217–280.

————. 1982. "The French Presentational as a Base–Generated Structure". *Studies in Language* 6.193–219.

————. 1992a. "French Inalienable Binding". Laeufer & Morgan 1992.367–384.

————. 1992b. "On the Economy of Romance Nonlexical Datives". Hirschbühler & Koerner 1992.123–134.

————. 1992c. "Case Marking and French Psych Verbs". *Lingvisticae Investigationes* 16.21–40.

Herslund, Michael, Ole Mørdrup & Finn Sørensen eds. 1983. *Analyses grammaticales du français*. (=*Revue Romane* numéro spécial 24.). Copenhagaen: Akademisk Forlag (Etudes Romanes de l'Université de Copenhague).

Herslund, Michael. 1983. "Le datif de la possession inalienable en français".
    Herslund et al. 1983.99–116.

———. 1988. *Le datif en français*. Louvain: Peeters.

Hirschbühler, Paul. 1988. "The Middle and the Pseudo-Middle in French".
    Birdsong 1988.97–111.

——— & Konrad Koerner, eds. 1992. *Romance Languages and Modern
    Linguistic Theory*. Amsterdam & Philadelphia: John Benjamins.

Hockett, Charles F. 1958. *A Course in Modern Linguistics*. New York:
    MacMillan.

Hopper, Paul & Sandra Thompson. 1980. "Transitivity in Grammar and
    Discourse". *Language* 56.251–299.

Hornstein, Norbert and David Lightfoot. 1987. "Predication and Pro". *Lan-
    guage* 63.23–52.

Huang, C-T. James. 1984. "On the Distribution and Reference of Empty
    Pronouns". *Linguistic Inquiry* 15.531–574.

Hyams, Nina. 1986. *Language Acquisition and the Theory of Parameters*.
    Dordrecht: Reidel.

Jackendoff, Ray. 1972. *Semantic Interpretation in Generative Grammar*.
    Cambridge, Mass.: MIT Press.

———. 1975. "Morphological and Semantic Regularities in the Lexicon".
    Language 51.639–671.

———. 1977. *X' Syntax: A study of phrase structure*. Cambridge, Mass.:
    MIT Press.

———. 1987. "The Status of Thematic Relations in Linguistic Theory".
    Linguistic Inquiry 18.369–412.

———. 1990. *Semantic Structures*. Cambridge, Mass., Mass.: MIT Press.

———. 1992. *Consciousness and the Computational Mind*. Cambridge,
    Mass., Mass.: MIT Press.

Jaeggli, Osvaldo. 1982. *Topics in Romance Syntax*. Dordrecht: Foris.

———. 1986a. "Arbitrary Plural Pronominals". *Natural Language and Lin-
    guistic Theory* 4.43–76.

———. 1986b. "Passive". *Linguistic Inquiry* 17.587–622.

———. 1986c. "Three Issues in the Theory of Clitics: Case, doubled NPs and
    extraction". Borer 1986.15–42.

——— & Kenneth Safir, eds. 1989. *The Null Subject Parameter*. Dordrecht:
    Reidel.

Johns, Alana. 1992. "Deriving Ergativity". *Linguistic Inquiry* 23.57–88.

Johnson, Marta, ed. 1978. *Recycling the Prague Linguistic Circle*. Ann
    Arbor: Karoma.

Junker, Marie-Odile. 1988. "Transitive, Intransitive and Reflexive Uses of
    Adjectival Verbs in French". Birdsong & Montreuil 1988.189–199.

——— & France Martineau. 1987. "Les possessions inaliénables dans les
    constructions objet". *Revue Romane* 22.194–209.

——— & ———. 1992. "The Structure of Infinitives". *Probus* 4.127–153.

Kaisse, Ellen. 1985. *Connected Speech: The interaction of syntax and
    phonology*. Orlando, Fla.: Academic Press.

Kayne, Richard. 1975. *French Syntax: The transformational cycle*. Cambridge, Mass.: MIT Press.

———. 1979. "Rightward NP Movement in French and English". *Linguistic Inquiry* 10.710–719.

———. 1983a. "Le datif en français et en anglais". Herslund et al. 1983.86–97.

———. 1983b. "Connectedness". *Linguistic Inquiry* 14.223–249.

———. 1983c. "Chains, Categories External to S and French Complex Inversion". *Natural Language and Linguistic Theory* 1.109–137.

———. 1984. *Connectedness and Binary Branching*. Dordrecht: Foris.

———. 1989a. "Null Subjects and Clitic Climbing". Jaeggli & Safir 1989.239–261.

———. 1989b. "Facets of Romance Past Participle Agreement". *Dialect Variation and the Theory of Grammar* ed. by Paola Benicà, 85–103. Dordrecht: Foris.

———. 1991. "Romance Clitics, Verb Movement and Pro". *Linguistic Inquiry* 22.647–686.

———. 1993. "Toward a Modular Theory of Auxiliary Selection". *Studia Linguistica* 47.3–31.

———. 1994. *The Antisymmetry of Syntax*. Cambridge, Mass.: MIT Press.

——— & Jean-Yves Pollock. 1978. "Stylistic Inversion, Successive Cyclicity and Move NP in French". *Linguistic Inquiry* 9.595–622.

Keenan, Edward L. 1976. "Towards a Universal Definition of 'Subject'". *Subject and Topic* ed. by Charles Li, 303–333. New York: Academic Press.

Kempchinsky, Paula. 1988. "Possessor Raising in Spanish". Unpub. ms., Univ. of Iowa, Iowa City.

———. 1992a. "An Adjunct Extraction Paradox in Spanish". Laeufer & Morgan 1992.329–346.

———. 1992b. "Clausal Complements and Case Theory in Romance". *Probus* 4.17–51.

———. 1992c. "The Spanish Possessive Dative Construction: Theta role assignment and proper government". Hirschbühler & Koerner 1992.135–150.

Keyser, Samuel Jay, ed. 1978. *Recent Transformational Studies in European Languages*. Cambridge, Mass.: MIT Press.

——— & Thomas Roeper. 1992. "The Abstract Clitic Hypothesis". *Linguistic Inquiry* 23.89–126.

Kirschner, Carl & Janet Decesaris. 1989. *Studies in Romance Linguistics*. Amsterdam & Philadelphia: John Benjamins.

Kim, Young-joo & Richard Larson. 1989. "Scope Interpretation and the Syntax of Psych-Verbs". *Linguistic Inquiry* 20.681–688.

Koopman, Hilda & Dominique Sportiche. 1991. "The Position of Subjects". *Lingua* 85.211–258.

Koster, Jan. 1978. "Conditions, Empty Nodes and Markedness". *Linguistic Inquiry* 9.551–594.

————. 1984. "On Binding and Control". *Linguistic Inquiry* 15.417–459.

Klausenburger, Jürgen. 1984. *French Liaison and Linguistic Theory*. Wiesbaden: Steiner.

Labelle, Marie. 1992a. "La structure argumentale des verbes locatifs à base nominale". *Lingvisticae Investigationes* 16.267–315.

————. 1992b. "Change of State and Valency". *Journal of Linguistics* 28.375–414.

Laeufer, Christiane & Terrell Morgan, eds. 1992. *Theoretical Analyses in Romance Linguistics*. Amsterdam & Philadelphia: John Benjamins.

Lakoff, George. 1970. *Irregularity in Syntax*. New York: Holt, Rinehart & Winston.

Lamarche, Jacques. 1991. "Problems for N⁰ Movement to NumP". *Probus* 3.215–236.

Lamiroy, Béatrice. 1983. *Les verbes de mouvement en français et español*. Amsterdam & Philadelphia: John Benjamins.

————. 1991 . "Binding Properties of French *en*". Georgopolis & Ishihara1991.397–414.

Larson, Richard. 1988. "On the Double Object Construction". *Linguistic Inquiry* 19.335–392.

Lasnik, Howard. 1988. "Subjects and the Theta–Criterion". *Natural Language and Linguistic Theory* 6.1–17.

————. 1992. "Case and Expletives: Notes towards a parametric account". *Linguistic Inquiry* 23.381–406.

————. 1993. "Lectures on Minimalist Syntax". Unpub. ms., Univ. of Connecticut, Storrs.

————. 1994. "Case and Expletives Revisited: On Greed and other human failings". Unpub. ms., Univ. of Connecticut, Storrs.

———— & Mamoru Saito. 1984. "On the Nature of Proper Government". *Linguistic Inquiry* 15.235–255.

———— & ————. 1992. *Move Alpha*. Cambridge, Mass.: MIT Press.

Leclère, Christian. 1976. "Datifs syntaxiques et datif éthique". *Recherches linguistiques à Montréal* 5.27–59.

————. 1978. "Sur une classe de verbes datifs". *Langue Française* 39.66–75.

Lefebvre, Claire. 1988. "Past Participle Agreement in French: Agreement = Case". Birdsong & Montreuil 1988.233–251.

Legendre, Géraldine. 1989a. "Inversion with Certain French Experiencer Verbs". *Language* 65.752–782.

————. 1989b. "Unaccusativity in French". *Lingua* 79.95–164.

————. 1990. "French Impersonal Constructions". *Natural Language and Linguistic Theory* 8.81–128.

Levin, Beth & Malka Rappaport [Hovav]. 1986. "The Formation of Adjectival Passives". *Linguistic Inquiry* 17.623–661.

————. 1995. *Unaccusativity: At the syntax–lexical semantics interface*. Cambridge, Mass.: MIT Press.

Lobeck, Anne. 1991. "Phrase Structure of Ellipsis in English". Rothstein 1991.81–103.

————. 1995. *Functional Heads, Licensing and Identification*. New York: Oxford Univ. Press.

Lois, Ximena. 1990. "Auxiliary Selection and Past Participle Agreement in Romance". *Probus* 2.233–255.

Longobardi, Giuseppe. 1994. "Reference and Proper Names: A theory of N–movement in syntax and Logical Form". *Linguistic Inquiry* 25.609–665.

Manzini, Maria. 1986. "On Italian *si*". Borer 1986.241–262.

————. 1992. *Locality: A theory and some of its empirical consequences*. Cambridge, Mass.: MIT Press.

————. 1994. "Locality, Minimalism and Parasitic Gaps". *Linguistic Inquiry* 25.481–508.

Marantz, Alec. 1984. *On the Nature of Grammatical Relations*. Cambridge, Mass.: MIT Press.

————. 1989. "Clitics and Phrase Structure". Baltin & Kroch 1989.99–116.

————. 1995. "A Reader's Guide to 'A Minimalist Program for Linguistic Theory'". Webelhuth 1995.349–382.

Martin, Robert. 1970. "La transformation impersonnelle". *Revue de linguistique romane* 34 (nos. 135–136).377–394.

Martineau, France. 1989. *La montée du clitique en moyen français: Une étude de la syntaxe des constructions infinitives*. Unpub. Ph.D. Dissertation, Univ. of Ottawa.

————. 1994. "The Expression of Subjunctive in Older French". *Catalan Working Papers in Linguistics* 3/2.45–70.

Martinet, André. 1955. *Économie des changements phonétiques*. Berne: A. Francke.

————. 1962. *A Functional View of Language*. Oxford: Clarendon Press.

————. 1975. *Studies in Functional Syntax / Etudes de syntaxe fonctionnelle*. Munich: Wilhelm Fink.

————. 1985. *Syntaxe générale*. Paris: Armand Collin.

Martinon, Philippe. 1927. *Comment on parle en français*. Paris: Larousse.

Massam, Diane. 1989. "Part / Whole Constructions in English". Fee & Hunt 1989.236–246.

Masullo, Pascual. 1992. *Incorporation and Case Theory in Spanish: A cross-linguistic perspective*. Unpub. Ph.D. Dissertation, Univ. of Washington, Seattle.

Mazzola, Michael, ed. 1994. *Issues and Theories in Romance Linguistics*. Washington D.C.: Georgetown Univ. Press.

May, Robert & Jan Koster, eds. 1981. *Levels of Syntactic Representation*. Dordrecht: Foris.

Mendikoetxea, Anaya. 1994. "Impersonality in Nonfinite Contexts: The Spanish *se* construction in control and raising environments". Mazzola 1994.385–401.

———— & Adrian Battye. 1990. "Arb *se / si* in Transitive Contexts: A comparative study". *Rivista di Grammatica Generativa* 15.161–198.

Milner, Jean-Claude. 1978. *De la syntaxe à l'interprétation*. Paris: Seuil.

————. 1982. *Ordres et raisons de langue*. Paris: Seuil.

Milsark, Gary Lee. 1976. *Existential Sentences in English*. Bloomington, Ind.:
  Indiana University Linguistics Club. [Reproduction of unpub. Ph.D.
  Dissertation, M.I.T., Cambridge, Mass., 1974.]
Mithun, Marianne. 1991. "Active/Agentive Case Marking and its Mo-
  tivations". *Language* 67.510–546.
Morin, Yves–Charles. 1978. "Interprétation des pronoms et des réfléchis en
  français". *Cahiers de linguistique de l'Université du Québec* 8.337–376.
Moritz, Luc & Daniel Valois. 1994. "Pied-Piping and Specifier–Head
  Agreement". *Linguistic Inquiry* 25.667–708.
Napoli, Donna Jo. 1988. "Subjects and External Arguments: Clauses and
  nonclauses". *Linguistics and Philosophy* 11.323–354.
————. 1989. *Predication Theory: A case study for indexing theory.*
  Cambridge: Cambridge Univ. Press.
Newmeyer, Frederick J. 1983. *Grammatical Theory, its Limits and its
  Possibilities*. Chicago: Univ. of Chicago Press.
————. 1986. *Linguistic Theory in America*. 2nd ed. Orlando, Fla.: Aca-
  demic Press.
————. 1987. "The Current Convergence in Linguistic Theory: Some im-
  plications for second language acquisition research". *Second Language
  Research* 3.1–19.
————. 1992. "Iconicity and Generative Grammar". *Language* 68: 756–796.
Obenauer, Hans–Georg. 1984. "On the Identification of Empty Categories".
  Linguistic Review 4.153–202.
Olarrea, Antxon. 1994. "Notes on the Optionality of Agreement". Unpub.
  ms., Univ. of Washington, Seattle.
Olié, Annie. 1984. "L'hypothèse de l'inaccusatif en français". *Lingvisticae
  Investigationes* 8.363–401.
Olsson, Hugo. 1984. "La construction *Je lui trouve mauvaise mine* en français
  moderne". *Studia Neophilologica* 56.183–213.
Otero, Carlos P. 1983. "Towards a Model of Paradigmatic Grammar". *Qua-
  derni di Semantica* 4.134–144, 311–326.
————. 1985. "Arbitrary Subjects in Finite Clauses". Bordelois, Contreras &
  Zagona 1985.81–109.
————. 1995 [1991]. "Head Movement, Cliticization, Precompilation and
  Word Insertion". Freidin 1995.296–337.
Ouhalla, Jamal. 1991. *Functional Categories and Parametric Variation*.
  London: Routledge.
Parodi, Claudia. 1994. "On Case and Agreement in Spanish and English DPs".
  Mazzola 1994.285–302.
Pearce, Elizabeth. 1990. *Parameters in Old French Syntax: Infinitival
  complements*. Dordrecht: Kluwer.
Perlmutter, David. 1989. "Multiattachment and the Unaccusative Hypothesis:
  The Perfect Auxiliary in Italian". *Probus* 1.63–119.
———— & Paul Postal. 1977. "Toward a Universal Characterization of Pas-
  sivization". *Studies in Relational Grammar*, vol. I, ed. by David Perlmut-
  ter, 3–29. Chicago: Univ. of Chicago Press.

Pesetsky, David. 1987. "Binding Problems with Experiencer Verbs". *Linguistic Inquiry* 18.126–140.
———. 1993. "Topic ... Comment". *Natural Language and Linguistic Theory* 11.557–558.
———. 1995. *Zero Syntax: Experiencers and cascades.* Cambridge, Mass.: MIT Press.
Picallo, M. Carme. 1984. "The INFL Node and the Null Subject Parameter". *Linguistic Inquiry* 15.75–102.
Pijnenburg, Hans & Aafke Hulk. 1989. "Datives in French Causatives". *Probus* 1.259–282.
Pinker, Stephen. 1989. *Learnability and Cognition: The acquisition of argument structure.* Cambridge, Mass.: MIT Press.
———. 1994. *The Language Instinct: How the mind creates language.* New York: Harper Collins.
Pollock, Jean–Yves. 1978 "Trace Theory and French Syntax". Keyser 1978. 65–112.
———. 1979. "Réanalyse et constructions impersonnelles". *Recherches linguistiques* 8.72–130.
———. 1981. "On Case and Impersonal Constructions". May & Koster 1981.219–252.
———. 1985. "On Case and the Syntax of Infinitives in French". Guéron, Obenauer & Pollock 1985.293–326.
———. 1986. "Sur la syntaxe de *en* et le paramètre du sujet nul". Ronat & Couquaux 1986.211–246.
———. 1989a. "Verb Movement, Universal Grammar and the Structure of IP". *Linguistic Inquiry* 20.365–424.
———. 1989b. "Opacity, Genitive Subjects and Extraction from NP in English and French". *Probus* 1.151–162.
Postal, Paul. 1971. *Cross–Over Phenomena.* New York: Holt, Rinehart & Winston.
———. 1983. "On Characterizing French Grammatical Structure". *Linguistic Analysis* 11.361–417.
———. 1984. "French Indirect Object Cliticization , and SSC / BT". *Linguistic Analysis* 14.111–172.
———. 1985. "La dégradation de prédicat et un genre négligé de montée". *Recherches Linguistiques* 13.33–68.
———. 1986. "Why Irish Raising is not Anomalous". *Natural Language and Linguistic Theory* 4.333–356.
Pullum, Geoffrey. 1988. "Citation Etiquette Beyond Thunderdome". *Natural Language and Linguistic Theory* 6.579–588.
Quicoli, Carlos. 1976. "Conditions on Quantifier Movement in French". *Linguistic Inquiry* 7.583–608.
———. 1980. "Clitic Movement in French Causatives". *Linguistic Analysis* 6.131–186.
Radford, Andrew. 1988. *Transformational Grammar: A first course.* Cambridge: Cambridge Univ. Press.

Raposo, Eduardo. 1985. "Some Asymmetries in the Binding Theory in Romance". *Linguistic Review* 5.75–110.

───── & Juan Uriagereka. 1990. "Long Distance Case Assignment". *Linguistic Inquiry* 21.505–537.

Rappaport, Malka, Mary Laughren & Beth Levin. 1987. "Levels of Lexical Representation". (=*Lexicon Project Working Papers*, 20.) Cambridge, Mass.: Center for Cognitive Science, MIT.

─────& Beth Levin. 1988. "What to Do with Theta Roles". Wilkins 1988.7–36.

Reed, Lisa. 1991. "The Thematic and Syntactic Structure of French Causatives". *Probus* 3.317–360.

─────. 1992a. "Remarks on Word Order in Causative Constructions". *Linguistic Inquiry* 23.164–172.

─────. 1992b. "On Clitic Case Alternations in French Causatives". Hirschbühler & Koerner 1992.205–224.

Reinhart, Tanya & Eric Reuland. 1993. "Reflexivity". *Linguistic Inquiry* 24. 657–720.

Ritter, Elizabeth & Sara Rosen. 1993. "Deriving Causation". *Natural Language and Linguistic Theory* 11.519–555.

Rivero, Maria–Luisa. 1990. "The Location of Nonactive Voice in Albanian and Modern Greek". *Linguistic Inquiry* 21.135–146.

Rizzi, Luigi. 1978. "A Restructuring Rule in Italian Syntax". Keyser 1978. 113–158.

─────. 1986a. "Null Objects in Italian and the Theory of *pro*". *Linguistic Inquiry* 17.501–557.

─────. 1986b. "On Chain Formation". in Borer 1986.65–95.

─────. 1990. *Relativized Minimality*. Cambridge, Mass.: MIT Press.

───── & Ian Roberts. 1989. "Complex Inversion in French". *Probus* 1.1–30.

Roberge, Yves. 1988. "Clitic–Chains and the Definiteness Requirement in Doubling Constructions". Birdsong & Montreuil 1988.353–369.

─────. 1990. *The Syntactic Recoverability of Null Arguments*. Kingston, Ont. & Montreal: McGill–Queens Univ. Press.

Roberts, Ian. 1987. *The Representation of Implicit and Dethematized Subjects*. Dordrecht: Foris.

Rochemont, Michael. 1986. *Focus in Generative Grammar*. Amsterdam & Philadelphia: John Benjamins.

───── & Peter Culicover. 1990. *English Focus Constructions and the Theory of Grammar*. Cambridge: Cambridge Univ. Press.

Ronat, Mitsou & Daniel Couquaux, eds. 1986. *La grammaire modulaire*. Paris: Editions de Minuit.

─────. 1990. *The Syntactic Recoverability of Null Arguments*. Kingston: McGill–Queens Univ. Press.

Rooryck, Johan. 1988. "Critères formels pour le datif nonlexical en français". *Studia Neophilologica* 60.97–107.

─────. 1992. "On the Distinction between Raising and Control". Hirschbühler & Koerner 1992.225–250.

————. 1995. "On the Interaction between Raising and Focus in Sentential Complementation". Paper presented at the Twenty–Fifth Linguistic Symposium on Romance Languages, Univ. of Washington, Seattle.

Rosen, Carol. 1980. *The Relational Structure of Reflexive Clauses: Evidence from Italian.* Unpub. Ph.D. Dissertation, Harvard Univ.

————. 1984. "The Interface between Semantic Roles and Initial Grammatical Relations". *Studies in Relational Grammar,* vol. II, ed. by David Perlmutter & Carol Rosen, 38–77. Chicago: Univ. of Chicago Press.

Rothemberg, Mira. 1974. *Les verbes à la fois transitifs et intransitifs en français contemporain.* The Hague: Mouton.

Rothstein, Susan. 1992a. "Case and NP Licensing". *Natural Language and Linguistic Theory* 10.119–139.

————, ed. 1992b. *Perspectives on Phrase Structure, Heads and Licensing.* (= *Syntax and Semantics,* 25.) Orlando, Fla.: Academic Press.

Rouveret, Alain & Jean–Roger Vergnaud. 1980. "Specifying Reference to the Subject: French causatives and conditions on representations". *Linguistic Inquiry* 11.97–202.

Ruwet, Nicolas. 1972. *Théorie syntaxique et syntaxe du français.* Paris: Seuil.

————. 1982. "Le datif épistémique en français et la condition d'opacité de Chomsky". *Grammaire des insultes,* 172–204. Paris: Seuil.

————. 1983. "Montée et controle: Une question à revoir?". Herslund et al. 1983.17–37.

————. 1989. "Weather Verbs and the Unaccusative Hypothesis". Kirschner & Decesaris 1989.313–346.

————. 1990. "*En* et *y*: Deux clitiques pronominaux anti–logophoriques". *Langages* 97.51–81.

Sachs, Hilary. 1991. "French Symmetric Adjectives and the Thematic Role Hierarchy". Unpub. ms., Univ. of Tennessee.

————. 1992. *Thematic Roles and lui Cliticization in French.* Unpub. Ph.D. Dissertation, Cornell Univ., Ithaca, N.Y.

Safir, Ken. 1987. "The Syntactic Projection of Lexical Thematic Structure". *Natural Language and Linguistic Theory* 5.561–601.

Saltarelli, Mario. 1992. "The Subject of Psych–Verbs and Case Theory". Hirschbühler & Koerner 1992.251–268.

Sandfeld, Kristian. 1929. *Syntaxe du français contemporain: I. Les pronoms.* Paris: Champion.

Saussure, Ferdinand de. 1931. *Cours de linguistique générale.* 3rd. ed. Paris: Payot.

Speas, Margaret. 1990. *Phrase Structure in Natural Language.* Dordrecht: Kluwer.

Sportiche, Dominique. 1981. "Bounding Nodes in French". *Linguistic Review* 1.219–246.

————. 1988. "A Theory of Floating Quantifiers and its Corollaries for Constituent Structure". *Linguistic Inquiry* 19.425–449.

————. 1989. "Conditions on Silent Categories". Unpub. ms., Univ. of Calif., Los Angeles.

————. 1992. "Clitic Constructions". Unpub. ms., Univ. of Calif., Los Angeles.

————. 1993a. "Sketch of a Reductionist Approach to Syntactic Variation and Dependencies". Unpub. ms., Univ. of Calif., Los Angeles.

————. 1993b. "Subject Clitics in French and Romance Complex Inversion and Clitic Doubling". Unpub. ms., Univ. of Calif., Los Angeles.

Stowell, Tim. 1981. *Elements of Phrase Structure*. Unpub. Ph.D. Dissertation, M.I.T., Cambridge, Mass.

————. 1983. "Subjects across Categories". *The Linguistic Review* 2.285–312.

————. 1989. "Subjects, Specifiers and X–bar Theory". Baltin & Kroch 1989.232–262.

Strozer, Judith. 1976. *Clitics in Spanish*. Unpub. Ph.D. Dissertation, Univ. of Calif., Los Angeles.

————. 1994. *Language Acquisition after Puberty*. Washington D.C.: Georgetown Univ. Press.

Suñer, Margarita. 1982. *Syntax and Semantics of Presentational Spanish Sentence Types*. Washington D.C.: Georgetown Univ. Press.

————. 1988. "The Role of Agreement in Clitic Doubled Constructions". *Natural Language and Linguistic Theory* 6.391–434.

————. 1990. "Impersonal *se* Passives and the Licensing of Empty Categories". *Probus* 2.209–231.

Tellier, Christine. 1991. *Licensing Theory and French Parasitic Gaps*. Dordrecht: Kluwer.

————. 1994. "The *have / be* Alternation: Attributives in French and English". Unpub. ms., Univ. de Montréal.

———— & Daniel Valois. 1993. "Binominal *chacun* and Pseudo–opacity". *Linguistic Inquiry* 24.575–583.

Terzi, Arhonto. 1994. "Clitic Climbing from Finite Clauses and Long Head Movement". *Catalan Working Papers in Linguistics* 3:2.97–122. Barcelona.

Torrego, Esther. 1984. "On Inversion in Spanish and Some of its Effects". *Linguistic Inquiry* 15.103–129.

Tranel, Bernard. 1992. "On Suppletion and French Liaison". Hirschbühler & Koerner 1992.269–308.

Travis, Lisa. 1984. *Parameters and Effects of Word Order Variation*. Unpub. Ph.D. Dissertation, M.I.T., Cambridge, Mass.

Tremblay, Mireille. 1989. "French Possessive Adjectives as Dative Clitics". Fee & Hunt 1989.399–413.

————. 1990. "An Argument Sharing Approach to Ditransitive Constructions". Halpern 1990.549–564.

Tr[o]ubetskoy, Nikolai S. 1949 [1939]. *Principes de phonologie*. Transl. by Jean Cantineau. Paris: Klincksieck.

————. 1968 [1935]. *Introduction to the Principles of Phonological Descriptions*. Transl. by L.A. Murray. The Hague: Martinus Nijhoff.

Uriagereka, Juan. 1995. "Aspects of the Syntax of Clitic Placement in Western Romance". *Linguistic Inquiry* 26.79–123.

Valois, Daniel. 1991. *The Internal Syntax of DP*. Unpub. Ph.D. Dissertation, Univ. of Calif., Los Angeles.

Van Valin, Robert D. Jr. 1990. "Semantic Parameters of Split Intransitivity". *Language* 66.221–260.

Vergnaud, Jean–Roger. 1974. *French Relative Clauses*. Unpub. Ph.D. Dissertation, M.I.T., Cambridge, Mass.

———. 1985. *Dépendances et niveaux de représentation en syntaxe*. Amsterdam & Philadelphia: John Benjamins.

——— & Maria–Luisa Zubizarreta. 1992. "The Definite Determiner and the Inalienable Constructions in French and in English". *Linguistic Inquiry* 23.595–652.

Villalba, Xavier. 1994. "Clitic Climbing in Causative Constructions". *Catalan Working Papers in Linguistics* 3:2.123–152. Barcelona.

Vinet, Marie-Thérèse. 1988. "Implicit Arguments and Control in Middles and Passives". Birdsong & Montreuil 1988.427–437.

Wagner, Robert Léon & Jacqueline Pinchon. 1962. *Grammaire du français classique et moderne*. Paris: Hachette.

Wanner, Dieter & Douglas A. Kibbee, eds. 1991. *New Analyses in Romance Linguistics*. Amsterdam & Philadelphia: John Benjamins.

Webelhuth, Gert. 1992. *Principles and Parameters of Syntactic Saturation*. New York: Oxford Univ. Press.

———, ed. 1995. *The Principles and Parameters Approach to Syntactic Theory: A synopsis*. London: Basil Blackwell.

Wehrli, Eric. 1986. "On Some Properties of French Clitic *se*". Borer 1986. 263–284.

White, Lydia. 1989. *Universal Grammar and Second Language Acquisition*. Amsterdam & Philadelphia: John Benjamins.

Wilkins, Wendy, ed. 1988. *Thematic Relations (= Syntax and Semantics, 21.)* San Diego, Cal.: Academic Press.

Willems, Dominique. 1981. *Syntaxe, lexique et sémantique: Les constructions verbales*. Gent: Rijksuniversiteit te Gent.

Williams, Edwin. 1980. "Predication". *Linguistic Inquiry* 11.208–238.

———. 1981. "Argument Structure and Morphology". *Linguistic Review* 1.81–114.

———. 1987. "Implicit Arguments, the Binding Theory and Control". *Natural Language and Linguistic Theory* 5.151–180.

———. 1989. "The Anaphoric Nature of Theta Roles". *Linguistic Inquiry* 20. 425–456.

———. 1994. *Thematic Structure in Syntax*. Cambridge, Mass.: MIT Press.

Zagona, Karen. 1982. *Government and Proper Government of Verbal Projections*. Unpub. Ph.D. Dissertation, Univ. of Washington, Seattle.

———. 1988a. *Verb Phrase Syntax: A parametric study of English and Spanish*. Dordrecht: Kluwer.

————. 1988b. "Proper Government of Antecedentless VP in English and Spanish". *Natural Language and Linguistic Theory* 6.95–128.

————. 1990. "*mente* Adverbs, Compound Interpretation and the Projection Principle". *Probus* 2.1–30.

————. 1992. "Tense Binding and the Construal of Present Tense". Laeufer & Morgan 1992.385–398.

————. 1994. "Perfectivity and Temporal Arguments". Mazzola 1994.523–546.

————, ed. Forthcoming. *Proceedings of the Twenty–Fifth Linguistic Symposium on Romance Languages.* Amsterdam & Philadelphia: John Benjamins.

Zamir, Jan R., Jean–Philippe Robert Mathy & Rosemary McCluskey. 1992. *750 French Verbs and their Uses.* New York: John Wiley.

Zaring, Laurie. 1991. "On Prepositions and Case Marking in French". *Canadian Journal of Linguistics* 36.363–377.

————. 1993. "On a Type of Argument Island in French". *Natural Language and Linguistic Theory* 11.121–174.

————. 1994. "On the Relationship between Subject Pronouns and Clausal Arguments". *Natural Language and Linguistic Theory* 12.515–569.

Zipf, George Kingsley. 1949. *The Principle of Least Effort.* Cambridge, Mass.: Addison–Wesley Press.

Zribi-Hertz, Anne. 1978. "Le poulet a cuit, le poulet s'est cuit: Une opposition aspectuelle parmi les verbes neutres du français". *Studies in French Linguistics* 1, 1.75–113.

————. 1982. "La construction *se*–moyen du français et son statut dans le triangle: moyen–passif–réfléchi". *Lingvisticae Investigationes* 6.345–401.

————. 1993. "On Stroik's Analysis of English Middle Constructions". *Linguistic Inquiry* 24.583–589.

Zubizarreta, Maria-Luisa. 1985. "The Relation between Morphophonology and Morphosyntax: The case of Romance causatives". *Linguistic Inquiry* 16.247–289.

————. 1987. *Levels of Representation in the Lexicon and in the Syntax.* Dordrecht: Foris.

————. 1992. "Word Order in Spanish and the Nature of Nominative Case". Unpub. ms., Univ. of Southern California, Los Angeles.

INDEX OF AUTHORS

INDEX OF SUBJECTS

In the CURRENT ISSUES IN LINGUISTIC THEORY (CILT) series (edited by: E.F. Konrad Koerner, University of Ottawa) the following volumes have been published thus far or are scheduled to appear in the course of 1995:

1.   KOERNER, Konrad (ed.): *The Transformational-Generative Paradigm and Modern Linguistic Theory.* 1975.
2.   WEIDERT, Alfons: *Componential Analysis of Lushai Phonology.* 1975.
3.   MAHER, J. Peter: *Papers on Language Theory and History I: Creation and Tradition in Language. Foreword by Raimo Anttila.* 1979.
4.   HOPPER, Paul J. (ed.): *Studies in Descriptive and Historical Linguistics. Festschrift for Winfred P. Lehmann.* 1977.
5.   ITKONEN, Esa: *Grammatical Theory and Metascience: A critical investigation into the methodological and philosophical foundations of 'autonomous' linguistics.* 1978.
6.   ANTTILA, Raimo: *Historical and Comparative Linguistics.* 1989.
7.   MEISEL, Jürgen M. & Martin D. PAM (eds): *Linear Order and Generative Theory.* 1979.
8.   WILBUR, Terence H.: *Prolegomena to a Grammar of Basque.* 1979.
9.   HOLLIEN, Harry & Patricia (eds): *Current Issues in the Phonetic Sciences. Proceedings of the IPS-77 Congress, Miami Beach, Florida, 17-19 December 1977.* 1979.
10. PRIDEAUX, Gary D. (ed.): *Perspectives in Experimental Linguistics. Papers from the University of Alberta Conference on Experimental Linguistics, Edmonton, 13-14 Oct. 1978.* 1979.
11. BROGYANYI, Bela (ed.): *Studies in Diachronic, Synchronic, and Typological Linguistics: Festschrift for Oswald Szemérenyi on the Occasion of his 65th Birthday.* 1979.
12. FISIAK, Jacek (ed.): *Theoretical Issues in Contrastive Linguistics.* 1981.   Out of print
13. MAHER, J. Peter, Allan R. BOMHARD & Konrad KOERNER (eds): *Papers from the Third International Conference on Historical Linguistics, Hamburg, August 22-26 1977.* 1982.
14. TRAUGOTT, Elizabeth C., Rebecca LaBRUM & Susan SHEPHERD (eds): *Papers from the Fourth International Conference on Historical Linguistics, Stanford, March 26-30 1979.* 1980.
15. ANDERSON, John (ed.): *Language Form and Linguistic Variation. Papers dedicated to Angus McIntosh.* 1982.
16. ARBEITMAN, Yoël L. & Allan R. BOMHARD (eds): *Bono Homini Donum: Essays in Historical Linguistics, in Memory of J.Alexander Kerns.* 1981.
17. LIEB, Hans-Heinrich: *Integrational Linguistics. 6 volumes. Vol. II-VI n.y.p.* 1984/93.
18. IZZO, Herbert J. (ed.): *Italic and Romance. Linguistic Studies in Honor of Ernst Pulgram.* 1980.
19. RAMAT, Paolo et al. (eds): *Linguistic Reconstruction and Indo-European Syntax. Proceedings of the Colloquium of the 'Indogermanischhe Gesellschaft'. University of Pavia, 6-7 September 1979.* 1980.
20. NORRICK, Neal R.: *Semiotic Principles in Semantic Theory.* 1981.
21. AHLQVIST, Anders (ed.): *Papers from the Fifth International Conference on Historical Linguistics, Galway, April 6-10 1981.* 1982.
22. UNTERMANN, Jürgen & Bela BROGYANYI (eds): *Das Germanische und die Rekonstruktion der Indogermanischen Grundsprache. Akten des Freiburger Kolloquiums der Indogermanischen Gesellschaft, Freiburg, 26-27 Februar 1981.* 1984.
23. DANIELSEN, Niels: *Papers in Theoretical Linguistics. Edited by Per Baerentzen.* 1992.
24. LEHMANN, Winfred P. & Yakov MALKIEL (eds): *Perspectives on Historical Linguistics. Papers from a conference held at the meeting of the Language Theory Division, Modern Language Assn., San Francisco, 27-30 December 1979.* 1982.
25. ANDERSEN, Paul Kent: *Word Order Typology and Comparative Constructions.* 1983.
26. BALDI, Philip (ed.): *Papers from the XIIth Linguistic Symposium on Romance Languages, Univ. Park, April 1-3, 1982.* 1984.

27. BOMHARD, Alan R.: *Toward Proto-Nostratic. A New Approach to the Comparison of Proto-Indo-European and Proto-Afroasiatic. Foreword by Paul J. Hopper.* 1984.

28. BYNON, James (ed.): *Current Progress in Afro-Asiatic Linguistics: Papers of the Third International Hamito-Semitic Congress, London, 1978.* 1984.

29. PAPROTTÉ, Wolf & René DIRVEN (eds): *The Ubiquity of Metaphor: Metaphor in language and thought.* 1985 (publ. 1986).

30. HALL, Robert A. Jr.: *Proto-Romance Morphology. = Comparative Romance Grammar, vol. III.* 1984.

31. GUILLAUME, Gustave: *Foundations for a Science of Language.*

32. COPELAND, James E. (ed.): *New Directions in Linguistics and Semiotics.* Co-edition with Rice University Press who hold exclusive rights for US and Canada. 1984.

33. VERSTEEGH, Kees: *Pidginization and Creolization. The Case of Arabic.* 1984.

34. FISIAK, Jacek (ed.): *Papers from the VIth International Conference on Historical Linguistics, Poznan, 22-26 August. 1983.* 1985.

35. COLLINGE, N.E.: *The Laws of Indo-European.* 1985.

36. KING, Larry D. & Catherine A. MALEY (eds): *Selected papers from the XIIIth Linguistic Symposium on Romance Languages, Chapel Hill, N.C., 24-26 March 1983.* 1985.

37. GRIFFEN, T.D.: *Aspects of Dynamic Phonology.* 1985.

38. BROGYANYI, Bela & Thomas KRÖMMELBEIN (eds): *Germanic Dialects:Linguistic and Philological Investigations.* 1986.

39. BENSON, James D., Michael J. CUMMINGS, & William S. GREAVES (eds): *Linguistics in a Systemic Perspective.* 1988.

40. FRIES, Peter Howard (ed.) in collaboration with Nancy M. Fries: *Toward an Understanding of Language: Charles C. Fries in Perspective.* 1985.

41. EATON, Roger, et al. (eds): *Papers from the 4th International Conference on English Historical Linguistics, April 10-13, 1985.* 1985.

42. MAKKAI, Adam & Alan K. MELBY (eds): *Linguistics and Philosophy. Festschrift for Rulon S. Wells.* 1985 (publ. 1986).

43. AKAMATSU, Tsutomu: *The Theory of Neutralization and the Archiphoneme in Functional Phonology.* 1988.

44. JUNGRAITHMAYR, Herrmann & Walter W. MUELLER (eds): *Proceedings of the Fourth International Hamito-Semitic Congress.* 1987.

45. KOOPMAN, W.F., F.C. Van der LEEK , O. FISCHER & R. EATON (eds): *Explanation and Linguistic Change.* 1986

46. PRIDEAUX, Gary D. & William J. BAKER: *Strategies and Structures: The processing of relative clauses.* 1987.

47. LEHMANN, Winfred P. (ed.): *Language Typology 1985. Papers from the Linguistic Typology Symposium, Moscow, 9-13 Dec. 1985.* 1986.

48. RAMAT, Anna G., Onofrio CARRUBA and Giuliano BERNINI (eds): *Papers from the 7th International Conference on Historical Linguistics.* 1987.

49. WAUGH, Linda R. and Stephen RUDY (eds): *New Vistas in Grammar: Invariance and Variation. Proceedings of the Second International Roman Jakobson Conference, New York University, Nov.5-8, 1985.* 1991.

50. RUDZKA-OSTYN, Brygida (ed.): *Topics in Cognitive Linguistics.* 1988.

51. CHATTERJEE, Ranjit: *Aspect and Meaning in Slavic and Indic. With a foreword by Paul Friedrich.* 1989.

52. FASOLD, Ralph W. & Deborah SCHIFFRIN (eds): *Language Change and Variation.* 1989.

53. SANKOFF, David: *Diversity and Diachrony.* 1986.

54. WEIDERT, Alfons: *Tibeto-Burman Tonology. A comparative analysis.* 1987

55. HALL, Robert A. Jr.: *Linguistics and Pseudo-Linguistics.* 1987.

56. HOCKETT, Charles F.: *Refurbishing our Foundations. Elementary linguistics from an advanced point of view.* 1987.

57. BUBENIK, Vít: *Hellenistic and Roman Greece as a Sociolinguistic Area.* 1989.

58. ARBEITMAN, Yoël. L. (ed.): *Fucus: A Semitic/Afrasian Gathering in Remembrance of Albert Ehrman.* 1988.

59. VAN VOORST, Jan: *Event Structure.* 1988.

60. KIRSCHNER, Carl & Janet DECESARIS (eds): *Studies in Romance Linguistics. Selected Proceedings from the XVII Linguistic Symposium on Romance Languages.* 1989.

61. CORRIGAN, Roberta L., Fred ECKMAN & Michael NOONAN (eds): *Linguistic Categorization. Proceedings of an International Symposium in Milwaukee, Wisconsin, April 10-11, 1987.* 1989.

62. FRAJZYNGIER, Zygmunt (ed.): *Current Progress in Chadic Linguistics. Proceedings of the International Symposium on Chadic Linguistics, Boulder, Colorado, 1-2 May 1987.* 1989.

63. EID, Mushira (ed.): *Perspectives on Arabic Linguistics I. Papers from the First Annual Symposium on Arabic Linguistics.* 1990.

64. BROGYANYI, Bela (ed.): *Prehistory, History and Historiography of Language, Speech, and Linguistic Theory. Papers in honor of Oswald Szemérenyi I.* 1992.

65. ADAMSON, Sylvia, Vivien A. LAW, Nigel VINCENT and Susan WRIGHT (eds): *Papers from the 5th International Conference on English Historical Linguistics.* 1990.

66. ANDERSEN, Henning and Konrad KOERNER (eds): *Historical Linguistics 1987.Papers from the 8th International Conference on Historical Linguistics,Lille, August 30-Sept., 1987.* 1990.

67. LEHMANN, Winfred P. (ed.): *Language Typology 1987. Systematic Balance in Language. Papers from the Linguistic Typology Symposium, Berkeley, 1-3 Dec 1987.* 1990.

68. BALL, Martin, James FIFE, Erich POPPE &Jenny ROWLAND (eds): *Celtic Linguistics/ Ieithyddiaeth Geltaidd. Readings in the Brythonic Languages. Festschrift for T. Arwyn Watkins.* 1990.

69. WANNER, Dieter and Douglas A. KIBBEE (eds): *New Analyses in Romance Linguistics. Selected papers from the Linguistic Symposium on Romance Languages XVIIII, Urbana-Champaign, April 7-9, 1988.* 1991.

70. JENSEN, John T.: *Morphology. Word structure in generative grammar.* 1990.

71. O'GRADY, William: *Categories and Case. The sentence structure of Korean.* 1991.

72. EID, Mushira and John MCCARTHY (eds): *Perspectives on Arabic Linguistics II. Papers from the Second Annual Symposium on Arabic Linguistics.* 1990.

73. STAMENOV, Maxim (ed.): *Current Advances in Semantic Theory.* 1991.

74. LAEUFER, Christiane and Terrell A. MORGAN (eds): *Theoretical Analyses in Romance Linguistics.* 1991.

75. DROSTE, Flip G. and John E. JOSEPH (eds): *Linguistic Theory and Grammatical Description. Nine Current Approaches.* 1991.

76. WICKENS, Mark A.: *Grammatical Number in English Nouns. An empirical and theoretical account.* 1992.

77. BOLTZ, William G. and Michael C. SHAPIRO (eds): *Studies in the Historical Phonology of Asian Languages.* 1991.

78. KAC, Michael: *Grammars and Grammaticality.* 1992.

79. ANTONSEN, Elmer H. and Hans Henrich HOCK (eds): *STAEF-CRAEFT: Studies in Germanic Linguistics. Select papers from the First and Second Symposium on Germanic Linguistics, University of Chicago, 24 April 1985, and Univ. of Illinois at Urbana-Champaign, 3-4 Oct. 1986.* 1991.

80. COMRIE, Bernard and Mushira EID (eds): *Perspectives on Arabic Linguistics III. Papers from the Third Annual Symposium on Arabic Linguistics.* 1991.

81. LEHMANN, Winfred P. and H.J. HEWITT (eds): *Language Typology 1988. Typological Models in the Service of Reconstruction.* 1991.

82. VAN VALIN, Robert D. (ed.): *Advances in Role and Reference Grammar*. 1992.
83. FIFE, James and Erich POPPE (eds): *Studies in Brythonic Word Order*. 1991.
84. DAVIS, Garry W. and Gregory K. IVERSON (eds): *Explanation in Historical Linguistics*. 1992.
85. BROSELOW, Ellen, Mushira EID and John McCARTHY (eds): *Perspectives on Arabic Linguistics IV. Papers from the Annual Symposium on Arabic Linguistics*. 1992.
86. KESS, Joseph F.: *Psycholinguistics. Psychology, linguistics, and the study of natural language*. 1992.
87. BROGYANYI, Bela and Reiner LIPP (eds): *Historical Philology: Greek, Latin, and Romance. Papers in honor of Oswald Szemerényi II*. 1992.
88. SHIELDS, Kenneth: *A History of Indo-European Verb Morphology*. 1992.
89. BURRIDGE, Kate: *Syntactic Change in Germanic. A study of some aspects of language change in Germanic with particular reference to Middle Dutch*. 1992.
90. KING, Larry D.: *The Semantic Structure of Spanish. Meaning and grammatical form*. 1992.
91. HIRSCHBÜHLER, Paul and Konrad KOERNER (eds): *Romance Languages and Modern Linguistic Theory. Selected papers from the XX Linguistic Symposium on Romance Languages, University of Ottawa, April 10-14, 1990*. 1992.
92. POYATOS, Fernando: *Paralanguage: A linguistic and interdisciplinary approach to interactive speech and sounds*. 1992.
93. LIPPI-GREEN, Rosina (ed.): *Recent Developments in Germanic Linguistics*. 1992.
94. HAGÈGE, Claude: *The Language Builder. An essay on the human signature in linguistic morphogenesis*. 1992.
95. MILLER, D. Gary: *Complex Verb Formation*. 1992.
96. LIEB, Hans-Heinrich (ed.): *Prospects for a New Structuralism*. 1992.
97. BROGYANYI, Bela & Reiner LIPP (eds): *Comparative-Historical Linguistics: Indo-European and Finno-Ugric. Papers in honor of Oswald Szemerényi III*. 1992.
98. EID, Mushira & Gregory K. IVERSON: *Principles and Prediction: The analysis of natural language*. 1993.
99. JENSEN, John T.: *English Phonology*. 1993.
100. MUFWENE, Salikoko S. and Lioba MOSHI (eds): *Topics in African Linguistics. Papers from the XXI Annual Conference on African Linguistics, University of Georgia, April 1990*. 1993.
101. EID, Mushira & Clive HOLES (eds): *Perspectives on Arabic Linguistics V. Papers from the Fifth Annual Symposium on Arabic Linguistics*. 1993.
102. DAVIS, Philip W. (ed.): *Alternative Linguistics. Descriptive and theoretical Modes*. 1995.
103. ASHBY, William J., Marianne MITHUN, Giorgio PERISSINOTTO and Eduardo RAPOSO: *Linguistic Perspectives on Romance Languages. Selected papers from the XXI Linguistic Symposium on Romance Languages, Santa Barbara, February 21-24, 1991*. 1993.
104. KURZOVÁ, Helena: *From Indo-European to Latin. The evolution of a morphosyntactic type*. 1993.
105. HUALDE, José Ignacio and Jon ORTIZ DE URBANA (eds): *Generative Studies in Basque Linguistics*. 1993.
106. AERTSEN, Henk and Robert J. JEFFERS (eds): *Historical Linguistics 1989. Papers from the 9th International Conference on Historical Linguistics, New Brunswick, 14-18 August 1989*. 1993.
107. MARLE, Jaap van (ed.): *Historical Linguistics 1991. Papers from the 10th International Conference on Historical Linguistics, Amsterdam, August 12-16, 1991*. 1993.
108. LIEB, Hans-Heinrich: *Linguistic Variables. Towards a unified theory of linguistic variation*. 1993.
109. PAGLIUCA, William (ed.): *Perspectives on Grammaticalization*. 1994.
110. SIMONE, Raffaele (ed.): *Iconicity in Language*. 1995.

111. TOBIN, Yishai: *Invariance, Markedness and Distinctive Feature Analysis. A contrastive study of sign systems in English and Hebrew.* 1994.

112. CULIOLI, Antoine: *Cognition and Representation in Linguistic Theory. Translated, edited and introduced by Michel Liddle.* 1995.

113. FERNÁNDEZ, Francisco, Miguel FUSTER and Juan Jose CALVO (eds): *English Historical Linguistics 1992. Papers from the 7th International Conference on English Historical Linguistics, Valencia, 22-26 September 1992.*1994.

114. EGLI, U., P. PAUSE, Chr. SCHWARZE, A. von STECHOW, G. WIENOLD (eds): *Lexical Knowledge in the Organisation of Language.* 1995.

115. EID, Mushira, Vincente CANTARINO and Keith WALTERS (eds): *Perspectives on Arabic Linguistics. Vol. VI. Papers from the Sixth Annual Symposium on Arabic Linguistics.* 1994.

116. MILLER, D. Gary: *Ancient Scripts and Phonological Knowledge.* 1994.

117. PHILIPPAKI-WARBURTON, I., K. NICOLAIDIS and M. SIFIANOU (eds): *Themes in Greek Linguistics. Papers from the first International Conference on Greek Linguistics, Reading, September 1993.* 1994.

118. HASAN, Ruqaiya and Peter H. FRIES (eds): *On Subject and Theme. A discourse functional perspective.* 1995.

119. LIPPI-GREEN, Rosina: *Language Ideology and Language Change in Early Modern German. A sociolinguistic study of the consonantal system of Nuremberg.* 1994.

120. STONHAM, John T. : *Combinatorial Morphology.* 1994.

121. HASAN, Ruqaiya, Carmel CLORAN and David BUTT (eds): *Functional Descriptions. Transitivity and the construction of experience.* 1995.

122. SMITH, John Charles and Martin MAIDEN (eds): *Linguistic Theory and the Romance Languages.* 1995.

123. AMASTAE, Jon, Grant GOODALL, Mario MONTALBETTI and Marianne PHINNEY: *Contemporary Research in Romance Linguistics. Papers from the XXII Linguistic Symposium on Romance Languages, El Paso//Juárez, February 22-24, 1994.* 1995.

124. ANDERSEN, Henning: *Historical Linguistics 1993. Selected papers from the 11th International Conference on Historical Linguistics, Los Angeles, 16-20 August 1993.* 1995.

125. SINGH, Rajendra (ed.): *Towards a Critical Sociolinguistics.* n.y.p.

126. MATRAS, Yaron (ed.): *Romani in Contact. The history, structure and sociology of a language.* 1995.

127. GUY, Gregory R., John BAUGH, Deborah SCHIFFRIN and Crawford FEAGIN (eds): *Towards a Social Science of Language. Papers in honor of William Labov. Volume 1: Variation and change in language and society.* n.y.p.

128. GUY, Gregory R., John BAUGH, Deborah SCHIFFRIN and Crawford FEAGIN (eds): *Towards a Social Science of Language. Papers in honor of William Labov. Volume 2: Social interaction and discourse structures.* n.y.p.

129. LEVIN, Saul: *Semitic and Indo-European: The Principal Etymologies. With observations on Afro-Asiatic.* 1995.

130. EID, Mushira (ed.) *Perspectives on Arabic Linguistics. Vol. VII. Papers from the Seventh Annual Symposium on Arabic Linguistics.* 1995.

131. HUALDE, Jose Ignacio, Joseba A. LAKARRA and R.L. Trask (eds): *Towards a History of the Basque Language.* 1995.

132. HERSCHENSOHN, Julia: *Case Suspension and Binary Complement Structure in French.* 1996.

133. ZAGONA, Karen (ed.): *Grammatical Theory and Romance Languages. Selected papers from the 25th Linguistic Symposium on Romance Languages (LSRL XXV) Seattle, 2-4 March 1995.* n.y.p.

134. EID, Mushira (ed.): *Perspectives on Arabic Linguistics Vol. VIII. Papers from the Eighth Annual Symposium on Arabic Linguistics.* n.y.p.

135. BRITTON Derek (ed.): *Papers from the 8th International Conference on English Historical Linguistics.* n.y.p.